LUTHER'S THEOLOGY OF THE CROSS

For Joanna

LUTHER'S THEOLOGY OF THE CROSS

Martin Luther's Theological Breakthrough

Alister E. McGrath

Basil Blackwell

First published 1985
First published in paperback 1990
Reprinted 1993, 1994

Blackwell Publishers, the publishing imprint of
Basil Blackwell Ltd
108 Cowley Road
Oxford OX4 1JF, UK

Basil Blackwell Inc.
238 Main Street
Cambridge, Massachusetts 02142
USA

British Library Cataloguing in Publication Data
A CIP catalogue record for this book is available from the
British Library.

Library of Congress Cataloging in Publication Data
McGrath, Alister E., 1953–
Luther's theology of the cross.
Bibliography: p. 182
Includes index.
1. Justification — History of doctrines — 16th century.
2. Jesus Christ — Crucifixion. 3. Jesus Christ — History
of doctrines — 16th century. 4. Luther, Martin, 1483–
1546. I. Title.
BR333.5J8M38 1985   234'.7'0924   84–20345
ISBN 0–631–17549–0 (pbk)

Typeset by System 4 Associates, Farnham Common, Buckinghamshire
Printed and bound in Great Britain by Hartnolls Limited, Bodmin, Cornwall
This book is printed on acid-free paper

Contents

Contents

Contents

Acknowledgements

LUTHER scholarship is a corporate enterprise, in which each successive study draws increasingly upon the established findings of those which precede it. It will thus be clear that the present study owes an incalculable amount to the labours of others. I wish to express particular thanks to those who have helped me at various times and in various ways: Professor A. G. Dickens, Prof. Dr Leif Grane, Prof. Dr Bengt Hägglund, Prof. Dr Heiko A. Oberman, Professor Gordon Rupp and Professor David C. Steinmetz. While they may not agree with my conclusions, I could not have reached them without their assistance.

I also owe sincere thanks to many others for their kindness and encouragement: to Robert Morgan and Edward Yarnold, for their invaluable advice; to the staff of the Bodleian library, for their patience in obtaining obscure works; to those to whom I lectured on or taught about Luther, who probably imparted more to me than I ever did to them; to the publishers, for their efficiency and encouragement; to the staff of Wycliffe Hall, especially Geoffrey Shaw, for forging such an outstanding environment in which to study and to teach; to my family, for tolerating the benign influence of Luther upon our life with such good humour. Luther knew the value of a good wife to her husband: I am sure he would approve my dedicating this small work to mine.

Abbreviations

WA   D. M. Luthers Werke. Kritische Gesamtausgabe. (Weimar, 1883-   )

WABr   D. M. Luthers Werke. Kritische Gesamtausgabe: Briefwechsel.

WADB   D. M. Luthers Werke. Kritische Gesamtausgabe: Deutsche Bibel.

WATr   D. M. Luthers Werke. Kritische Gesamtausgabe: Tischreden.

Introduction

CRUX SOLA EST NOSTRA THEOLOGIA
(WA 5.176.32-3)

The years 1517 and 1519 are generally regarded as being of decisive importance in the career of Martin Luther, and the history of the Reformation as a whole. The first witnessed Luther's posting of the Theses on Indulgences at Wittenberg, and the second the historic Leipzig disputation with Johannes Eck. It is all too easy for the historian to pass over the intervening year, 1518, as being little more than the necessary interval between these two pivotal events, a valley nestling between two mountains. In April of that year, however, at the invitation of Johannes von Staupitz, Luther presided over the traditional public disputation at the assembly of the Augustinian Congregation at Heidelberg. In the course of that disputation, a new phrase was added to the vocabulary of Christendom — the 'theology of the cross'. In the *theologia crucis*, we find Luther's developing theological insights crystallised into one of the most powerful and radical understandings of the nature of Christian theology which the church has ever known.

Crux probat omnia. For Luther, Christian thinking about God comes to an abrupt halt at the foot of the cross. The Christian is forced, by the very existence of the crucified Christ, to make a momentous decision. Either he will seek God elsewhere, or he will make the cross itself the foundation and criterion of his thought about God. The 'crucified God' — to use Luther's daring phrase — is not merely the foundation of the Christian faith, but is also the key to a proper understanding of the nature of God. The Christian can only speak about the glory, the wisdom, the righteousness and the strength of God as they are revealed in the crucified Christ. For Luther, the cross presents us with a riddle — a riddle whose solution defines the distinctively Christian understanding of both man and God. If God *is* present in the cross, then he is a God whose presence is hidden from us. As Luther observed, citing Isaiah 45.15, 'Truly you are a hidden God!' And yet the unfolding of that hidden presence of God in the scene of dereliction upon the cross holds the key to Luther's protracted search for a gracious God. No one would dream of seeking God in the 'disgrace, poverty, death and everything else that is shown to us in the suffering Christ' — nevertheless, God is there, hidden and yet revealed, for those who care to seek him.

The present study is an attempt to unfold the intricacies of the development of Luther's *theologia crucis* over the formative years 1509-19, and to indicate the manner in which Luther's developing insights into man's justification *coram Deo* are encapsulated in the concept of the 'theology of the cross'. This development can only be understood in the light of the late medieval theological context within which these insights took place. Luther's transition from being a typical theologian of the late Middle Ages to the pioneer of a new reforming theology is a subject of enormous historical and theological interest, whose complexity is more than outweighed by its inherent fascination. The present study is therefore essentially an investigation of the development of Luther's doctrine of justification over the years 1509-19, viewed in particular relation to his late medieval theological context. In the course of this study, many of the questions which are the subject of continuing debate among Luther scholars — such as the *date* and the *nature* of Luther's theological breakthrough — will be examined and reviewed in the light of the most recent scholarship.

Before we begin to show how a theologian of the late Middle Ages became a theologian of the cross, one further comment is necessary. The theology of the cross has assumed a new significance and urgency in the present century, in the aftermath of two world wars and with the ever-increasing threat of a third. It must never be forgotten that the theology of the cross is far more than an historical idea. The increasing recognition of the shallowness and naïveté of much Christian thinking about God and man has caused many to begin to retrace the steps taken by Luther before them, and to join him as he kneels at the foot of the cross, and adores the God who is 'hidden in suffering'. If the present study assists to increase that number, it will more than have served its purpose.

PART I

THE BACKGROUND

Luther as a Late Medieval Theologian 1509-14

1

The Dawn of the Reformation
at Wittenberg

BY the end of the Middle Ages, the need for reform and renewal within the Christian church was so obvious that it could no longer be ignored. The Middle Ages had seen the political power of the church, and particularly that of the papacy, reach previously unknown heights. While the spiritual authority of the pope within the church had long been recognised, the medieval period witnessed the extension of such claims to the secular sphere. [1] Even if the force of the claims made on behalf of the papacy to absolute spiritual and temporal authority was greatly diminished by the absence of effective executive powers by which they might have been enforced, [2] the fact remains that such claims were made and recognised, at least in part.

The political success of the church during the Middle Ages was not, however, without its cost. To the faithful, the Christian church remained the visible embodiment of Christ upon earth; to an increasing number of sceptics, within its ranks as well as outside them, it appeared as a vast legal, judicial, financial, administrative and

[1] The extension of this claim to *indirect* power over secular rulers 'by reason of sin' to include *direct* power in temporal affairs appears to be particularly associated with Innocent III: see B. Tierney, ' "Tria quippe distinguit iudicia..." ': A Note on Innocent III's Decretal *Per Venerabilem*', *Speculum* 37 (1962), pp. 48-59. It may be noted that the popes themselves were more modest in their claims to authority than those who campaigned on their behalf, such as Augustus Triumphus of Ancona. For the best study, see L. Buisson, *Potestas und Caritas: Die päpstliche Gewalt im Spätmittelalter* (Köln, 1958).

[2] For the development of papal authority in the medieval period in general, see further G. le Bas, 'Le droit romain au service de la domination pontificale', *Revue historique de droit français et étranger* 27 (1949), pp. 377-98; W. Ullmann, *Medieval Papalism: The Political Theories of the Medieval Canonists* (London, 1949); M. J. Wilks, *The Problem of Sovereignty: The Papal Monarchy with Augustus Triumphus and the Publicists* (Cambridge, 1963).

diplomatic machine, [3] whose spiritual concerns were frequently difficult
to detect, to say the least. By the end of the medieval period, the
spirituality of the church was at a low ebb, despite the perceptible
quickening in piety due to the propagation of the *devotio moderna* by
the Windesheim congregation of the Brethren of the Common Life. [4]
The secular interests of the clergy, the widespread absence of bishops
from their dioceses and the financial difficulties of the curia are further
examples of factors which combined to compromise the moral and
spiritual authority of the church at the time in so serious a manner.
There remains, however, a further factor which is of particular
significance to our study. It is becoming increasingly clear that there
was considerable confusion within the late medieval church, undoubtedly exacerbated by a largely uneducated clergy, on matters of
doctrine, and the doctrine of justification in particular. It is precisely this widespread confusion at the beginning of the sixteenth
century which appeared to have occasioned and catalysed Luther's
theological reflections during the years 1509-19, with which we are
here concerned.

The importance of the doctrine of justification is best appreciated
when the nature of Christianity itself is considered. The central
teaching of the Christian faith is that reconciliation has been effected
between God and sinful man through Jesus Christ, and that this reconciliation is a present actuality for those within the church, and a present
possibility for those outside it. The essence of the Christian faith is
thus located in the saving action of God towards mankind in Jesus
Christ. The Christian doctrine of justification is primarily concerned
with the question of how this saving action may be appropriated by
the individual — in other words, with the question of what man must
do if he is to enter into fellowship with God. [5] The hope of salvation in

[3] For a fascinating insight into the financial experimentations of the Avignon
papacy, see Y. Renouard, *Les relations des papes d'Avignon et des compagnies commerciales
et bancaires de 1316 à 1378* (Paris, 1941).

[4] The recent study of R. R. Post, *The Modern Devotion: Confrontation with Reformation
and Humanism* (Leiden, 1968), calls into question much of the traditional understanding of the nature and influence of this movement, particularly in relation to its
supposed diffusion of humanist ideals in the Low Countries. As Oberman has pointed
out, there appears to be a connection between the *devotio moderna* and the *via moderna*,
at any rate in the persons of Gabriel Biel, Wendelin Steinbach and Peter Braun:
H. A. Oberman, *Werden und Wertung der Reformation: Vom Wegestreit zum Glaubenskampf*
(Tübingen, 1977), pp. 56-7.

[5] For an introduction, see Alister McGrath, 'Der articulus iustificationis als

Christ is a leading characteristic of the faith of the Christian church throughout its entire history, which lends particular urgency to the question posed by the doctrine of justification: what man must *do* if he is to be saved? If the hope of salvation is to be taken seriously, the question of how that salvation may be achieved must be taken with an equal seriousness. The practical importance of this question may be illustrated with reference to the fate of a small group of Italian noblemen at the beginning of the sixteenth century.

In 1510 Paolo Giustiniani, the leader of a small group of Paduan-educated humanists, entered the hermitage of Camaldoli, near Arezzo, soon to be followed by most of the remainder of this circle of humanists. The circle had shared a common concern for personal holiness and ultimate salvation, in common with many of their contemporaries. After intense personal anguish. Giustiniani decided that his only hope for salvation lay in the ascetic monastic life as a means of expiating his sins. Our interest here, however, concerns Gasparo Contarini, one of the members of the circle who chose to remain in the world. In 1957 Hubert Jedin, searching through the archives of the hermitage at Camaldoli, discovered the correspondence between Contarini and Giustiniani,[6] and thus enabled us to enter into the mind of a man who was passionately concerned for his own salvation, and yet unwilling to enter a monastery. It is clear from this correspondence that Contarini went through a period of deep depression after his friends entered the hermitage. The question which appears to have caused Contarini particular anguish was the following: if his friends doubted whether *they* could ever atone for their sins by leading lives of austere piety, what hope could there be for Contarini, who had chosen to avoid such a life by remaining in the world?

On Easter Eve 1511, in near despair, Contarini happened to fall into conversation with a priest, and as a result began to rethink his

---

axiomatischer Grundsatz des christlichen Glaubens', *Zeitschrift für Theologie und Kirche* 81 (1984), pp. 383-94. For the full discussion of the development of the Christian doctrine of justification within the western theological tradition, from the earliest times to the present day, see Alister E. McGrath, *Iustitia Dei: A History of the Christian Doctrine of Justification* (2 vols: Cambridge, 1986).

[6] H. Jedin, 'Contarini und Camaldoli', *Archivio per la storia della pietà* 2 (1959), pp. 51-117. Unfortunately, Giustiniani's replies to Contarini have never been traced, if they survive. The term 'satisfaction', used frequently in the course of this correspondence, is used in the sense established by Anselm of Canterbury, meaning 'a penalty imposed by God for the offence of sin': See F. Hammer, *Genugtuung und Heil: Absicht, Sinn und Grenzen der Erlösungslehre Anselms von Canterbury* (Wien, 1966).

dilemma. We do not know who this priest was, and cannot be entirely certain of the exact substance of his advice to Contarini. Nevertheless, it is clear that Contarini had now resolved his dilemma. In his mercy, God had permitted his only son, Jesus Christ, to make satisfaction for the sins of the world, so that in Contarini's words:

Even if I did all the penances possible, and many more besides, they would not be enough to atone for my past sins, let alone to merit salvation . . . [Christ's] passion is sufficient, and more than sufficient, as a satisfaction for sins committed, to which human weakness is prone. Through this thought, I changed from great fear and anguish to happiness. I began to turn with my whole heart to this greatest good which I saw, for love of me, on the cross, his arms open and his breast opened right up to his heart. Thus I — the wretch who lacked the courage to leave the world and do penance for the satisfaction of my sins! — turned to him, and asked him to allow me to share in the satisfaction which he, the sinless one, had performed for us. He was quick to accept me and to permit his Father to totally cancel the debt which I had contracted, and which I was incapable of satisfying by myself.

Now, since I have such a one to pay my debt, shall I not sleep securely in the midst of the city, even though I have not satisfied the debt which I had contracted? Yes! I shall sleep and wake as securely as if I had spent my entire life in the hermitage![7]

The question with which Contarini and his circle had wrestled, with such a variety of results, is the question which we have identified as lying at the heart of the Christian doctrine of justification: what must I *do* to be saved? Contarini and Giustiniani came to very different conclusions — *but which corresponded to the teaching of the church on the matter?* The simple fact is that there was such confusion at the time that this vital question could not be answered by anyone with any degree of conviction. The Contarini-Giustiniani correspondence is of considerable interest, as it bears witness to a spiritual dilemma practically identical to that faced by the young Luther,[8] also occasioned by confusion within the church over the doctrine of justification.

The doctrine of justification had been the subject of considerable

---

[7] Jedin, *Contarini und Camaldoli*, p. 64.

[8] Jedin elsewhere compares Contarini's experience with the young Luther's 'Turmerlebnis': H. Jedin, 'Ein Turmerlebnis des jungen Contarinis', in *Kirche des Glaubens — Kirche der Geschichte: Ausgewählte Aufsätze und Vorträge* I (Freiburg, 1966), pp. 167-80.

debate within the early western church during the course of the Pelagian controversy.[9] In 418 the Council of Carthage undertook a preliminary clarification of the church's teaching on justification in response to this controversy.[10] Its pronouncements were, however, vague at several points which were to prove of significance, and these were revised at what is generally regarded as being the most important council of the early church to deal with the doctrine of justification — the Second Council of Orange, convened in 529.[11] No other council was convened to discuss the doctrine of justification between that date and 1545, when the Council of Trent assembled to debate that doctrine, among many others. There was thus a period of over a millennium during which the teaching office of the church remained silent on the issue of justification.[12] This silence serves to further enhance the importance of the pronouncements of Orange II on the matter, as these thus come to represent the definitive teaching of the Christian church on the doctrine of justification during the medieval period, before the Council of Trent was convened. Recent scholarship has established that no theologian of the Middle Ages ever cites the decisions of Orange II, or shows the slightest awareness of the existence of such decisions. For reasons which we simply do not understand, from the tenth century until the assembly of the Council of Trent in 1545, the theologians of the western church appear to be unaware of the existence of such a council, let alone of its pronouncements.[13] The theologians of the Middle Ages were thus obliged to base their teaching on justification on the canons of the Council of Carthage, which were simply incapable of bearing the strain which

[9] The best recent study of Pelagius' theology of grace is that of G. Greshake, *Gnade als konkrete Freiheit: Eine Untersuchung zur Gnadenlehre des Pelagius* (Mainz, 1972). Most modern studies have emphasised Pelagius' orthodox *intentions*, particularly in relation to the need to encourage a human response to the divine initiative in justification: see R. F. Evans, *Pelagius: Inquiries and Reappraisals* (New York, 1968).

[10] H. Denzinger, *Enchiridion Symbolorum* (Barcelona, 24/25th edn, 1948) D. 101-108.

[11] D. 174-200. For the problems raised by the fact that this was a *local*, rather than an *ecumenical*, council, see *Problems of Authority: An Anglo-French Symposium*, ed. J. M. Todd (London, 1964), pp. 63-4.

[12] While no council was ever convened over the specific issue of justification, it may be pointed out that questions relating to the doctrine were occasionally touched upon by other magisterial pronouncements — e.g. in the profession of faith sent by Leo IX to the Bishop of Antioch in 1053 (D. 680-6).

[13] This was first pointed out by H. Bouillard, *Conversion et grâce chez Thomas d'Aquin* (Paris, 1944), pp. 99-123. See further M. Seckler, *Instinkt und Glaubenswille nach Thomas von Aquin* (Mainz, 1961), pp. 90-133.

came to be placed upon them.[14] The increasing precision of the technical terms employed within the theological schools inevitably led to the somewhat loose terms used by the Council of Carthage being interpreted in a manner quite alien to that intended by those who originally employed them.

For reasons such as these, there was considerable confusion within the later medieval church concerning the doctrine of justification. This confusion undoubtedly did much to prepare the way for the Reformation, in that the church was simply not prepared for a major debate on justification, and was unable to respond to Luther's challenge when it finally came.[15] How can a sinner enter into fellowship with a holy and righteous God? How can the troubled conscience find peace by discovering a gracious God? Luther was not the only one to ask such questions, and was not the only one to find himself confused by the variety of answers given. In practice, it may be noted that the questions which were to torment the young Luther and others so appear to have been asked but rarely in the later medieval period, the predominance of external (and, it seems, largely superficial) forms of the religious life tending to rob such questions of their force.

Possessed of a tired spirituality, morally bankrupt, doctrinally confused: each succeeding study of the later medieval period confirms this depressing evaluation of the then prevailing state of the Christian church in Europe. It may, however, be pointed out that the catholic system of church order is such that its emphasis upon the *institution* of the church, with its associated ecclesiastical apparatus, means that a prolonged period of spiritual mediocrity or even decline can be sustained without undue damage, to await spiritual renewal and regeneration at a future date. If the life-blood of the Christian faith appeared to cease to flow through her veins, at least the church was able to retain her outward structures for the day when renewed

[14] For example as illustrated by Gabriel Biel's use of Canon 5: A. E. McGrath, 'The Anti-Pelagian Structure of "Nominalist" Doctrines of Justification', *Ephemerides Theologicae Lovanienses* 57 (1981), pp. 107-19, *in fine*.
[15] This point is particularly emphasised by Joseph Lortz, *Die Reformation in Deutschland* (2 vols: Freiburg, 4th edn, 1962) Vol. I, pp. 137-8. For studies of the Christian church in the later medieval period which bear witness to this confusion, see J. Toussaert, *Le sentiment religieux en Flandre à la fin du Moyen Age* (Paris, 1963); M. Bowker, *The Secular Clergy in the Diocese of Lincoln* (Cambridge, 1968); P. Heath, *The English Parish Clergy on the Eve of the Reformation* (London, 1969).

spiritual fervour would revitalise her, raising her from her knees and propelling her forward to meet the challenges and opportunities of a new age. It was this hope which sustained those working for reform and renewal within the late medieval church.

Although earlier popes had occasionally imposed and supervised programmes of reform within the church,[16] the dawn of the sixteenth century saw this initiative in the process of passing to numerous small groups and individuals, usually working independently of each other, although with similar objectives. It is becoming increasingly clear that the final decade of the fifteenth century witnessed a remarkable upsurge in reforming and renewing activity within the church, frequently with the approval of, and occasionally even at the instigation of, the institutional church itself. This upsurge in activity gained ground throughout Europe during the first two decades of the sixteenth century, before the spectre of a new heresy — Lutheranism — caused a frightened church to begin the systematic suppression of these groups and their ideals during the third and fourth decades of that century. Whatever positive impact Luther's stand at Wittenberg may have had upon the catholic church as a whole, it had the universally negative effect of bringing practically all of those working for reform and renewal under suspicion of heresy. Such was the odium which came to be attached to the name of Martin Luther that similarities, however slight, between Luther and contemporary catholic writers tended to be regarded as evidence of heresy on the part of the latter, rather than orthodoxy on the part of the former.[17]

The revival within the late fifteenth century is particularly associated with Spain, then newly won back from the Moor. The sudden development of Spanish mysticism during the final decade of the century remains unexplained, although the unique character of the Spanish cultural context, enriched by Christian, Moslem and Jew alike, unquestionably did much to promote and sustain it. The vitality of this

---

[16] C. Schmitt, *Un pape réformateur et un défenseur de l'unité de l'église: Benoit XII et l'Ordre des Frères Mineurs* (Quaracchi, 1959), Of interest in this respect is the belief which arose in Italy during the thirteenth century concerning *papa angelicus* (or *pastor angelicus*) — the reforming pope who, it was believed, would restore apostolic simplicity and zeal within the church, and thus inaugurate a new era in its history.

[17] See A. Selke de Sánchez, 'Algunos datos nuevos los primeros alumbrados: el edicto de 1525 y su relación con el processo de Alcaraz', *Bulletin Hispanique* 54 (1952), pp. 125-52; O. Ortolani, *Pietro Carnesecchi: Son Estratti dagli Atti del Processo del Santo Officio* (Firenze, 1963); E. L. Gleason, 'Sixteenth Century Italian Interpretations of Luther', *Archiv für Reformationsgeschichte* 60 (1969), pp. 160-73.

movement was harnessed through the Cisnerian reform of the Spanish church, leading to a revival of religious vocations and a new concern for religious education, which found its most concrete and enduring expression in the establishment of the University of Alcalá de Henares.[18] Through Europe, a new interest developed in the writings of St Paul, apparently due at least in part to the considerable influence of the Italian humanism of the *Quattrocento*, with its celebrated intention to return *ad fontes*, to base itself upon the title deeds of Christendom, rather than its later medieval expressions.[19] In England, John Colet drew attention to the Pauline emphasis upon the necessity of a personal encounter of the soul with Christ;[20] In Paris, Lefèvre d'Etaples contemplated Paul's teaching on the supremacy of faith in the spiritual life;[21] in the Lowlands, Erasmus of Rotterdam propounded his *philosophia Christi* as the basis for collective renewal within the church, capturing the hearts as well as the minds of the intellectual élite of Europe as he did so.[22] In Italy itself, the movement usually known as 'Evangelism', characterised by its preoccupation with the question of personal salvation, became highly influential in certain circles: if its allegedly aristocratic bias hindered its progress among the population as a whole, it certainly assisted its progress within the higher échelons of the church.[23] This preoccupation

[18] See J. N. Bakhuizen van den Brink, *Juan de Valdés réformateur en Espagne et en Italie* (Genève, 1969); J. C. Nieto, *Juan de Valdés and the origins of the Spanish and Italian Reformation* (Geneva, 1970).
[19] For an excellent introduction, see R. Cessi, 'Paolinismo preluterano', *Renconditi dell' Accademia nazionale dei Lincei*, Series 8, 12 (1957), pp. 3-30. See further the following chapter of the present study.
[20] S. Jayne, *John Colet and Marsilio Ficino* (Oxford, 1963); J. K. McConica, *English Humanists and Reformation Politics* (Oxford, 1965).
[21] R. M. Cameron, 'The Charges of Lutheranism brought against Jacques Lefèvre d'Etaples', *Harvard Theological Review* 63 (1970), pp. 119-49.
[22] For an excellent discussion of the nature and influence of Erasmianism, see McConica, *English Humanists*, pp. 13-43. For the best analysis to date of Erasmus' *Enchiridion*, see R. Stupperich, 'Das Enchiridion Militis Christiani des Erasmus von Rotterdam nach seiner Entstehung, seinem Sinn und Charakter', *Archiv für Reformationsgeschichte* 69 (1978), pp. 5-23.
[23] The original study is that of E. M. Jung, 'On the Nature of Evangelism in Sixteenth Century Italy', *Journal of the History of Ideas* 14 (1953) pp. 511-27. For more recent studies, see P. McNair, *Peter Martyr in Italy: An Anatomy of Apostasy* (Oxford, 1967), pp. 1-50; D. Fenlon, *Heresy and Obedience in Tridentine Italy: Cardinal Pole and the Counter Reformation* (Cambridge, 1972), pp. 1-23. The allegedly aristocratic nature of the movement has been called into question: E. Pommier, 'La societé vénetienne et la réforme protestante au XVIᵉ siècle', *Bolletino dell' Istituto di Storia della Società e dello Stato Veneziano* 1 (1959), pp. 3-26.

with personal salvation is well illustrated by Contarini's spiritual experience of 1511, noted above. While Luther was still a prisoner within the matrix of late medieval theology, others had already broken free from it, anticipating in many respects his own spiritual breakthrough.

The reform of the church and the renewal of spirituality: these two themes lay at the heart of the rising tide of dissatisfaction on the part of laity and clergy alike over the state of the church of their day. The demands for reform and renewal took many forms, with an equally great variation in the results which they achieved. A seemingly insignificant addition to these demands was a list of theses for academic disputation nailed to the main north door of the castle church at Wittenberg at about noon on 31 October 1517.[24] Wittenberg was not an important university, and Martin Luther was hardly known outside the somewhat restricted university circles of Erfurt and Wittenberg. History suggests, however, that great upheavals in the affairs of men arise out of relatively small matters, even if their ultimate roots lie much deeper. The fuel for the Reformation had been piled up for many years: it happened to be Luther's posting of the ninety-five theses

[24] For the background to this event, see H. Bornkamm, *Luthers geistige Welt* (Gütersloh, 3rd edn, 1959), pp. 41-57. On the content of the theses, see E. Kähler, 'Die 95 Thesen: Inhalt und Bedeutung', *Luther. Zeitschrift der Luther-Gesellschaft* 38 (1967), pp. 114-24. Recently, there has been intensive debate concerning the date on which the theses were posted — and, indeed, whether they were posted at all. Although the majority opinion is that the theses definitely were posted, and that they were posted on 31 October 1517, three important minority opinions must be noted:

(1) The theses were posted on 1 November 1517: H. Volz, *Martin Luthers Thesenanschlag und dessen Vorgeschichte* (Weimar, 1959).
(2) The theses date from as late as December 1517: K. Honzelmann, *Urfassung und Drucke der Ablassthesen Martin Luthers und ihre Veröffentlichung* (Paderborn, 1966).
(3) The theses were not posted at all: E. Iserloh, *Luther zwischen Reform und Reformation. Der Thesenanschlag fand nicht statt* (Münster, 3rd edn, 1968). This opinion is by far the least probable, and does not appear to follow logically from the evidence assembled in its support.

For a reliable discussion of these opinions in the light of the best evidence, see H. Bornkamm, 'Thesen und Thesenanschlag Luthers', in *Geist und Geschichte der Reformation*, eds H. Liebing and K. Scholder (Berlin, 1966), pp. 179-218; H. A. Oberman, *Werden und Wertung der Reformation*, p. 190, n. 89. For a useful collection of pertinent contemporary documents, see W. Köhler, *Dokumente zum Ablassstreit von 1517* (Tübingen, 2nd edn, 1934).

on indulgences which eventually sparked off the conflagration which proved to be the greatest intellectual and spiritual upheaval yet known in Europe. Whereas a reforming ecumenical council could have defused the situation by imposing reform where it was so obviously needed, the absence of any such eventuality led to Luther's protest against the theology of indulgences developing into a serious and a still unresolved schism within the church.

The posting of theses for academic disputation, even where these related to theological matters, was a commonplace in German university life at the time. In October 1514 Johannes Eck — later to be Luther's antagonist at the Leipzig disputation of 1519 — posted a series of theses at Ingolstadt for public academic disputation.[25] These theses related to the vexed question of usury,[26] an issue in many respects more contentious than that of indulgences, and one which certainly aroused passions in ecclesiastical financial circles. It was probably on account of this latter consideration that Gabriel von Eyb, who then held simultaneously the offices of bishop of Eichstätt and chancellor of the university of Ingolstadt, intervened to prevent the proposed disputation from taking place.[27] Not to be deprived of his disputation, however, Eck referred his theses to the universities of Cologne, Heidelberg, Freiburg, Tübingen and Mainz, as well as to Ingolstadt,[28] in order that they might receive further consideration.

Such disputations were not unknown at Wittenberg, nor was Luther's without its precedents. On 26 April 1517, less than six months before Luther posted his theses, Andreas Bodenstein von Karlstadt, then dean of the theology faculty at Wittenberg, posted 151 theses for disputation. These theses were of a highly controversial nature, reflecting Karlstadt's own discovery of the *vera theologia* of St Augustine earlier the same year, and chiefly concern the doctrine of

---

[25] Oberman, *Werden und Wertung der Reformation*, p. 177.

[26] G. F. von Pölnitz, 'Die Beziehungen des Johannes Eck zum Augsburger Kapital', *Historisches Jahrbuch der Görresgesellschaft* 60 (1940), pp. 685-706. For useful historical background to the issues involved, see T. P. McLaughlin, 'The Teaching of the Canonists on Usury', *Medieval Studies* 1 (1939), pp. 81-147; 2 (1940), pp. 1-22; R. de Roover, *La pensée économique des scolastiques: Doctrines et méthodes* (Montréal/Paris, 1971).

[27] Oberman, *Werden und Wertung der Reformation*, p. 184.

[28] von Pölnitz, *Beziehungen des Johannes Eck*, p. 694. Oberman has published the submission to Tübingen, along with other pertinent material: Oberman, *Werden und Wertung der Reformation*, pp. 426-30.

justification. [29] In terms of their theological substance, particularly when seen in the light of the then prevailing theology of the *via moderna*, they are of far greater weight than Luther's theses on indulgences. Furthermore, Karlstadt's high standing in the faculty and the university as a whole lent added weight to the challenge directed against the *Gabrielistae*. What is of particular interest, however, is the date on which Karlstadt chose to publish his theses, and the place where they were posted. The castle church at Wittenberg possessed an imposing collection of sacred relics, which were publicly displayed several times during the course of the year. Like many churches at the time, the castle church had been granted the right to bestow a partial or plenary indulgence upon those present at the exhibition of the relics, with the inevitable result that such exhibitions were well attended and the subject of considerable local interest. It was on the eve of one such occasion that Karlstadt posted his theses. As the main north door of the castle church served as a university notice board, Karlstadt could be sure that his proposed disputation would not pass unnoticed by those who thronged the area that evening and the following morning. Contemporary records, however, indicate that the Feast of All Saints (1 November) was regarded as the most important occasion upon which the Wittenberg relics were displayed. [30] It was on this occasion that Luther posted his theses, in precisely the same manner already employed by Karlstadt, to direct

[29] On these theses, see E. Kähler, *Karlstadt und Augustin: Der Kommentar des Andreas Bodenstein von Karlstadt zu Augustins Schrift De Spiritu et Litera* (Halle, 1952), pp. 4*-7*. Luther was delighted with these theses, as he made clear in a letter of 6 May 1517 to Christoph Scheurl in Nuremberg: WABr 1.94.16-19. It is clear, however, that Karlstadt's theology of justification is far closer to that of St Augustine than was Luther's. In particular, the following points of difference between the two reformers should be noted: (1) Luther's Christocentrism is absent from Karlstadt's theses: Karlstadt is primarily concerned with a theology of *grace*, not a theology of *Christ*; (2) it is clear that faith does not have the significance for Karlstadt which it so obviously has for Luther; (3) Luther's dialectic between Law and Gospel is absent, being replaced by a dialectic between Letter and Spirit. In every respect, these differences between Karlstadt and Luther reflect identical differences between Augustine and Luther, and indicate Karlstadt's faithfulness to the theology of the great African bishop. These differences, however, do not appear to have been noticed or commented upon at the time — which is hardly surprising, considering the pace at which events began to move that year.

[30] The most important of these is Andreas Meinhardi's *Dialogus illustrate ac augustissime urbis Albiorenae vulgo Vittenberg dicte* (Leipzig, 1508), whose sixth chapter describes the events of All Saints' Day at the Castle Church.

attention to his proposed public disputation on indulgences.

The circumstances which surrounded Luther's posting of the ninety-five theses are, in many respects, comparable to those attending Eck's attempt to provoke a disputation on usury, or Karlstadt's attempt to provoke one on Augustine's doctrine of justification. The revised statutes of the theology faculty at Wittenberg (1508) make it clear that such disputations were a normal part of university life at the time. Such disputations were not restricted to those held on Friday mornings during university terms (*disputationes ordinariae*), intended primarily as a means of theological education, or those stipulated as a necessary ordeal for those intending to proceed to higher degrees. The *exercitia disputationum* appears to have been regarded as of such importance as to justify occasional *disputationes quodlibeticae*,[31] which fitted into neither of these categories. In calling for public university disputations upon subjects of their choosing, Luther — and, before him, Eck and Karlstadt — did nothing more than arrange for a perfectly legitimate university disputation, following a well-established procedure. Far from defying the church of his day, Luther merely posted a legitimate university notice in its appropriate place. Those who see the death-knell of the medieval church in the hammer-blows which resounded on the door of the castle church as Luther posted his theses are, regrettably, substituting romance for history.

Like Eck, Luther failed to provoke a public disputation: all the evidence suggests, however, that this failure reflected an absence of interest in the subject in university circles, rather than any serious attempt on the part of the church authorities to suppress what might have proved to be an embarrassing debate. Indeed, had Luther succeeded in provoking a public disputation on the matter, it would almost certainly have been seen as little more than a local dispute between the

[31] See the important study of Ernst Wolf, 'Zur wissenschaftsgeschictlichen Bedeutung der Disputationen an der Wittenberger Universität im 16. Jahrhundert', in *Peregrinatio II: Studien zur reformatorischen Theologie, zum Kirchenrecht und zur Sozialethik* (München, 1965), pp. 38-51. Further light has been cast upon the role and nature of disputations at Wittenberg at the time by the discovery in 1976 of the protocol to the disputations at Wittenberg between members of the Wittenberg theological faculty and a group of Saxon Franciscans, which took place 3-4 October 1519: G. Hammer, 'Militia franciscana seu militia Christi: Das neugefundene Protokoll einer Disputation des sächsischen Franziskaner mit Vertretern der Wittenberger theologischen Fakultät am 3. und 4. Oktober 1519', *Archiv für Reformationsgeschichte* 69 (1978), pp. 51-81; 70 (1979), pp. 59-105.

Augustinian and Dominican orders over a minor issue, in which both parties had a vested interest. It must be pointed out that Luther's theses are far less radical than is frequently imagined: Luther did not question the authority of the pope or the existence of purgatory, and actually *affirmed* his belief in the notion of apostolic pardons. In a matter surrounded by much theological confusion and considerable popular feeling, most of Luther's theses were quite unexceptionable. Furthermore, a critique of the theology of indulgences which parallels that of Luther in several respects was drawn up by the theology faculty at Paris in May of the following year, without occasioning any serious charge of impropriety, let alone heresy.[32] It may also be pointed out that Luther himself later stated that the whole question of indulgences was quite insignificant in comparison with the greater question of man's justification before God,[33] thus suggesting that the posting of the theses on indulgences was *not* the beginning of the Reformation, viewed in terms of the *theological* issues at stake. Nevertheless, the *historical* fact remains that it was out of the aftermath of the posting of these theses that the movement known as the Reformation began, with Martin Luther being widely recognised as its leading figure.

Once the Reformation had begun in earnest, a third demand was added to those already widely in circulation throughout Europe. For Luther, the reformation of morals and the renewal of spirituality, although of importance in themselves, were of secondary significance in relation to the *reformation of Christian doctrine*. Well aware of the frailty of human nature, Luther criticised both Wycliffe and Huss for confining their attacks on the papacy to its moral shortcomings, where they should have attacked the theology on which the papacy was ultimately based. For Luther, a reformation of morals was secondary

[32] As pointed out, with useful documentation, by Oberman, *Werden und Wertung der Reformation*, p. 192 n. 90.

[33] WA 18.786.28-9. Luther here praises Erasmus for locating the real theological issue at stake (the bondage of the will, a fundamental aspect of Luther's teaching on justification), instead of concentrating upon peripheral matters, such as indulgences. For the opinion that the doctrine of the *servum arbitrium* and the remaining aspects of Luther's teaching on justification are related as the two sides of the one coin, see G. L. Plitt, 'Luthers Streit mit Erasmus über den freien Willen in den Jahren 1524-1525', *Studien der evangelisch-protestantischen Geistlichen des Grossherzogthums Baden* 2 (1876) pp. 205-14.

to a reformation of doctrine.[34] It was clear, of course, that once irreversible schism with the catholic church had taken place, the reformers would be obliged to revise the accepted ecclesiologies if they were to avoid the stigma of being branded as schismatics. It may, however, be pointed out that Luther himself entertained a profound distaste for schism in the period between the posting of the theses and the Leipzig disputation of mid-1519. In early 1519, Luther wrote thus of schism: 'If, unfortunately, there are things in Rome which cannot be improved, there is not — nor can there be! — any reason for tearing oneself away from the church in schism. Rather, the worse things become, the more one should help her and stand by her, for by schism and contempt nothing can be mended.'[35] Even though the Leipzig disputation would do much to alter Luther's views on the relative demerits of schism, it may be noted that the assumption underlying both the *Confessio Augustana* (1530) and the Colloquy of Regensburg (1541) was that the estrangement of the evangelical faction from the catholic church was still to be regarded as temporary. It was only after the failure of Regensburg that the possibility of a permanent schism within the church became increasingly a probability, so that ecclesiological questions began to come to the fore within the evangelical faction.[36] It is therefore necessary to emphasise that the essential factor which led to this schism in the first place, and thus to the rethinking of the accepted ecclesiologies, was Luther's fundamental conviction that the church of his day had lapsed into some form of Pelagianism, thus compromising the gospel, and that the church itself was not prepared to extricate itself from this situation.

For Luther, the entire gospel could be encapsulated in the Christian

[34] WATr 1.624: 'Doctrina et vita sunt distinguenda. Vita est mala apud nos sicut apud papistas; non igitur dimicamus et damnamus eos. Hoc nesciverunt Wikleff et Hus, qui vitam impugnarunt.' WATr 4.4338: 'Sed doctrina non reformata frustra fit reformatio morum.'

[35] WA 2.72.35-37. Luther's attitudes to the papacy and schism over the years 1517-20 are notoriously difficult to follow: see R. Bäumer, *Martin Luther und der Päpst* (Münster, 1970). For a more sympathetic and penetrating analysis, see S. H. Hendrix, *Luther and the Papacy: Stages in a Reformation Conflict* (Philadelphia, 1981).

[36] Ecclesiological developments are particularly associated with Martin Bucer: J. Courvoisier, *La notion d'église chez Bucer dans son développement historique* (Paris, 1933). For evangelical ecclesiologies in general, see H. Strohl, *La notion d'église chez les réformateurs* (Paris, 1936).

article of justification[37] — the affirmation that man, sinner though
he is and sinner though he will remain throughout his history, really
can enter into a gracious relationship with God through the death
and resurrection of Jesus Christ. The sacerdotal and sacramental
systems of the church have their proper and legitimate place, but
cannot be allowed to interpose between the sinner and the living God
who calls him to faith through the Word. For Luther, Jesus Christ
is the righteousness of God, revealing at one and the same time God's
condemnation of sin and remedy for it. Through the creative power
of the Holy Spirit and the hearing of the Word of the gospel, the sinner
shares in the divine righteousness through faith. In comparison with
this, matters such as the authority of the pope, the nature of purgatory
and the propriety of indulgences were seen by Luther as being quite
insignificant and irrelevant. Even as late as 1535, Luther stated
unequivocally that he was still prepared to acknowledge the authority
of the pope on condition that he acknowledge in turn that the sinner
had free forgiveness of sins through the death and resurrection of Jesus
Christ, and not through the observance of the traditions of the
church.[38]

Was Luther really stating anything other than the common Christian
gospel? Was not the extent of theological diversity within late medieval
catholicism already so great that such opinions could be accommodated
without difficulty? Need this have led to irreversible schism? Was the
Reformation actually the consequence of a fundamental misunderstanding of Luther's frequently intemperate and occasionally obscure
pronouncements?[39] Such questions cannot be answered with any

[37] For an excellent introduction to Luther's doctrine of justification and its theological
significance, see B. Hägglund, *Was ist mit Luthers 'Rechtfertigungs'-Lehre gemeint?*
(Vortragsreihe der Luther-Akademie-Ratzeburg 4: Ratzeburg, 1982).
[38] WA 40 I.357.18-22: 'Papa, ego voli tibi osculari pedes teque agnoscere summum
pontificem, si adaveris Christum meum et permiseris, quod per ipsius mortem
et resurrectionem habeamus remissionem peccatorum et vitam aeternam, non per
observationem tuarum traditionum. Si hoc cesseris, non adimam tibi coronam et
potentiam tuam.'
[39] The current ecumenical dialogue is obliged to proceed upon this assumption,
in one form or another: H. Küng, *Rechtfertigung. Die Lehre Karl Barths und eine katholische
Besinnung* (Einsiedeln, 1957); H. J. McSorley, *Luthers Lehre vom unfreien Willen nach
seiner Hauptschrift De servo arbitrio im Lichte der biblischen und kirchlichen Tradition* (München,
1967). For a critique of Küng's thesis, see A. E. McGrath, 'Justification: Barth,
Trent and Küng', *Scottish Journal of Theology* 34 (1981), pp. 517-29; idem., 'ARCIC
II and Justification: Some Difficulties and Obscurities relating to Anglican and Roman
Catholic Teaching on Justification', *Anvil* 1 (1984), pp. 27-42.

degree of confidence. The fact remains, however, that Luther himself regarded the Reformation as having begun over, and to have chiefly concerned, the correct understanding of the Christian doctrine of justification, and that this concern is evident in his writings throughout his later career, including some of the confessional material of the Lutheran church. The Smalkald Articles of 1537 assert that everything in the evangelical struggle against the papacy, the world and the devil hangs upon the Christian article of justification. [40] Similarly, in the same year Luther prefaced an academic disputation with the assertion that the article of justification was not merely supreme among other Christian doctrines, but that it also upheld and controlled them. [41] In the struggle for the reformation of Christian doctrine, the evangelical case was held to rest entirely upon this single article.

It will therefore be clear that a study of the development of Luther's doctrine of justification over the crucial years 1509-19, culminating in the statement of the *theologia crucis*, is of enormous interest to historians and theologians alike. The importance of the matter to historians will be evident. Given that Luther's understanding of the doctrine of justification is clearly of such fundamental importance in relation to so significant an historical movement as the Reformation, it is obviously of considerable interest to establish how this particular understanding emerged, what factors appear to have been instrumental in effecting it, and how it relates to previous understandings of the same matter. It has always been important for intellectual historians to establish the sources of an author's thought. The character, distinctiveness and ultimate significance of an intellectual achievement such as that of Luther are invariably better understood when those who have influenced his ideas, either positively or negatively, are identified.

---

[40] *Die Bekenntnisschriften der evangelisch-lutherischen Kirche* (Göttingen, 1952), 416.22-3: 'Et in hoc articulo sita sunt et consistunt omnia, quae contra papam, diabolum et mundum in vita nostra docemus, testamur et agimus.'

[41] WA 39 I.205.2-5: 'Articulus iustificationis est magister et princeps, dominus, rector et iudex super omnia genera doctrinarum, qui conservat et gubernat omnem doctrinam ecclesiasticam et erigit conscientiam nostram coram Deo.' On this, see E. Wolf, 'Die Rechtfertigungslehre als Mitte und Grenze reformatorischer Theologie', *Evangelische Theologie* 9 (1949-50), pp. 298-308. It may be noted that Karl Barth was severely critical of this magisterial understanding of the *articulus iustificationis*, for reasons which shed much greater light on his own theology than that of Luther: Alister E. McGrath, 'Karl Barth and the *articulus iustificationis*: The Significance of his Critique of Ernst Wolf within the Context of his Theological Method', *Theologische Zeitschrift* 39 (1983), pp. 349-61.

Luther cannot be regarded merely as a protagonist in German and European history: the ideas which led him to assume this role, their origins and significance, must be taken into account if a proper understanding and evaluation of Luther's historical significance is to emerge. [42] It is understandably difficult for a liberal historian, with a distaste for dogma and theology, and who would much have preferred a reformation of the church along humanist lines, to come to terms with the theological issues at stake in Luther's revolt. Nevertheless, Luther the man cannot be isolated from Luther the theologian, nor can his actions be isolated from the ideas which ultimately inspired them.

The importance of the matter to the theologian is somewhat greater, for two reasons. First, it is clearly important to establish precisely what Luther's teaching on so crucial a matter as justification actually is, and how the various strands of this teaching are woven together in the *theologia crucis*. There is, however, reason to suggest that the second reason is the more significant. Can the distinctive teachings of the Reformation, and supremely their chief article, that of justification, be considered to be truly catholic? If it can be shown that the chief teaching of the Reformation, the article by which the church stands or falls, [43] was a theological novelty, unknown to the Christian church throughout the first fifteen hundred years of her existence, it will be

[42] If this is not done, the Reformation will appear as merely one episode in the essentially continuous development of intellectual history in the period 1300-1600, without proper appreciation of its genuinely radical and innovatory character. For an excellent discussion of this important point, see Heiko A. Oberman, 'Reformation: Epoche oder Episode', *Archiv für Reformationsgeschichte* 68 (1977), pp. 56-111.
[43] See F. Loofs, 'Der articulus stantis et cadentis ecclesiae', *Theologische Studien und Kritiken* 90 (1917), pp. 323-400. In this study, Loofs argues that the phrase, 'the article by which the church stands or falls' — referring to the article of justification — only came into use in the eighteenth century. In fact, as we have shown on the basis of an exhaustive analysis of the dogmatic works of the period, the phrase appears to have come into circulation at the beginning of the seventeenth century, and is used by *Reformed*, as well as by *Lutheran*, theologians. Thus the Reformed theologian J. H. Alsted begins his discussion of the justification of man before God with the following statement: 'Articulus iustificationis dicitur articulus stantis et cadentis ecclesiae' (*Theologia scholastica didacta* [Hanoviae, 1618], p. 711). There is thus every reason to suggest that the phrase represents a common *modus loquendi theologicus* by the beginning of the seventeenth century. Precursors of the phrase can, of course, be found in the writings of Luther himself — e.g. WA 40 III.352.3: '...quia isto articulo stante stat Ecclesia, ruente ruit Ecclesia.'

clear that the Protestant claim to have *reformed* the church cannot be taken seriously: far from having *re*formed Christian doctrine, Luther would have *de*formed it to a point at which it could no longer be considered catholic or Christian. This point was made with particular force by the theologians of the Counter Reformation, such as Bossuet:

The Church's doctrine is always the same...the Gospel is never different from what it was before. Hence, if at any time someone says that the faith includes something which yesterday was not said to be of the faith, it is always *heterodoxy*, which is any doctrine different from *orthodoxy*. There is no difficulty about recognising false doctrine: there is no argument about it: it is recognised at once, whenever it appears, merely because it is new. [44]

If, on the other hand, it can be shown that Luther restored or recovered an authentically catholic understanding of justification from the distortions of the later medieval period, the reform of doctrine which he initiated and sustained on the basis of this understanding of justification must be taken with the utmost seriousness. It is therefore of considerable theological importance, not only to establish precisely what Luther's developing views on justification, culminating in the theology of the cross, actually were, but also the precise nature of that development, and what factors were instrumental in effecting that development. [45]

---

[44] *Première instruction pastorale* xxvii; cited by O. Chadwick, *From Bossuet to Newman: The Idea of Doctrinal Development* (Cambridge, 1957), p. 17. For the general point at issue, see Alister E. McGrath, 'Forerunners of the Reformation? A Critical Examination of the Evidence for Precursors of the Reformation Doctrines of Justification', *Harvard Theological Review* 75 (1982), pp. 219-42.

[45] It will be clear that these considerations necessitate the examination of the relationship between the origins of Luther's theology and the origins of the Reformation itself. For an excellent introduction to this difficult area, see Heiko A. Oberman, 'Headwaters of the Reformation: *Initia Lutheri — Initia Reformationis*', in *Luther and the Dawn of the Modern Era. Papers for the Fourth International Congress for Luther Research*, ed. H. A. Oberman (Leiden, 1974), pp. 40-88. It is important in this respect to appreciate that by late 1517 Luther was a member of a theological faculty which was dedicated to theological reform, and that Luther insisted, not only that other members of that faculty held views on grace and works indentical to his own, but that in some cases, they had actually held these views before he himself arrived at them: WABr 1.170.20-29 (May 1518). The importance of Karlstadt's conversion to Augustinianism in early 1517, resulting in the posting of the 151 theses of April 1517, is often overlooked, but was actually vital to the initiation of the Reformation, given Karlstadt's position as dean of the faculty at the time.

The present study is based upon the assumption that the genuinely creative and innovative aspects of Luther's *theologia crucis* can only be properly appreciated if Luther is regarded as having begun to teach theology at Wittenberg on 22 October 1512 *as a typical theologian of the later Middle Ages*, and as having begun to break away from this theological matrix over a number of years. [46] There is still a disturbing tendency on the part of some Luther scholars to approach the later medieval period from the standpoint of the later Luther, projecting Luther's perceived theological concerns and prejudices onto this earlier period. Not only does this impede a proper understanding of the theology of the later medieval period; it also prevents a proper understanding of Luther's own theological development, which can only be properly evaluated in the light of the theological currents prevalent in the later Middle Ages. The tendency to regard the study of the theology of the later medieval period as serving as little more than a prologue to that of the Reformation has recently been reversed, with increasing emphasis being placed upon the importance of the later medieval period as a field of study in its own right. As a consequence, we now possess a far greater understanding of the complexities of the theology of the later medieval period than has ever been possible before, and are thus in a favourable position to attempt an informed evaluation of Luther's initial relationship to this theology, and also the nature of his subsequent break with it.

Luther was not a man without beginnings, a mysterious and lonely figure of destiny who arrived at Wittenberg already in possession of the *vera theologia* which would take the church by storm, and usher in a new era in its history. Although it is tempting to believe that Luther suffered a devastating moment of illumination, in which he suddenly became conscious of the *vera theologia* and of his own divine mission to reform the church on its basis, all the evidence which we possess points to Luther's theological insights arising over a prolonged period at Wittenberg, under the influence of three main currents of thought: humanism, the 'nominalism' of the *via moderna*, and the theology of his own Augustinian Order. It is these three currents of thought, in the forms which they assumed at Erfurt, and particularly

---

[46] This assumption is supported by many considerations, as will become clear during the course of this study. For the time being, it is sufficient to recall Luther's celebrated statement: 'When I became a doctor [i.e., 19 October 1512], I did not yet know that we cannot expiate our sins' (WA 45.86.18-19).

at Wittenberg, which appear to define the confluence from which Luther's *theologia crucis* would emerge. Although Luther's early theology can be shown to reflect well-established thought-patterns of the later medieval period, this serves to emphasise, rather than to detract from, his theological genius. There comes a point at which Luther can no longer be explained on the basis of his origins and his environment, and when he began to pursue a course significantly different from the thought-world of his contemporaries, as the cruciality of the cross of Christ embedded itself more and more deeply in Luther's theological reflections. Whether for good or for ill, the consequences of this break with the past are still with us. The present study is an attempt to gather together the developing strands of the theology of the cross as they make their appearance, setting them in their context and assessing their significance. It is an attempt, not to praise or damn Luther, but simply to understand him.

2

Headwaters of the Reformation at Wittenberg: *Studia Humanitatis, Via Moderna, Schola Augustiniana Moderna*

IN 1502 Frederick the Wise, Elector of Saxony, founded a university at Wittenberg to rival that of neighbouring Leipzig. The circumstances surrounding the foundation were somewhat unusual, in that it was founded without initial ecclesiastical approval, and hence without access to the traditional sources of income.[1] Furthermore, while other German universities of the period had high-ranking ecclesiastical dignitaries as their chancellors, Wittenberg had to be content with Goswin of Orsoy, a minor ecclesiastic with an apparent talent for mediocrity. Despite these inauspicious beginnings, the Elector's new university would soon rise from its initial obscurity to attain international fame, although for reasons which Frederick could hardly have foreseen or desired. All this, however, lay in the future. When Luther returned to Wittenberg in the late summer of 1511, he found an Augustinian priory and a university in which three particularly significant elements of later medieval thought were well established. It is these three elements — *studia humanitatis*, the *via moderna*, and the *schola Augustiniana moderna* — with which we are concerned in the present chapter. Luther had already encountered the latter two in the specific forms which they assumed at Erfurt and Wittenberg, and would encounter and exploit the first during his second Wittenberg period. In the present chapter, we propose to consider these three elements as the background to Luther's theological development, before considering the nature and character of that development itself.

[1] See W. Friedensburg, *Geschichte der Universität Wittenberg* (Halle, 1917).

From its foundation, the University of Wittenberg enjoyed particularly close links with the Augustinian Order in general, and the
Black Cloister at Wittenberg in particular. At the foundation of the
university, Elector Frederick had called Johannes von Staupitz, then
prior of the Augustinian Cloister at Munich, to become the first dean
of the faculty of theology, and also to take up one of the two chairs
which were reserved for members of the Order.[2] Although Staupitz
had to relinquish his teaching duties the following year, in order to
take up his new responsibilities as vicar-general of his Order,[3] close
links between the Order and the university were maintained, with
over one hundred Augustinians being matriculated, and seventeen
becoming members of the university teaching staff, during the period
in which Staupitz held the office of vicar-general.

Although the Augustinian Order had had a long and distinguished
association with the humanist movement in Italy,[4] the driving force
in establishing Wittenberg as a centre for the *studia humanitatis* was
unquestionably Christoph Scheurl.[5] Following a well-established
precedent, Scheurl left his native Germany at the age of sixteen to
study law at Bologna.[6] While there, it is clear that he took the opportunity to immerse himself in the learning and culture of the late
Renaissance, and particularly the art of rhetoric. In 1505 a Saxon was
appointed rector of the University of Bologna, and Scheurl used this
occasion to deliver an oration in praise of the contributions of his native
Germany to human civilisation. Although the original version of this
oration has not survived, an expanded version of the text was published
in 1506 as *Libellus de laudibus Germaniae et ducum Saxoniae*.[7] In style and

[2] One was the chair of biblical studies in the faculty of theology; the other was
the chair of moral philosophy in the faculty of arts.
[3] For an excellent introduction to the history of the order in Germany up to the
beginnings of the Reformation, see E. Wolf, 'Die Augustiner-Eremiten in
Deutschland bis zur Reformation', in *Mittelalterliches Erbe — Evangelische Verantwortung.
Vorträge und Ansprachen zum Gedenken der Gründung des Tübinger Augustinerklosters 1262*
(Tübingen, 1962), pp. 25-44.
[4] See R. Arbesmann, *Der Augustiner-Eremitenorder und der Beginn der humanistischen
Bewegung* (Würzburg, 1965). For the role of the religious orders in general in diffusing
humanist ideals, see P. O. Kristeller, 'The Contribution of Religious Orders to
Renaissance Thought and Learning', *American Benedictine Review* 21 (1970), pp. 1-55.
[5] For a biography, see W. Graf, *Doktor Christoph Scheurl von Nürnburg* (Leipzig, 1870).
[6] For an indication of the popularity of Bologna as a centre for German students
during the period, see G. C. Knod, *Deutsche Studenten in Bologna (1289-1562):
Biographischer Index zu den Acta nationis Germanicae universitatis Bononiensis* (Berlin, 1899).
[7] See R. Kautsch, 'Des Chr. Scheurls *Libellus de laudibus Germaniae*', *Repertorium*

content, the work is typical of the humanism of the *Quattrocento*. Favourable reports of the oration were not slow in spreading north of the alps, and Scheurl soon found himself regarded as a leading figure in the humanist movement. After receiving his doctorate in laŵ at Bologna in December 1506, Scheurl returned to Saxony to take up a lectureship at Wittenberg, which had been promised to him by the Elector the previous year.[8] The university annals for April 1507 duly record the presence of 'Christoferus Scheurl Nurembergen, utriusque Juris Doctor Bononien' among the university teaching staff.[9] Scheurl's reputation, however, appears to have preceded him to Wittenberg: the next entry in the university annals records his election as rector of Wittenberg university in May 1507,[10] a matter of weeks after his arrival. Under his influence, the university would change direction significantly, with increased emphasis being placed upon the *studia humanitatis*.[11]

The personal influence of the early rectors of the university upon the university curriculum is also attested by certain significant alterations to the university statutes in 1508. In the autumn of 1507, Scheurl was succeeded as rector by Jodocus Trutvetter, newly arrived from Erfurt. Although we know little of Trutvetter's early years, it is clear that by 1504 he was regarded by many as being the leading figure, not merely within the theological faculty at Erfurt, but also within the university as a whole. His election as rector of the university immediately after his arrival at Wittenberg parallels that of Scheurl some six months previously, and appears to reflect a desire on the part of the members of the new university to attract attention to it by installing well-known figures as rector.

Scheurl and Trutvetter formed a close attachment, as is evident from their extensive correspondence. Trutvetter, however, brought

---

für Kunstwissenschaft 21 (1898), pp. 286-7. The second edition, published in 1508, was dedicated to Frederick the Wise.

[8] G. Bauch, 'Christoph Scheurl in Wittenberg', *Neue Mitteilungen aus dem Gebiet historischer-antiquarischer Forschungen* 21 (1903), pp. 33-42; p. 34. Cf. Scheurl's letter to Sixt Tucher: *Christoph Scheurl's Briefbuch. Ein Beitrag zur Geschichte der Reformation und ihre Zeit*, ed. F. von Soden and J. K. F. Knaake (2 vols: Potsdam, 1867-72), Volume I, Letter No. 4, pp. 5-8.

[9] Scheurl took up his appointment on 13 April 1507: See *Album Academiae Vitebergensis*, ed. C. E. Foerstermann (Leipzig, 1841), p. 20.

[10] *Album*, p. 21. See also Bauch, p. 36.

[11] For a study of this, see M. Grossmann, *Humanism in Wittenberg 1485-1517* (Nieuwkoop, 1975).

more than his reputation to Wittenberg: he also brought the new philosophy of the *via moderna*. Along with Bartholomäus Arnoldi of Usingen, Trutvetter had been instrumental in fostering the *via moderna* at Erfurt.[12] Trutvetter himself singled out Johannes Buridan and Gabriel Biel as his most influential teachers,[13] and this influence can be seen in his extant works.

The distinction between the *via antiqua* and *via moderna* dates from the second half of the fourteenth century. The former is usually taken to refer to the well-established Thomist and Scotist schools, characterised by their metaphysical realism, while the latter is usually held to refer to the new philosophy associated with men such as William of Ockham, Marsilius of Inghen and Gregory of Rimini, characterised by their metaphysical nominalism. This distinction will be developed further in the present chapter at the appropriate point. By the end of the fifteenth century, several German universities, such as Heidelberg,[14] found themselves having to teach according to both the *via antiqua* and the *via moderna*. Wittenberg, however, was initially committed to the *via antiqua* alone. For the first five years of its existence, the *via moderna* does not appear to have made any inroads into the curriculum of the university. For example in May 1507, Scheurl — then newly elected as rector — published his *Rotulus doctorum Wittemberge profitentum*, in which he catalogued the doctors then teaching at Wittenberg, as well as their subjects and hours of lecturing. Although Scheurl intended the document to publicise the academic excellence of Wittenberg at a time when student members were dangerously low, the document is of particular interest to us in that it offers us an invaluable insight into the early teaching patterns of

[12] For an excellent analysis of the development of the *via moderna* at Erfurt, see W. Urban, 'Die "via moderna" an der Universität Erfurt am Vorabend der Reformation', in *Gregor von Rimini: Werk und Wirkung bis zur Reformation*, ed. H. A. Oberman (Berlin/New York, 1981), pp. 311-330. For biographies of Arnoldi and Trutvetter, see N. Paulus, *Der Augustiner Bartholomäus Arnoldi von Usingen, Luthers Lehrer und Gegner: Ein Lebensbild* (Freiburg, 1893); G. Plitt, *Jodokus Trutfetter von Eisenach, der Lehrer Luthers in seinem Wirken geschildert* (Erlangen, 1876). It is important to appreciate that it was the faculty of *arts*, not *theology*, which was dominated by the *via moderna* at Erfurt — the university records point to a number of Thomists and Scotists present on the theology faculty: See L. Grane, *Contra Gabrielem: Luthers Auseinandersetzung mit Gabriel Biel in der Disputatio contra scholasticam theologiam* (Gyldendal, 1962), p. 16, n. 31.

[13] F. W. Kampschulte, *Die Universität Erfurt in ihrem Verhältnis zu dem Humanismus und der Reformation: I. Der Humanismus* (Trier, 1858), pp. 43-5.

[14] G. Ritter, *Via antiqua und via moderna auf den deutschen Universitäten des XV. Jahrhunderts* (Heidelberg, 1922).

the university prior to the reforms of 1508. The lectures offered by the faculty of arts are carefully distinguished, according to whether they are given *secundum viam Thomae or secundum viam Scoti*. The following entry is instructive:

In artibus per duas opiniones celeberrimas ordinarii et extraordinarii:
Hora sexta antemeridina:
Magister Nicolaus Amsdorff theologie baccalaureus in via Scoti.
Magister Andreas de Carlstadt theologie baccalaureus in via sancti Thomae. [15]

As well as introducing us to two names which will feature prominently in any history of the Reformation, and indicating the early start to the daily teaching programme at Wittenberg, the entry serves to illustrate the careful distinction made between the two schools of the *via antiqua* within the faculty of arts. No other *viae* are noted or referred to within the document, allowing us to conclude with a reasonable degree of certainty that, in its early years, Wittenberg was committed to the *via antiqua*.

Early in 1508 the Elector asked Scheurl, by then dean of the faculty of law, to revise the statutes of the university. Scheurl's final revisions included the establishment of new statutes, not merely for the university as a whole, but for each individual faculty. The new statutes for the faculty of arts reveal a highly significant addition. Originally, members of that faculty had been obliged to teach according to the *via Thomae* or the *via Scoti*: the new *statuta collegii artistarum* oblige members of that faculty to teach according to one of three *viae* — the *via Thomae*, the *via Scoti*, and the *via Gregorii*. [16] What are we to understand by this additional *via*? The situation has been somewhat confused by alterations made to one of the original manuscripts of the statutes, where an unknown later writer systematically substituted 'Guilelmus' for 'Gregorius' at its every occurrence, [17] thus indicating that, in

[15] W. Friedensburg, *Urkundenbuch der Universität Wittenberg, Teil I (1502-1611)* (Magdeburg, 1926), p. 15.
[16] *Statuta* cap 10; *Urkundenbuch*, p. 56: '. . . Magistri deputentur ad lecciones ordinarias per reformatores indifferenter profiteatur via Thome, Scoti, Gregorii'. Cf. *Statuta* cap. 3; *Urkundenbuch* p. 53: '. . . incipiendo scilicet ab eo qui primum in senatum est ascriptus, quicumque ille fuerit, seu religiosus seu secularis, Thome, Scotho sive Gregorio mancipatus. . .'
[17] *Urkundenbuch* p. 58, note 't'. The earlier edition of T. Muther, *Die Wittenberger Universität- und Fakultätstatuten von Jahre MDVIII* (Halle, 1867) substituted 'Guilelmo' for 'Gregorio' at cap. 3 (Muther, p. 41), and 'Guilelmi' for 'Gregorii' at cap. 10

the opinion of this unknown writer, the *via Gregorii* was none other
than the *via moderna*, the school of thought particularly associated
with William (Guilelmus) of Ockham, among others. It is somewhat
more difficult to ascertain how Scheurl intended the phrase to be interpreted: all the indications are, however, that it is indeed the *via moderna*
which is being referred to. The following considerations indicate this
conclusion:

First, it is clear that Scheurl himself knew of one major new school
of thought in early sixteenth-century Germany, and that he regarded
Jodocus Trutvetter as one of its chief exponents. This is made clear
in a letter written by him, dated 12 August 1513, in which he refers
to Trutvetter as *modernorum princeps*, using the correct term (*modernus*)
for a follower of the *via moderna*.[18] The personal presence of Trutvetter
at Wittenberg as rector of the university, and Scheurl's close friend-
ship with him, strongly suggest that this third *via* is intended to
correspond to the school of thought of which Trutvetter was a noted
representative. If the statutes are thus interpreted *e mente auctoris*, there
are excellent reasons for concluding that the *via moderna* is intended.

Secondly, if the *via moderna* is *not* intended, what is? There were
only three major schools of thought in early sixteenth-century
Germany: the *via Thomae*, the *via Scoti* and the *via moderna*. It is highly
improbable that Scheurl would have altered the statutes to include
a previously unrecognised *via* if it did not correspond to the *via* already
highly influential in the arts faculties of other universities, such as
Paris, Erfurt and Heidelberg — that is, the *via moderna*. Even if it
could be demonstrated that there was a coherent *schola Augustiniana*
at Wittenberg at this time, it is highly unlikely that Scheurl would
incorporate it into the faculty statutes in preference to the *via moderna*,
given the increasingly high standing of this *via* within the German
university context of the late fifteenth and early sixteenth centuries.
We shall return to this point in a following section.

Thirdly, the *via moderna* was known by various synonyms at the
time. Ritter has drawn our attention to the fact that the *via moderna*
was known as the *via Marsiliana* at Heidelberg, after Marsilius of

---

(Muther, p. 45). Muther's edition, however, was based on only one of the two sources
available, and his reconstruction of the statutes is therefore somewhat conjectural.
The second source lacks the substitution.

[18] *Christoph Scheurl's Briefbuch*, Vol. I, Letter No. 80, pp. 123-5. Note also the following: '...propterea quod vos qui sectam illam modernam amplectimini...'.

Inghen.[19] If the term *via Gregorii* were to have been derived in a similar manner, it would obviously have been named after Gregory of Rimini, the *antesignanus nominalistarum*, as an earlier generation of scholars dubbed him. In terms of his logic and metaphysics, the 'standard-bearer of the nominalists' was regarded by his contemporaries and successors as being among the group of personalities particularly associated with the *via moderna*.[20] Of particular interest in this respect is the fact that Marsilius of Inghen — unquestionably a *modernus* — frequently refers to Gregory as *magister noster*,[21] implying a certain degree of continuity between their teachings. Although Gregory's *theology*, particularly his doctrine of justification, is such as to set him at some distance from Ockham *cum suis*, it must be emphasised that his logic and metaphysics are thoroughly Ockhamist. As we are here dealing with the statutes of the faculty of *arts*, not those of the faculty of *theology*, it is perfectly legitimate to argue that the *metaphysical* school associated with Gregory of Rimini — that is, the *via moderna* — is here designated as the *via Gregorii*. While it is not at all clear why Scheurl should have chosen the phrase *via Gregorii* in the first place, it seems evident that the *via moderna* is intended.

There is, however, no further reference to the *via Gregorii* in subsequent archives of the university for the period 1508-19, even in the one document where such reference would be expected. On 9 April 1516 the university, finding itself in an increasingly difficult financial situation, approached Frederick the Wise over the question of placing

[19] G. Ritter, *Studien zur Spätscholastik I: Marsilius von Inghen und die okkamistische Schule in Deutschland* (Heidelberg, 1921), p. 46.

[20] The names usually associated with the *Nominalium via et modernorum doctrina* include Marsilius of Inghen, Johannes Buridan, William of Ockham, Robert Holcot, Gregory of Rimini, Pierre d'Ailly and Gabriel Biel. On this, see R. Paqué, *Das Pariser Nominalistenstatut: Zur Entstehung des Realitätsbegriffs der neuzeitlichen Naturwissenschaft* (Berlin, 1970), p. 22, nn. 13-14.

[21] Ritter, *Marsilius von Inghen* p. 11 n. 4 (*'frater magister noster'*) and p. 38, n. 3 (*'Gregorius magister noster'*). Recently, an attempt has been made to distance Gregory from the epistemology of the *via moderna*: See Jósef Worek, 'Agustinismo y aristotelismo tomista en la doctrina gnoseológica de Gregorio Ariminense', *La Ciudad de Dios* 177 (1964) pp. 435-68; 635-82. Worek argues that Gregory is essentially Augustinian in his epistemology, while conceding a strong Aristotelian influence. Worek's thesis, unfortunately, appears to be based upon a crucial textual misreading, arising from the abbreviated form of the original manuscript text. On paleographical grounds, Worek's references to *conceptum speculativum* should be replaced by *conceptum specificum* (e.g. pp. 642-3). The consequences of this alteration for Worek's thesis will be obvious.

the university's finances on a more secure footing.[22] In his rather
guarded reply to this request, Frederick asked the university to provide
him with details of the university teaching staff and their commit-
ments,[23] which the university duly supplied.[24] This latter document
is similar in many respects to Scheurl's *Rotulus* of 1507, giving details
of lecturers and lectures alike. Amsdorf, we discover, is still lecturing
at 6 a.m. *in Scoto*! There is, however, no reference whatsoever to the
via Gregorii. Three members of the faculty of arts are prepresented
as lecturing *secundum viam Thomae*, and three (including Amsdorf)
secundum viam Scoti, the remainder of the faculty not being designated
as committed to one particular *via*.[25] While it is clear that the absence
of any reference to the *via Gregorii* cannot be taken as demonstrating
that the *via* was unrepresented on the faculty, such absence certainly
indicates that the third *via* had failed to gain a status comparable to
those of the *via antiqua*. While the possibility that at least one member
of the faculty of arts taught *secundum viam Gregorii inter alia* cannot be
excluded, it appears certain that no member of that faculty taught
exclusively according to that *via*. It is therefore clear that the *via Gregorii*
— which we here regard as synonymous with the *via moderna* — does
not appear to have displaced lecturers from their traditional loyalties
within the faculty. Such displacements, it must be emphasised, were
not unknown within that faculty: Karlstadt, who in 1507 lectured
secundum viam Thomae, later became a Scotist,[26] although it may be
pointed out that, by doing so, he still remained within the *via antiqua*.
Does the absence of any reference to the *via moderna* within the faculty
of arts at this time indicate that Wittenberg was still committed to

[22] *Urkundenbuch* No. 55; pp. 74-6.
[23] *Urkundenbuch* No. 56; p. 76.
[24] *Urkundenbuch* No. 57; pp. 76-81. This document is dated 22 September 1517 —
i.e., a week before Luther posted the 95 Theses.
[25] *Urkundenbuch* No. 57; pp. 77-8.
[26] This is related by Karlstadt himself in the preface to his commentary on
Augustine's *de spiritu et litera*. In his dedicatory epistle to Staupitz, Karlstadt relates
his intellectual pilgrimage: '...quia sectam Capreolinam et Scotisticam manifesta
interpretatione successive profitebar...' (E. Kähler, *Karlstadt und Augustin: Der
Kommentar des Andreas Bodenstein von Karlstadt zu Augustins Schrift De spiritu et litera* (Halle,
1951), 3.19-21.).
On Capreolus and the neo-Thomist school, to which Karlstadt here refers, see
M. Grabmann, 'Johannes Capreolous O.P., der "Princeps Thomistarum", und seine
Stellung in der Geschichte der Thomistenschule', in *Mittelalterliches Geistesleben III*,
ed. L. Ott (München, 1956), pp. 370-410.

the *via antiqua?* This question may be answered unequivocally in the negative. The lecture list submitted to Frederick by the university indicates that at least one lecturer in the faculty of *theology* was lecturing *secundum viam modernam.* It appears that Amsdorf, in addition to lecturing within the faculty of arts, undertook some lecturing within the faculty of theology *vice* Karlstadt. In a highly significant entry, Amsdorf is represented as lecturing '*in Gabriele*', an unequivocal reference to Gabriel Biel, the then most influential theologian of the *via moderna.* [27] The observation that Amsdorf lectured *secundum viam Scoti* in the faculty of arts, and *secundum viam modernam* in the faculty of theology, suggests that the *via moderna* may have gained a greater following at Wittenberg than might at first appear to be the case.

The relevance of this discussion to our study lies in the fact that the new academic year at Wittenberg in 1508 saw Martin Luther taking up the Augustinian chair of moral philosophy within the faculty of arts. The new statutes of that faculty had then just come into force, and Luther would have been *permitted*, but not *obliged*, to teach according to the *via Gregorii.* Luther was no stranger to the *via moderna*, having been taught by Arnoldi and Trutvetter at Erfurt; furthermore, in 1507, when he began to study theology seriously, he came once more under the influence of the *via moderna*, particularly through Johannes Nathin, his regent of studies at the Erfurt priory, and to a lesser extent through the then prior at Erfurt, Johannes de Paltz. [28] As part of his theological education within the order, he would have read the seminal works of Pierre d'Ailly and William of Ockham, and particularly Gabriel Biel's *Collectorium circa quattuor sententiarum libros.* [29] Luther frequently refers to Ockham with approval, and appears to take a certain delight

---

[27] *Urkundenbuch* No. 57, p. 77.

[28] On Paltz, see B. Lohse, *Mönchtum und Reformation: Luthers Auseinandersetzung mit dem Mönchsideal des Mittelalters* (Göttingen, 1963); M. Ferdigg, 'Die vita et operibus et doctrina Joannis de Paltz O.E.S.A.', *Analecta Augustiniana* 30 (1967), pp. 210-321; 31 (1968) pp. 155-318.

[29] He would, of course, have studied Biel's *Lectura super canonem missae* while preparing for ordination. In a provocative study, Louis Saint-Blanc argued that d'Ailly mediated the influence of Gregory of Rimini, rather than William of Ockham, to the young Luther: 'La théologie de Luther et un noveau Plagiat de Pierre d'Ailly', *Positions Luthériennes* 4 (1956), pp. 61-77. This conclusion has been rejected by H. A. Oberman, who rightly points out that d'Ailly's plagiarism in respect of Gregory of Rimini's *Prologue* is not matched by a rejection of Ockham on the points involved: *The Harvest of Medieval Theology: Gabriel Biel and Late Medieval Nominalism.* (Cambridge, Mass., 1963), pp. 199-201.

in calling him *Magister meus*.[30] Furthermore, there are reasons for believing that Trutvetter was implicated in Luther's move from Erfurt to Wittenberg, thus suggesting a certain degree of affinity in outlook between the two men.

If the distinction between the *via antiqua* and the *via moderna* is held to reside in the epistemological realism of the former and nominalism of the latter, Luther appears to have remained an adherent of the *via moderna* throughout his life. In its strict epistemological sense, the term 'nominalism' refers to the epistemological contention that all things which exist are only particulars — that is, there is no genuine or objective identity in things which are not in themselves identical.[31] Contemporary sources indicate that this position was known as 'Terminism' at the beginning of the sixteenth century,[32] and there are excellent grounds for preferring this term to 'Nominalism'. In a fragment of Luther's *Table-Talk*, recorded by Lauterbach, the reformer indicated that he wished to be considered *Terminista modernus*.[33] Luther is represented as arguing that the term *humanitas* does not refer to a 'common humanity which exists in all men' (the realist position), but to all men *individually* (the terminist position). Setting aside Ockham's distinction between *terminus conceptus* and *terminus prolatus* as requiring more mental effort than is usually possible over a dinner table, Luther's discussion of the differences between the two schools is both accurate and revealing, and prompts the following question: does this evident influence of the *via moderna* extend to Luther's early *theology* as well as to his *epistemology*?

Before we pursue this question in a later section of this chapter, a third source of influence on the young Luther must be considered. In September 1505 Luther joined the Order of the Hermits of St Augustine, usually referred to simply as the 'Augustinian Order'. As part of his discipline, he was obliged to begin serious theological study under the direction of his superiors. Furthermore, during the entire

[30] e.g. WA 38.160.3; 39 I.420.27; 30 II.300.10. Luther himself appears to have regarded the terms *moderni* and *Occamistae* as essentially synonymous: cf. WA 1.509.13-14; 5.371.36-37; 6.194.37-195.5 Cf. Grane, *Contra Gabrielem*, pp. 265 and 377, *contra* K. Holl, *Gesammelte Aufsätze zur Kirchengeschichte I* (Tübingen, 1928), p. 49 n.2.
[31] D. M. Armstrong, *Nominalism and Realism: Universals and Scientific Realism* (2 vols: Cambridge, 1978) Vol. I, pp. 12-57.
[32] H. A. Oberman, *Werden und Wertung der Reformation* (Tübingen, 1977), p. 49 n. 80.
[33] WATr 5.6419. The text is reprinted by Oberman, *Werden und Wertung*, p. 425.

period covered by our study, Luther remained a member of the Augustinian Order, and the definitive statement of the *theologia crucis* of 1518 took place in a disputation conducted by Luther *before members of that same Order*. The question of what influence this Augustinian background had upon Luther's theological development is of considerable interest. The modern study of this question dates from the first years of the present century, when Carl Stange argued that the taking of monastic vows implied the recognition of the authority of the official doctors of the Order in question. In the case of the Dominicans, Stange argued, this doctor was St Thomas Aquinas; in the case of the Franciscans, Duns Scotus; in the case of the Augustinians, Giles of Rome and Gregory of Rimini.[34] Stange supported this contention by appealing to a remark due to Jerome Dungersheim: Egydius Rhomanus ordinis heremitarum s. Augustini, quem et Luther professus est. According to Stange, the sense of this statement was that Luther had vowed canonical obedience to the teaching of Giles of Rome, of the Order of the Hermits of St Augustine.[35] This thesis, however, is quite absurd. The following evidence against it may be noted:

Luther does not appear to have any knowledge of the theology of Gregory of Rimini until the time of the Leipzig disputation in 1519.[36] If Gregory of Rimini was regarded as one of two doctors, whose authority was recognised by members of the Augustinian Order, it is very difficult to explain Luther's evident ignorance concerning him.

Furthermore, there is no evidence to support Stange's general contention concerning the magisterial authority of certain doctors within the individual Orders at the time, such as the authority of St Thomas Aquinas within the Dominican, and Duns Scotus within the Franciscan, Orders. As Hermelink correctly observed, the influence of the universities could not be disregarded in this connection. At Cologne, where the *via antiqua* was dominant in university circles, the Dominicans did indeed look to St Thomas as a magisterial authority — but at Vienna and Erfurt, where the *via moderna* was in the ascendancy,

---

[34] C. Stange, 'Über Luthers Beziehungen zur Theologie seines Ordens', *Neue kirchliche Zeitschrift* 11 (1900), pp. 574-85; 'Luther über Gregor von Rimini', *Neue kirchliche Zeitschrift* 13 (1902), pp. 721-7.
[35] Stange, 'Über Luthers Beziehungen', p. 578. For the use of *professus* in this sense, see *Revised Medieval Latin Word-List*, ed. R. E. Latham (London, 1973), p. 375.
[36] The evidence for this assertion is carefully presented by Leif Grane, 'Gregor von Rimini und Luthers Leipziger Disputation', *Studia Theologica* 22 (1968), pp. 29-49.

the Dominicans regarded William of Ockham as authoritative.[37] Furthermore, as the Tridentine proceedings on justification made clear,[38] the Franciscans were frequently divided amongst themselves over who the doctor of their Order actually was, and thus tended to divide into two camps: those who regarded Duns Scotus as authoritative, and those who recognised the rival claims of St Bonaventure.

Finally, Stange's interpretation of Jerome Dungersheim's statement, upon which his theory appears to be dependent, is open to another, more plausible, translation. The relative pronoun *quem* is understood by Stange to refer to *Egydius Rhomanus*, whilst Hermelink argued that it should be regarded as referring to *ordo*.[39] If the antecedent for *quem* is taken to be *ordo*, the following sense is yielded: Luther vowed canonical obedience to the Order of the Hermits of St Augustine, to which Giles of Rome also belonged — making no reference whatsoever to Luther's having vowed to regard Giles' teaching as authoritative.

A more cautious and reliable judgement would be that Luther was influenced by the personalities and currents of thought associated with the Erfurt and Wittenberg Augustinian priories, which may — or may not! — reflect wider and more general trends within the Augustinian Order itself at the time. At the Erfurt priory, Luther's colleagues within the Order appear to have been, in general, exponents of the *via moderna*, such as Bartholomäus Arnoldi of Usingen or Johannes Nathin. At Wittenberg, however, Luther came under the influence of Johannes von Staupitz, whose associations with the *via moderna* were considerably more distant. By Luther's own testimony, the influence of Staupitz upon his own theological and spiritual development was profound,[40] even if some of Luther's statements regarding his debt to Staupitz must be regarded as being quite unrealistic.[41] It is, however, extremely

---

[37] H. Hermelink, *Die theologische Fakultät in Tübingen vor der Reformation 1477-1534* (Stuttgart, 1906), pp. 95-6.

[38] Alister E. McGrath, *Iustitia Dei: A History of the Christian Doctrine of Justification* (3 vols: Cambridge, forthcoming) Vol. II, IV. 4.

[39] Hermelink, *Die theologische Fakultät*, p. 95 n. 1: 'Der Satz des Hieronymus Dungersheim: Egydius Rhomanus ordinis heremitarum s. Augustini, quem et Luther professus est, ist von Stange falsch ausgelegt, denn das Relativepronomen geht auf ordinis.'

[40] e.g. WATr 2.526 'Staupicius hat die doctrinam angefangen.'

[41] e.g. WATr 1.173 'Ex Erasmo nihil habeo. Ich hab al mein ding von Doctor Staupitz; der hatt mir occasionem geben.' It is possible that Luther is merely referring to the fact that his theological breakthrough came about as a consequence of the

difficult to establish the precise nature of Luther's relationship to Staupitz, for the following reasons:[42]

First, Staupitz's influence upon Luther appears to have been at its greatest during the period prior to 1512, for which we have practically no literary evidence relating to *either* of them.

Secondly, there is no surviving literary evidence that Luther ever heard Staupitz lecture or preach. Whatever influence Staupitz had upon the young Luther was mediated through conversations to which no third party was witness.

Thirdly, much of our evidence concerning their mutual relationship dates from the fourth decade of the century, and derives from the potentially unreliable *Table-Talk*. There is every possibility that this evidence is distorted, either through the effects of the passage of time on Luther's memory of events or his perception of their significance, or through the inherent unreliability of those who jotted down Luther's *dicta* as they ate. The *Table-Talk* can only be allowed to confirm what has already been established by other, more reliable, sources.

Lastly, the possibility that similarities between Luther and Staupitz reflect Luther's influence upon Staupitz, rather than *vice-versa*, cannot be excluded, and is actually indicated by Staupitz's final letter to Luther.[43] This point serves to emphasise the fundamental difficulty encountered in any attempt to evaluate the nature and extent of influences upon Luther, whether they originate from Staupitz or elsewhere: agreements between Luther and others simply cannot be interpreted uncritically as influence of these latter upon Luther, without additional supporting evidence.

Despite these difficulties, it is clearly of considerable interest to attempt an analysis of the influence of the Augustinian Order upon the development of Luther's *theologia crucis*. One possibility, which we shall consider in detail in the present chapter, is that there existed a 'medieval Augustinian tradition' on justification, perhaps in the form

---

biblical studies he was forced to undertake through Staupitz's insistence that he earn his doctor's cap: cf. WATr 1.885; 4.3924; 4.4091; 5.5371.

[42] We here follow the excellent study of D. C. Steinmetz, *Luther and Staupitz: An Essay in the Intellectual Origins of the Reformation* (Durham NC, 1980), pp. 3-34. See also his earlier study, *Misericordia Dei: The Theology of Johannes von Staupitz in its Late Medieval Setting* (Leiden, 1968).

[43] This letter is reprinted in T. Kolde, *Die deutsche Augustiner-Congregation und Johannes von Staupitz* (Gotha, 1879), pp. 446-7. In this letter, Staupitz refers to himself as *discipulus tuus*.

of a 'modern Augustinian school', which Luther encountered and fashioned into his own particular theology of justification. What is more certain is that Luther would have encountered both the humanist movement and the *via moderna within the Augustinian Order itself*, although in particular forms peculiar to the Erfurt or Wittenberg priories. Before pursuing this question further, however, it is appropriate to consider each of these three elements individually.

STUDIA HUMANITATIS

Any discussion of the movement usually known as 'humanism' must be prefaced by an attempt to clarify precisely what is meant by the term. The term *Humanismus* was coined in 1808 by the German educationalist F. J. Niethammer, to express an emphasis upon the Greek and Latin classics in secondary education.[44] Niethammer felt that this emphasis was threatened by the growing demands for a more practical and scientific education for the youth of modern Germany. The word thus came to be used extensively in this loose sense to refer to the revival of classical studies associated with the Italian Renaissance,[45] and hence, by association, to other such movements in northern Europe. The most characteristic and widespread aspect of the Italian Renaissance is generally agreed to be the 'humanist' movement, characterised by the general tendency of the age to attach great importance to classical studies, and in particular, to consider classical antiquity as the common standard by which all cultural activities were to be judged, and the common norm on which they should be modelled. Renaissance humanism, it must be emphasised, was not a philosophical system, nor was it even characterised by certain philosophical tendencies: it was essentially a cultural programme, which laid particular emphasis upon a specific genre of literary studies.

The term 'humanism', as noted above, appears to be a neologism coined in the nineteenth century, and is not found in the original 'humanist' sources of the fourteenth and fifteenth centuries. The term *humanista*, however, is frequently encountered in later fifteenth-century

---

[44] W. Rüegg, *Cicero und der Humanismus* (Zürich, 1946), pp. 1-4; A. Campana, 'The Origin of the Word "Humanist"', *Journal of the Warburg and Courtauld Institutes* 9 (1946), pp. 60-73.

[45] The term 'Renaissance' itself requires definition, a task which proves exceptionally difficult: *Zu Begriff und Problem der Renaissance*, ed. A. Buck (Darmstadt, 1969).

sources. Although the opinion that the humanist movement originated outside the schools and universities of Renaissance Italy still appears to be entertained in certain quarters, it must be emphasised that there is no evidence to support this contention. All the evidence we now possess indicates close links between humanism and the Italian universities, and it is precisely this association which appears to have led to the introduction of the term *humanista*. In contemporary sources, this term is used to designate a professional teacher of the *studia humanitatis*, [46] and appears to have been coined by analogy with *jurista*, *legista*, *artista* etc., which were used to designate university teachers of the subjects in question. The *studia humanitatis* was usually regarded as embracing the disciplines of grammar, rhetoric, poetry, history and moral philosophy. [47] Further, as Kristeller has pointed out, the university chairs usually held by men associated with the humanist movement were those of grammar and rhetoric. [48] The humanist movement did not originate in the fields of philosophical or scientific studies, but in the totally distinct and quite unrelated areas of grammatical and rhetorical studies. The humanists continued the earlier medieval tradition in these latter areas, but gave the received tradition a new sense of direction by pointing to classical standards as the end to be achieved, and classical studies as the means by which this end should be pursued.

This point is of particular importance in relation to two frequently encountered interpretations of the nature and significance of the humanist movement. According to the first of these, humanism was a movement devoted to classical scholarship and philology. There is, of course, no doubt that such scholarship was a hallmark of Renaissance humanism: nevertheless, it must be pointed out that such scholarship was not regarded as an end in itself, but the means to another end. The further question of *why* the humanists wished to study the classical period cannot be evaded. It may reasonably be pointed out that the writings of the humanists which are devoted to exhibiting or encouraging written or spoken eloquence far exceed in number those devoted to classical scholarship. This interpretation cannot adequately explain the great emphasis upon the *ars dictamini* and

---

[46] Or *studia humaniora*.
[47] See Charles Trinkaus, 'A Humanist's Image of Humanism. The Inaugural Orations of Bartolommeo della Fonte', *Studies in the Renaissance* 7 (1960), pp. 90-147.
[48] P. O. Kristeller, *Renaissance Thought and Its Sources* (New York, 1979), p. 97.

ars arengandi within contemporary humanist circles. It seems that the humanists of the *Quattrocento* were first and foremost professional rhetoricians who turned to the classical world of antiquity for inspiration and instruction from acknowledged masters of the past, and were *thence* obliged to study classical literature and philology as a means to that end.[49] The rhetorical concerns of the humanists were of paramount importance to them, and their classical learning incidental to them.

The second interpretation of humanism is considerably more ambitious, and correspondingly less convincing. According to this interpretation, humanism was the new philosophy of the Renaissance, which arose in conscious opposition to the scholasticism of the previous period. Historians of western thought have often asserted that the Renaissance was essentially an age of Platonism (whether of Augustinian or neo-Platonist origins), which stood in contrast to the Aristotelianism of the earlier medieval period. This view of humanism cannot be sustained, for a number of reasons. It cannot account for the stubborn persistence of scholastic philosophy during the Italian Renaissance, such as the Aristotelianism associated with Pomponazzi and Zabarella.[50] Furthermore, most Italian humanists showed little interest in philosophical matters in the first place. Thus Cicero was studied as an orator, and not as a philosopher.[51] The wide spectrum of philosophical affinities evident within Italian humanism of the *Quattrocento* is ultimately a reflection of the inescapable fact that philosophical matters were of purely incidental interest to the humanists, whose real interests lay elsewhere.

In dealing with humanism as it influenced or affected Luther, we are primarily concerned with northern European humanism, and its influence upon the universities of Erfurt and Wittenberg.[52] The question of the origins of German humanism has been one of the most

---

[49] H. H. Gray, 'Renaissance Humanism: The Pursuit of Eloquence', in *Renaissance Essays*, ed. P. O. Kristeller and P. P. Wiener (New York, 1968), pp. 199-216. This is *not* to say that humanism made no contribution to philosophy or theology: it is simply to say that the humanists were *primarily* men of letters.

[50] See E. Garin, 'Le traduzioni umanistiche di Aristotele nel secolo XV', *Atti e Memorie dell' Accademia Fiorentini di Scienze Morali 'La Colombaria'* 16 (1951) pp. 55-104; P. O. Kristeller, 'Renaissance Aristotelianism', *Greek, Roman and Byzantine Studies* 6 (1965) pp. 157-74.

[51] R. Sabbadini, *Storia del Ciceranismo* (Turino, 1885); Rüegg, *Cicero und der Humanismus*.

[52] See Kampschulte, *Die Universität Erfurt*; Grossmann, *Humanism at Wittenberg*.

contentious issues in Renaissance scholarship,[53] far surpassing in this respect the related question of its influence upon Luther.[54] It is possible to summarise the available evidence on this former question as follows: although indigenous factors did much to promote and sustain the development of northern European humanism, it is clear that the influence of Italian humanism was of decisive importance at every stage in that development. German interest in, knowledge of, and respect for classical culture and philosophy was largely engendered by the diffusion of Italian humanism north of the Alps. It is now generally recognised that there were three main channels by which Italian humanism was thus diffused north of the Alps:[55]

First, through the exchange of persons,[56] such as northern European students who studied in Italy before returning home to take up positions of responsibility. Christoph Scheurl is an excellent example of this phenomenon, in relation to Wittenberg.

Secondly, through the foreign correspondence of the Italian humanists.[57] The great humanist concern for written, as well as spoken, eloquence, led to epistolography assuming the status of an art form, a suitable vehicle for spreading the ideals of humanism abroad. The full extent of this foreign correspondence is only now becoming apparent, as the task of cataloguing and analysing humanist manuscripts contained in libraries throughout Europe continues.

Thirdly, through manuscripts and printed books.[58] An astonishing

[53] G. Ritter, 'Die geschichtliche Bedeutung des deutschen Humanismus', *Historische Zeitschrift* 127 (1922-23), pp. 393-453; H. Entner, 'Der Begriff "Humanismus" als Problem der deutschen Literaturgeschichtsschreibung', *Klio* 40 (1962), pp. 260-70; R. Newald, *Probleme und Gestalte des deutschen Humanismus* (Berlin, 1963); L. W. Spitz, *The Religious Renaissance of the German Humanists* (Cambridge, Mass., 1963); H. Entner, 'Probleme der Forschung zum deutschen Frühhumanismus 1400-1500', *Wissenschaftliche Zeitschrift der Ernst-Moritz-Arndt-Universität Greifswald* 15 (1966), pp. 587-90.

[54] See the important study of H. Junghans, 'Der Einfluß des Humanismus auf Luthers Entwicklung bis 1518', *Luther-Jahrbuch* 37 (1970), pp. 37-101. See also M. Burchdorf, *Der Einfluß des Erfurter Humanismus auf die Entwicklung Luthers bis 1510* (Leipzig, 1928); P. Kalkoff, 'Die Stellung der deutschen Humanismus zur Reformation', *Zeitschrift für Kirchengeschichte* 46 (1927), pp. 161-231; H. Lutz, 'Humanismus und Reformation: Alte Antworten auf neue Fragen', *Wort und Wahrheit* 27 (1972), pp. 65-77.

[55] P. O. Kristeller, 'The European Diffusion of Italian Humanism', in *Renaissance Thought II: Papers on Humanism and the Arts* (New York, 1965), pp. 69-88.

[56] Kristeller, *European Diffusion*, pp. 71-6.

[57] Kristeller, *European Diffusion*, pp. 76-8.

[58] Kristeller, *European Diffusion*, pp. 78-83.

number of humanist manuscripts found their way north of the Alps, a trend which became even more marked with the introduction of printing. The related practice of dedicating manuscripts or books to wealthy northern patrons greatly assisted in this diffusion. The library at Wittenberg is known to have contained numerous humanist works of this type, frequently dedicated to Frederick the Wise himself.

It is therefore of particular interest to observe that the most influential humanist writing in circulation in northern Europe during the first decades of the sixteenth century was unquestionably the *Enchiridion Militis Christiani* of Erasmus of Rotterdam, an indigenous product of northern Europe.[59] This work stands in the sharpest of contrasts to the scholasticism of later medieval theology in general. Its thesis, like that of many of Erasmus' early writings, was that the contemporary decay of the church could be remedied by a corporate return *ad fontes* to Scripture and the early writings of the fathers. Although the *Enchiridion* appears to have received a cool response initially, it appears to have become astonishingly popular in the years after 1515. In the first twelve years of its existence (1503-14), it was reprinted only once (1509); in the following six years, it was reprinted twenty-four times, and translated into several living languages. Erasmus knew that to command the printing presses of Europe was, in effect, to command the intellectual élite of Europe — a fact which Luther would exploit in the period around the Leipzig disputation, when demand for his works became near-insatiable. The proliferation of vernacular editions of the *Enchiridion* indicates how deep a chord of sympathy was struck by Erasmian ideals at the time.

In a prefatory epistle, written in 1518 to Paul Volz, a monastic reformer, Erasmus indicated that his intention in publishing the *Enchiridion* was to provide a simple and yet learned *philosophia Christi* for the educated layman.[60] Erasmus directed most of his criticism against scholastic theologians towards the specialised theological language they used, which made their writings unintelligible to the layman. Indeed, it is a hallmark of Erasmus' criticism of scholastic theologians, that their verbal formulations are singled out as being of greater importance

---

[59] See Stupperich, 'Das Enchiridion Militis Christiani des Erasmus von Rotterdam nach seiner Entstehung, Charakter und Sinn', *Archiv für Reformationsgeschichte* 69 (1978), pp. 5-23. For Erasmus' humanist theology, see A. Renaudet, *Erasme: sa pensée religieuse et son action d'après sa correspondence* (Paris, 1926).

[60] P. S. Allen, *Opus Epistolarum Des. Erasmi Roterodami* (12 vols: Oxford, 1906-58), Vol. III, Letter No. 858.

than the actual theological substance of these formulations.

In the *Enchiridion*, Erasmus lays great emphasis upon the need to study scripture incessantly, and to read commentaries upon them written by the fathers, rather than the schoolmen, as the former were much closer in time to the sources of doctrine than the latter. In general, Erasmus' interest in scripture and the fathers reflects the general humanist desire to return to antiquity, rather than any profound scepticism concerning the orthodoxy of later medieval theology. Although his personal creed remains elusive, Erasmus' method is clear: the Christian church must return to her sources, and break free from the scholasticism which so addled her of late. With this end in mind, Erasmus himself undertook extensive editorial work, including the publication of the *Novum Instrumentum omne* in 1516. This work not only included the full Greek text of the New Testament, but also a new Latin translation which differed from the Vulgate at points of potential theological significance, along with extensive notes justifying these alterations.[61] Erasmus' editions of patristic texts were notable in two respects. The first is their accuracy and comprehensiveness, which made them indispensable to scholars. It is, however, the second respect which particularly claims our attention: the works of St Augustine were not given any pride of place among these texts. This reflects Erasmus' marked preference for Jerome, whom he regarded as the essential embodiment of the ideals of the Renaissance. In a letter of 21 May 1515 to Leo X, Erasmus declared his intention to encourage the re-emergence of Jerome as *the* Christian theologian. As early as that year, Erasmus had defined Jerome, not Augustine, as *summus theologus*.[62] Although the western theological tradition may be regarded as essentially an extended commentary upon the works of St Augustine, particularly with respect to the theological renaissance of the twelfth century, Erasmus effectively called this foundation into question with his predilection for *noster Hieronymus*. The humanist concern for accurate texts was thus not without its theological overtones.

The importance of the increasing availability of editions of the works

---

[61] For the possible theological implications of these notes, see A. E. McGrath, 'Humanist Elements in the Early Reformed Doctrine of Justification', *Archiv für Reformationsgeschichte* 73 (1982), pp. 5-20.

[62] H. A. Oberman, *Werden und Wertung der Reformation*, pp. 93-5. Oberman's criticism of Charles Béné, *Erasme et Saint Augustin ou l'influence de Saint Augustin sur le humanisme d'Erasme* (Genève, 1969) is extremely valuable: p. 95, n. 50.

of St Augustine to the development of the Reformation at Wittenberg
may be illustrated with reference to the career of Andreas Bodenstein
von Karlstadt, initially opposed to Luther, and later one of his fiercest
defenders. On 25 September 1516 Luther presided over a disputation
on the occasion of the promotion of Bartholomäus Bernhardi of
Feldkirch, in Schwabia, to the degree of Bachelor of Divinity.[63]
Normally Karlstadt, as the dean of the faculty of theology, should
have been in the chair: for reasons which we do not know, his place
was taken on this occasion by Luther. In the course of this disputation,
Luther's protégé sharply attacked the teaching that a man can fulfil the
commandments of God by his own reason and strength. This outraged
Karlstadt and Lupinus (both of whom were present), who refused
to believe that Augustine could countenance such a teaching.[64] On
13 January 1517 Karlstadt set out for Leipzig, determined to equip
himself with a copy of Augustine's works, in order to refute Luther's
claims. The point we wish to make, incidentally, is the long delay
occasioned by the absence of readily available editions of Augustine's
works, with reference to which Karlstadt could have settled the matter
on the spot. The edition which Karlstadt finally managed to purchase
(probably the Paris edition of 1515) appears to have convinced him
that Luther was indeed right: on 26 April of that year, he defended
151 Augustinian theses, including many already associated with the
name of Martin Luther. It is therefore possible to argue that the delayal
of the Reformation at Wittenberg was partly due to the absence of
readily available editions of the works of St Augustine, so that the
vera theologia could be verified as essentially Augustinian in provenance.
After his enthusiastic discovery of Augustine, Karlstadt lectured to
the university on Augustine's *de spiritu et littera*, and took particular
delight in pointing out how students now had access to the bible and
editions of the fathers.

I congratulate you, fellow-students, that the truth of sacred letters once more
shines in our university . . . Rejoice that you may hear, learn and understand
the true bible from doctors of the church and from the bible itself, not from
the schoolmen or from vanities.[65]

[63] As Luther made clear, these theses represented his own position: WABr 1.65.18.
[64] WABr 1.65.29-66.1 'At illos implacabiliter offendit, praecipue Doctorem
Carlstadium, quod haec sciens negare audeam.' It was at this dispute that Luther
further outraged Karlstadt by denying that the treatise *de vera et falsa poenitentia* was
written by Augustine: WABr 1.65.24-5.
[65] Kähler, *Karlstadt und Augustin*, 9.29-10.5.

Although Karlstadt may be excused for failing to mention it, we must emphasise that the accessibility of the printed text of the Bible and the fathers was almost totally due to the efforts of the humanists. Similarly, the revival in the study of biblical languages, of decisive importance to the Reformation, was nearly totally due to the activity of humanist scholars.

The revival of biblical languages, Hebrew and Greek, in Germany is particularly associated with Johannes Reuchlin (1455-1522). Although his epitaph exaggerates somewhat when it credits him with having rescued the Hebrew and Greek languages from oblivion, [66] there is no doubt that Reuchlin did much to pave the way for the direct use of the Hebrew text of the Old Testament in biblical exegesis. It may also be noted in passing that Reuchlin illustrates the darker side of humanism: although the movement is usually regarded as encapsulating the higher ideals of humanity, its darker and irrational side is well illustrated by Reuchlin's obsession with the *cabala*, although it is probably best illustrated by the widespread fascination occasioned by the Faust legend. [67] The first guide to the Hebrew language to be published in northern Europe was Konrad Pellikan's *de modo legendi et intelligendi Hebraeum*, published at Strassburg in 1504, although written several years earlier. This work, a mere twenty pages in length, consisted of a grammar, a selection of passages for reading and translation, and a brief lexicon. [68] It was superseded by Reuchlin's *de rudimentis Hebraicis*, published in 1506, which was later supplemented by his edition of the seven penitential psalms, published in 1512. The humanist movement thus provided Luther with the tools which he required for his biblical studies, and he appears to have made the most of them.

[66] *Johannes Reuchlins Briefwechsel*, ed. L. Geiger (Stuttgart, 1875), p. 363: 'Musas elegantores . . . reştituit ac hebraicam simul et grecam linguam ab inheritu reduxit . . .' For knowledge of Hebrew in Germany at the time, see L. Geiger, *Das Studium der hebräischen Sprache in Deutschland* (Breslau, 1870); G. Bauch, 'Die Einführung des Hebräischen in Wittenberg mit Berücksichtigung der Vorgeschichte des Studiums der Sprache in Deutschland', *Monatschrift für Geschichte und Wissenschaft des Judentums* 48 (1904), pp. 22-32; 77-86; 145-60; 214-23; 283-99; 328-40; 461-90. On Greek, see G. Bauch, 'Die Anfänge des Studiums der griechische Sprache und Literatur in Norddeutschland', *Gesellschaft für deutsche Erziehungs- und Schulgeschichte* 6 (1896), pp. 47-98; 163-93.

[67] D. Harmening, 'Faust und die Renaissance-Magie: Zum ältesten Faust-Zeugnis (Johannes Trithemius an Johannes Virdung, 1507)', *Archiv für Kulturgeschichte* 55 (1973), pp. 56-79.

[68] S. Raeder, *Die Benutzung des masoretischen Textes bei Luther in der Zeit zwischen der ersten und zweiten Psalmenvorlesung* (Tübingen, 1967), pp. 2-3.

Luther's knowledge and use of the Hebrew language over the period
1509-19 has been the subject of intense scrutiny. [69] Although Luther
appears to have had initial difficulties with the language, these do
not appear to have prevented him from using the Hebrew text of the
Old Testament with increasing facility and skill, culminating in his
second course of lectures on the Psalter. Luther had purchased
Reuchlin's *de rudimentis* at Erfurt shortly before moving to Wittenberg
for the first time, and references to this work can be detected in the
Randbemerkungen of 1509-10. On the basis of an exhaustive analysis
of this work, Raeder concluded that Luther must have worked his
way through the vast bulk of Reuchlin's text. [70] It is also clear that
Luther made extensive use of Lefèvre d'Etaples' *Psalterium Quincuplex*
of 1509 during the course of the *Dictata super Psalterium* of 1513-15. [71]
The theological significance of a good knowledge of Hebrew in relation
to the doctrine of justification will be considered further in chapter
4. It may, however, be noted that Luther did not appear to possess
such a knowledge as he began to expound the Psalter for the first time
in 1513. By the time of the Romans lectures of 1515-16, it is clear
that his knowledge of Hebrew has improved, and he occasionally shows
first-hand knowledge of the original Hebrew texts of the Old Testament
in connection with passages of theological significance — for example,
Romans 4.18. [72] It is probably during the course of these lectures that
we find Luther most dependent upon humanist biblical scholarship
and philology: not only is he dependent upon humanist learning for
his knowledge of the Hebrew text of the Old Testament, but his
knowledge of the Greek text of the New Testament derives from
Lefèvre d'Etaples' *Epistola Divi Pauli* of 1512, which contained sections
of the Greek text, and Erasmus' *Novum Instrumentum omne* of 1516,
once this appeared. [73] Luther's use of the biblical languages, especially
Hebrew, is generally considered to be best illustrated from the Hebrews
lectures of Easter 1517 — Easter 1518. [74]

By late 1518, the influence of humanism at Wittenberg was probably

---

[69] S. Raeder, *Das Hebräische bei Luther untersucht bis zum Ende der ersten Psalmenvorlesung*
(Tübingen, 1961); idem., *Die Benutzung des masoretischen Textes*; idem., *Grammatica
Theologica: Studien zu Luthers Operationes in Psalmos* (Tübingen, 1977).
[70] Raeder, *Das Hebräische bei Luther*, pp. 62-3. Raeder further observes that Luther
does not appear to have understood Reuchlin correctly at every point: pp. 59-60.
[71] Raeder, *Das Hebräische bei Luther*, pp. 3-4.
[72] Raeder, *Die Benutzung des masoretischen Textes*, pp. 12-19.
[73] Raeder, *Die Benutzung des masoretischen Textes*, pp. 19-22.
[74] Raeder, *Die Benutzung des masoretischen Textes*, pp. 67-77.

at its peak. Earlier, Luther had written to Johannes Lang in near ecstasy over the changes which he had seen taking place at Wittenberg:

Our theology and St Augustine prosper and, by the work of God, reign in our university. Aristotle is in continual decline, perhaps to his future permanent ruin. Lectures on the *Sentences* are treated with disdain, and nobody can hope for an audience unless he puts forward this theology, that is, the bible or St Augustine, or some other doctor of authority in the church. [75]

Further developments took place in March 1518. When Karlstadt was won over to the *theologia nova* in early 1517, his influence and status were such that the entire theology faculty at Wittenberg was now committed to the programme of theological reform. The priorities of the *vera theologia* were such that adjustments were required to the university curriculum to accommodate this new emphasis upon the bible and St Augustine. In March 1518, a conference took place at Karlstadt's lodgings at which the nature and extent of these adjustments were decided. [76] Luther reported these alterations as including the introduction of lectures on Greek and Hebrew, and the abandonment of lectures on Petrus Hispanicus and Aristotle. [77] In essence, these reforms were humanist in nature, similar to those already being put into effect at other European universities at the time, such as Vienna. In terms of their *motivation*, however, the reforms reflected the theological basis of the *vera theologia* — the bible and the fathers, especially St Augustine. There were, of course, those who saw in the reforms within the theological faculty at Wittenberg the spirit of the Italian Renaissance, and were thus attracted there to teach. Their experience serves to illustrate that the *studia humanitatis* within that faculty was merely a means for the promotion of the *vera theologia*, rather than an end in itself. This point is well demonstrated by the brief appearance of Johannes Böschenstein at Wittenberg in November 1518. Contemporary sources indicate that Böschenstein was a typical Renaissance man of letters, who saw the Hebrew language as an end in itself, and quite unsympathetic towards those who saw Hebrew as nothing more than a tool for the study of the scriptures. 'As if we wanted to turn out orators for the Jews!': Luther's sarcastic comment concerning Böschenstein's motives for teaching

[75] WABr 1.99.8-13.
[76] WABr 1.153.3-154.1.
[77] WABr 1.155.41-5.

Hebrew gives us an invaluable insight into the real reasons for the new emphasis on the *studia humanitatis* at Wittenberg. [78]

By the time of the Leipzig disputation of 1519, it was clear that there were considerable affinities between Luther and the humanist movement, although these affinities often masked profound differences between them. [79] The following points of affinity may be noted:

Firstly, their mutual rejection of scholasticism. For the humanists, the scholastic theologians had made theology unintelligible by their use of arcane language and terms: a *simpler* theology was required. For Luther, the scholastics were perfectly intelligible, but their theology was unacceptable: a *reformation of doctrine* was required.

Secondly, their mutual desire to return to the early fathers of the church. Melanchthon saw the Leipzig disputation as a conflict between the early church and Aristotle, [80] a view which appears to have been common in humanist circles. For the humanists, the early fathers represented a simple, comprehensible form of Christianity, made respectable by their antiquity, which avoided the pointless speculation and unintelligible Latin of the scholastics. For Luther, the fathers stood for a form of Christianity which had since become corrupted by the accretions and distortions of the medieval period. If the church was to be reformed, a purer form of doctrine was required, and this was to be found in the writings of the fathers. An evident point of difference between the humanists, especially Erasmus, and Luther relates to the perceived status of Augustine. For the humanists in general, the early fathers represented a corporate understanding of the Christian faith: as the authority of the fathers rested in their *antiquity*, none could be

---

[78] WABr 1.288.34. See WABr 1.298 n. 3 for useful background material. The fate of Mosellanus in this respect is also instructive: U. M. Kremer, 'Mosellanus: Humanist zwischen Kirche und Reformation', *Archiv für Reformationsgeschichte* 73 (1982), pp. 20-34.

[79] See B. Moeller, 'Die deutschen Humanisten und die Anfänge der Reformation', *Zeitschrift für Kirchengeschichte* 70 (1959), pp. 46-61. The opinion that the humanists would have nothing to do with Luther until after the Leipzig Disputation of 1519 cannot be sustained. In 1518 Bucer remarked that Luther and Erasmus were in agreement on everything, except that Luther made explicit what Erasmus merely hinted at: *Die Reformation in Augenzeugenberichten*, ed. H. Junghans (Düsseldorf, 1967), pp. 214-38, especially pp. 214-5. Later, Bucer appears to have become aware of the divergence of opinion between Luther and Erasmus: F. Krüger, *Bucer und Erasmus: Eine Untersuchung zum Einfluß des Erasmus auf die Theologie Martin Bucers* (Wiesbaden, 1970). This awareness thus passes into his doctrine of justification, which is more moralist and pietist in character than Luther's: McGrath, *Humanist Elements*, pp. 10-14.

[80] Moeller, *Die deutschen Humanisten*, p. 53.

regarded as pre-eminent, although it is necessary to note Erasmus' predilection for Jerome as *summus theologus* in this respect. The Wittenberg theology faculty as a whole regarded Augustine as pre-eminent among the fathers, on the basis of the *nature of his theology*, which they regarded, at least initially, as the most faithful to scripture. The thoroughly Augustinian cast of the *vera theologia* at Wittenberg is one of its most characteristic features in the years 1517-19.

Thirdly, their mutual desire to return to Holy Scripture. The humanists respected scripture on account of its simplicity and antiquity, and interpreted the phrase *sola scriptura* in an inclusive sense, meaning 'not without scripture', thus permitting other sources of antiquity to be regarded as authoritative. For Luther, scripture was to be respected because through it the theologian had access to the Word of God: the phrase *sola scriptura* was to be interpreted in an exclusive sense, meaning 'through scripture, and *through scripture alone*'.[81]

Fourthly, their mutual interest in rhetoric. This affinity has only been fully recognised recently.[82] The great humanist emphasis upon eloquence was carried over into the Reformation, through the medium of preaching. The new emphasis upon the preaching of the Word of God, which is characteristic of the Reformation as a whole, led to intense interest on the part of the Reformers in the rhetorical arts. Whereas the humanists regarded eloquence, whether written or spoken, as an end in itself, the Reformers saw such eloquence as an invaluable means to an even greater end — the proclamation of the Word of God.[83] Throughout his life, Luther maintained a highly positive and appreciative attitude to rhetoric,[84] which he frequently contrasted with the dull

[81] Moeller, *Die deutschen Humanisten*, p. 54. It may be pointed out that it is Karlstadt, rather than Luther, who is associated with the enunciation of the *sola scriptura* principle, which later became the programmatic basis of the Zürich Reformation: see B. Moeller, 'Zwinglis Disputationen. Studien zu den Anfängen der Kirchenbildung und des Synodalwesens im Protestantismus', *Zeitschrift der Savigny-Stiftung für Rechtsgeschichte*, Kan. Abt. 56 (1970), pp. 275-324; 60 (1974), pp. 213-364. See further Moeller's later study, 'Die Ursprünge der reformierten Kirche', *Theologische Literaturzeitung* 100 (1975), pp. 642-53.

[82] W. J. Bouwsma, 'Renaissance and Reformation: An Essay in their Affinities and Connections', in *Luther and the Dawn of the Modern Era. Papers for the Fourth International Congress for Luther Research*, ed. H. A. Oberman (Leiden, 1974), pp. 127-49.

[83] G. W. Locher, 'Praedicatio verbi Dei est verbum Dei: Heinrich Bullinger zwischen Luther und Zwingli: Ein Beitrag zu seiner Theologie', *Zwingliana* 10 (1954), pp. 47-57, for a useful introduction.

[84] L. W. Spitz, 'Headwaters of the Reformation: *Studia Humanitatis, Luther Senior et Initia Reformationis*', in *Luther and the Dawn of the Modern Era*, pp. 89-116, especially pp. 104-6.

dialectic of scholasticism. If the method of dialectic lay at the heart of later medieval theology, that of rhetoric lay close to the heart of the new theology which was being forged at Wittenberg during the second decade of the sixteenth century.

It is clear that the influence of the humanist movement upon the theological development of the Reformation in general, and of the young Luther in particular, was considerable.[85] In the case of Luther, however, this influence relates primarily to the means by which this development took place, rather than to the substance of that development. Without access to the biblical texts in their original languages, without a working knowledge of those languages, and without access to the works of St Augustine, the Reformation could never have begun; without the support of the humanists during the fateful period after the Leipzig disputation, the Reformation could never have survived its first years; without attracting leading humanists, such as Melanchthon, Bucer and Calvin, and without the rhetorical skills to proclaim the new theology, the Reformation could never have been perpetuated. In all these respects, the Reformation owed its very existence to the humanist movement. Furthermore, the influence of humanism upon the social and political theology of the churches of the Reformation is universally recognised to be considerable. Nevertheless, the fact remains that Luther exploited the humanist movement for his own ends. While other reformers, such as Melanchthon, maintained cordial links with the movement, Luther distanced himself from it, until he finally broke what links he still had with the movement by publicly criticising Erasmus in the 1525 treatise *de servo arbitrio*.[86] When considered in relation to its *substance* over the period 1517-19, the *vera theologia* can be seen to have owed little to humanism; it is therefore somewhat ironical that the Reformation in general, and Luther's theological development in particular, owed so much to *studia humanitatis*.

The relationship between the *initia Lutheri theologiae* and the *initia Reformationis* is notoriously complex, so that what may be true of

---

[85] Moeller, *Die deutschen Humanisten*, p. 59: 'Ohne Humanismus, keine Reformation.'
[86] For two classic studies, see K. Zickendraht, *Der Streit zwischen Erasmus und Luther über die Willensfreiheit* (Leipzig, 1909); H. Humbertclaude, *Erasme et Luther: leur polémique sur le libre arbitre* (Paris, 1909). For the more positive attitude towards humanism adopted by most Protestants, see H. Liebing, 'Die Ausgänge des Europäischen Humanismus', in *Geist und Geschichte der Reformation*, eds H. Liebing and K. Scholder (Berlin, 1966) pp. 357-76.

Luther's *personal* theological development is not necessarily true of that of the Reformation as a whole. Nevertheless, it seems to us that the humanist movement can only be seen as the *essential catalyst* for the Reformation, rather than its *cause*. For Luther, the provision of this catalyst was nothing less than providential: God, in his wisdom and mercy, had provided *die Sprachen* through which the Reformation might come about. Nevertheless, the fact remains that, in the formative period under consideration, both in *substance* and in *motivation*, Luther's theology cannot conceivably be regarded as humanist: indeed, there are all too many points, such as the doctrine of the *servum arbitrium*, at which Luther's theology must be regarded as diametrically opposed to the spirit of the humanist movement — thus occasioning considerable embarrassment to the more humanist members of the evangelical faction, such as Philip Melanchthon. Although the tension between the *vera theologia* and humanism would not become evident until the third decade of the sixteenth century, it was already latent within the nature of the young Luther's theological development, both in regard to its substance (for example, the nature of his early difficulties concerning the concept of the 'righteousness of God', to be discussed in a later chapter), and its sources (for example, the tension over the status of St Augustine and Holy Scripture). If the *initia Reformationis* are seen to lie in the theological development of the young Luther over the period 1509-19, we are forced to the following conclusion: *humanism did not father the Reformation — it merely acted as midwife at its birth*. Nevertheless, the precise causal relationship between the *initia theologiae Lutheri* and the *initia Reformationis* is now appreciated to be of such complexity that the riddle of the nature and extent of humanist influence upon the origins of the Reformation may ultimately have to be declared insoluble.

VIA MODERNA

As we have already noted, a sharp distinction began to develop during the later part of the fourteenth century between the realist epistemology of the *via antiqua* and the nominalist epistemology of the *via moderna*. [87] Although it is correct to refer to the *via moderna* as 'nominalist' in relation

[87] Ritter, *Via Antiqua und Via Moderna*, p. 17.

to its epistemology, [88], the term 'nominalist' eventually came to acquire overtones which far exceeded the somewhat restricted sphere of epistemology. By the fourth decade of the present century, the term 'nominalist' was not so much *descriptive* as *perjorative*. In its descriptive sense, the term referred to the denial of the existence of extra-mental universals (that is, 'Terminism'); in its perjorative sense, the term referred to a variety of undesirable characteristics which were held to be associated with this denial, including (1) atomism, individualism, or particularism; (2) excessive emphasis upon the omnipotence of God; (3) voluntarism; (4) scepticism; (f) fideism. [89] A number of seminal studies since then have made this understanding of 'nominalism' quite untenable. [90] The publication of an ever-increasing number of treatises written by *moderni* has made it abundantly clear that a nominalist epistemology (that is, Terminism) can be associated with any one of an astonishing variety of theological positions, ranging from the ferocious anti-Pelagianism of Gregory of Rimini[91] and Hugolino of Orvieto[92] to the more optimistic estimation of man associated with Robert Holcot[93] and Gabriel Biel. [94] Of particular importance in the current rejection of the term 'nominalism' to refer to the theology of the *via moderna* was the

[88] There is, in fact, a problem associated with William of Ockham's 'nominalism', which is probably better designated as 'conceptual realism': Gordon Leff, *William of Ockham: The Metamorphosis of Scholastic Discourse* (Manchester, 1977), pp. 78-237. For the development of 'Terminism' in the earlier medieval period, see L. M. de Rijk, *Logica Modernorum: A Contribution to the History of Early Terminist Logic* (2 vols: Assen, 1962-7).

[89] See C. Michalski, 'Les courants philosophiques à Oxford et à Paris pendant le XIVe siècle', *Bulletin Internationale de l'Academie Polonaise des Sciences et des Lettres*, classe d'histoire et de philosophie 1919-1920 (Cracow, 1922), pp. 59-88. For further references see W. J. Courtenay, 'Nominalism and Late Medieval Religion', in *The Pursuit of Holiness in Late Medieval and Renaissance Religion* ed. C. Trinkaus and H. A. Oberman (Leiden, 1974), pp. 26-59. For more recent presentations of the traditional, and now discredited, interpretation, see: R. M. Torelló, 'El Ockhamismo y la decadencia escolástica en el siglo XIV', *Pensamiento* 9 (1953), pp. 199-228; 11 (1955) pp. 171-88; 259-83; J. R. Gironella, 'Para la historia del nominalismo y de la reacción antinominalista de Suárez', *Pensamiento* 17 (1961), pp. 279-310.

[90] For a list, see W, J. Courtenay, 'Nominalism and Late Medieval Thought: A Bibliographical Essay', *Theological Studies* 33 (1972), pp. 716-34.

[91] M. Schüler, *Prädestination, Sünde und Freiheit bei Gregor von Rimini* (Stuttgart, 1934).

[92] A. Zumkeller, 'Hugolino von Orvieto über Prädestination, Sünde und Verdienst', *Augustiniana* 4 (1954), pp. 109-56; 5 (1955) pp. 5-51.

[93] P. Molteni, *Roberto Holcot: Dottrina della grazia e della giustificazione* (Pinerola, 1968).

[94] W. Ernst, *Gott und Mensch am Vorabend der Reformation. Eine Untersuchung zur Moralphilosophie und -theologie bei Gabriel Biel* (Leipzig, 1972).

seminal essay of Erich Hochstetter.[95] In this essay, Hochstetter pointed out that the term 'nominalist' was applied to the followers of William of Ockham *by their opponents*, and was therefore suspect. Since then, the phrase *via moderna* has gained general acceptance as the most suitable designation for the movement in question, and this designation will therefore be employed throughout the present study.

During the past twenty years, considerable attention has been paid to the theological framework within which the theologians of the *via moderna* operated, especially their use of the dialectic between the two powers of God and the concept of covenantal causality, which is so characteristic a feature of their doctrines of justification. In the present section, we propose to delineate the main features of the doctrines of justification associated with the *via moderna*, and consider the intensely debated question of whether such doctrines can be said to be 'Pelagian'.

The most convenient point from which to begin our discussion of such doctrines of justification is the use made by the *moderni* of the dialectic between the two powers of God. This has been seriously misunderstood in the past,[96] and the present perpetuation of such misunderstandings is a serious obstacle to the correct appreciation of the nature of the theology of the *via moderna*. The distinction between the absolute and ordained powers of God had its origins in early scholasticism, with Peter Damien and Anselm of Canterbury, although it would not be used extensively until the fourteenth century. St Thomas Aquinas points out that while God is omnipotent, there are many things which he is perfectly capable of doing, but which he *elects* not to do. From an initial set of possibilities, limited only by the condition that the outcome must not involve contradiction, God selected a subset which he willed to actualise. St Thomas emphasised that God could have selected a different set of possibilities for actualisation had he desired to do so: however, having now willed to actualise a particular subset of possibilities, God abides by his decision, so that the remaining subset of unwilled possibilities must be set aside as only hypothetically possible.[97] God's absolute power (*potentia absoluta*) refers to the initial set of possibilities open to God, while

[95] E. Hochstetter, 'Nominalismus?', *Franciscan Studies* 9 (1949), pp. 370-403.
[96] e.g. G. M. Manser, 'Drei Zweifler auf dem Kausalitätsprinzip im XIV Jahrhundert', *Jahrbuch für Philosophie und spekulative Theologie* 27 (1912), pp. 291-305. A more recent misunderstanding is due to George Lindbeck, 'Nominalism and the Problem of Meaning as illustrated by Pierre d'Ailly on Predestination and Justification', *Harvard Theological Review* 52 (1959), pp. 43-60.
[97] *Summa Theologiae* 1a q.25 a.5 c.

his ordained power (*potentia ordinata*) refers to the subset of possibilities which God determined to actualise. Thus God cannot be said to act out of absolute necessity (*necessitas consequentis*), in that he was free to select any possibilities he cared to for actualisation, subject to the sole condition of non-contradiction (that is, God is unable to construct a triangle with four sides). Nevertheless, having selected which possibilities to actualise, God imposes upon himself a certain degree of restriction, in that he has freely chosen to be faithful to a certain ordering of his creation. The significance of the distinction between the two powers of God lies in the concept of necessity involved: how can God be said to act *reliably*, without simultaneously asserting that he acts of *necessity*? The dialectic between the two powers of God allowed the reliability of God's action to be upheld, without implying that God acts of necessity. God is understood to have imposed upon himself, by a free and uncoerced primordial decision, a certain self-limitation, in that he is faithful to the order which he himself has established. In that God is faithful to this ordained order, he may be said to be reliable; in that this order is itself the contingent consequence of a free decision of God, God cannot be said to act of absolute necessity, but merely by a conditional necessity (*necessitas coactionis* or *necessitas consequentiae*).

The theologians of the *via moderna* used the dialectic between the two powers of God for several purposes, including the defence of the divine freedom in the face of philosophical determinisms, similar to the Averroism against which the device was originally employed.[98] Of these, one of the most important is the attack on the necessity of an infused habit of grace in justification. Although such theologians, particularly Pierre d'Ailly, are often accused of using the dialectic between the two powers of God to undermine the normal channels of justification, it is clear that this judgement cannot be sustained.[99] While the *moderni* upheld the *de facto* necessity of such habits in justification, they drew attention to the contingent nature of this necessity. Within the framework of God's absolute power, they emphasised that God was at liberty to justify man by other means than an infused habit of grace. Although the conditional or *de facto* necessity of such habits in justification was not called into question, it was stressed that the implication of such habits in justification

---

[98] M. Grabmann, *Der lateinische Averroismus des 13. Jahrhunderts und seine Stellung zur christlichen Weltanschauung* (München, 1931). The older study of E. Renan, *Averroès et l'Averroisme* (Paris, 1852), is still useful here.

[99] e.g. W. J. Courtenay, 'Covenant and Causality in Pierre d'Ailly', *Speculum* 46 (1971), pp. 94-119.

was the result of the divine decision that they should be thus implicated, rather than because of any natural causal relationship between such habits and justification. Thus while Peter Aureole argued that there was a necessary connection between justification and the possession of a created habit of grace 'by the very nature of things' (*ex natura rei*),[100] Ockham argued that no such *natural* connection existed: if the two were related causally, it was because God had ordained that they should be thus related. While Aureole's concept of causality was *ontological*, Ockham's was *covenantal*, and this distinction is of central importance to the theologies of justification associated with the *moderni*. We shall return to this point shortly.

Ockham's use of the dialectic between the two powers of God to demonstrate the radical contingency of created habits in the ordained means of divine acceptation, while not questioning their *de facto* necessity, was misunderstood at a very early stage. In 1326 a commission of six theologians censured 51 articles culled from Ockham's works. The verdict of this commission has had a considerable effect on modern estimations of Ockham, and the charges of Pelagianism still pressed against him ultimately derive from this fourteenth-century investigation. It has often been suspected that Ockham's condemnation was the consequence of personal malice;[101] it is obvious, however, that the condemnation is the consequence of theological incompetence. This conclusion may be drawn on the basis of the report of the *magistri* involved, which was recently discovered in MS Vat. lat. 3075.[102] The four propositions which particularly concern us are those which are denounced as 'Pelagian or worse':[103]

(1) *De potentia sua absoluta* God may accept as meritorious man's good use of his will by his purely natural powers.

---

[100] See P. Vignaux, *Justification et prédestination au XIVe siècle* (Paris, 1934), pp. 43-95.
[101] C. K. Brampton, 'Personalities at the Process against Ockham at Avignon 1324-26', *Franciscan Studies* 25 (1966) pp. 4-25.
[102] A. Pelzer, 'Les 51 articles de Guillaume Occam censurés en Avignon en 1326', *Revue d'Histoire Ecclesiastique* 18 (1922), pp. 240-70. For a second version of this list, differing in numeration as well as content, see J. Koch, 'Neue Aktenstücke zu dem gegen Wilhelm Ockham in Avignon geführten Prozess', *Recherches de théologie ancienne et médiévale* 7 (1935), pp. 353-80; 8 (1936) pp. 79-93, 168-97.
[103] Pelzer, *Les 51 articles*, p. 251: 'Dicimus quod iste longus processus in predicto articulo contentus est erroneus et sapit Pelagianam vel peius.' Cf. Ockham, *In I Sent.* dist. xvii q.2.

(2) *De potentia absoluta* God may accept a man as worthy of eternal life without his possessing a habit of grace, or damn him without his having sinned.

(3) The third proposition states the same position.

(4) *De potentia absoluta* God can remit sin without the infusion of grace.

It is perfectly clear that these propositions are to be understood as hypothetical possibilities *de potentia Dei absoluta*, and do not pertain *de facto*. However, the *magistri* declined to draw this conclusion, regarding the addition of the phrase '*de potentia Dei absoluta*' as quite irrelevant to the substance of the propositions.[104] It is manifestly obvious that this is incorrect. Ockham merely exploits the tension between what is *de facto* and what might have been *de possibili* to demonstrate the radical contingency of the created order. Ockham insists that there is only one power in God[105] — in other words, that God has only one course of action open to him now, whatever the initial possibilities may have been. The charges of Pelagianism against him can only be sustained if, and only if, it can be shown that the possibilities noted above are *present* possibilities — that is, possibilities which pertain *de potentia ordinata*. The inclusion of the phrase '*de potentia absoluta*' in each of the above propositions refers to *discarded hypothetical possibilities*. It is simply impossible to concur with the verdict of the six *magistri*: their condemnation of Ockham, however, demonstrates the caution which must be exercised in discussing the theologies of justification associated with the *via moderna*, if they are to be understood correctly.

Luther himself does not use the dialectic between the two powers of God to any significant extent, although, as we shall argue in the following chapter, he incorporates several consequences of its application into his early theology of justification. One such consequence is the notion of a covenant (*pactum* or *testamentum*) between God and man, on the basis of which justification takes place.

Out of the initial set of possibilities open to him, God willed to enter into a 'covenant' or 'contract' with man, and it is this *pactum* which constitutes the fulcrum about which the doctrines of justification

---

[104] Pelzer, *Les 51 articles*, p. 252: 'Nec excusari per illam addicionem, quam ponit: de potentia absoluta, quia argumentum suum eque procedit absque illa condicione sicut cum illa. Propositio autem quam assumit, est heretica et conclusio heretica.'
[105] *Quodl.* VI q. 1. Cf. K. Bannach, *Die Lehre von der doppelten Machts Gottes bei Wilhelm von Ockham* (Wiesbaden, 1975).

associated with the *via moderna* turn. [106] As noted above, the theologians of the *via moderna* adopted a concept of causality which is *covenantal*, rather than *ontological*. According to this understanding of causality, one entity is related to another on the basis of an agreement between contracting parties, rather than on the basis of the entities themselves. Ockham illustrates this type of causality with reference to a small lead coin (*denarium plumbeum*). [107] Consider two different types of economic systems. In the one, gold is used as the coinage, having a considerable inherent value in its own right, by its very nature, on the basis of which it is accepted and recognised as currency. In other, small lead coins are used, having negligible inherent value. Nevertheless, the king of the country in question, who issued these coins in the first place, has promised to redeem these coins at a much greater value, fixed by him, and on the basis of which they are accepted as currency *with this greater ascribed value*. A similar situation exists today, where paper money, with negligible inherent value, has a much greater ascribed value on account of the covenant made by the issuing agency (such as a bank) to pay the bearer a certain sum in gold on demand. The two types of causality in question may therefore be illustrated with reference to these analogies as follows. The first corresponds to *ontological* causality, where gold coins purchase goods on account of their very nature, gold being inherently precious. The second corresponds to *covenantal* causality, in that the lead coins, which are inherently valueless, have a much greater value conferred upon them on account of the promise or covenant made by the king. The correlation between the coin and its value within the economic system thus rests upon the ordination of the king, which imposes a much greater ascribed value (*valor impositus*) upon the inherently worthless coin.

It is this principle which governs the thinking of the theologians of the *via moderna* on the causality of justification. Just as a major

---

[106] Heiko A. Oberman, 'Wir sind pettler. Hoc est verum. Bund und Gnade in der Theologie des Mittelalters und Reformation', *Zeitschrift für Kirchengeschichte* 78 (1967), pp. 232-52; M. Greschat, 'Der Bundesgedanke in der Theologie des späten Mittelalters', *Zeitschrift für Kirchengeschichte* 81 (1970), pp. 44-63; Courtenay, *Covenant and Causality*; B. Hamm, *Promissio, pactum, ordinatio: Freiheit und Selbstbindung Gottes in der scholastischen Gnadenlehre* (Tübingen, 1977) pp. 355-90.

[107] Ockham, *In IV Sent*. q.1 C:'... sicut si rex ordinaret quod quicumque acciperet denarium plumbeum haberet certum donum...' For the background to this analogy, see W. J. Courtenay, 'The King and the Leaden Coin: The Economic Background of "sine qua non" Causality', *Traditio* 28 (1972), pp. 185-209.

discrepancy can arise between the inherent value of a coin (*bonitas intrinseca*) and its ascribed value (*valor impositus*) within an economic system, given a firm and binding contract on the part of the issuing agency (the king or a bank), so a similar discrepancy can arise between the inherent moral value of human acts and their meritorious value, within the terms of the *pactum* between God and man. The *moderni* were able to maintain that (1) human moral acts were inherently of little value, and (2) that they were capable of meriting justification *de congruo*, by using the device of the covenant between God and man, by virtue of which God had ordained to accept man's inherently worthless moral actions as the means of his justification. Thus the *moderni* were able to avoid exalting human works to Pelagian proportions (by insisting that their inherent value was negligible), while still allowing them to bring about man's justification (by insisting that their ascribed value, under the terms of the *pactum*, was infinitely greater).

The principle of covenantal causality can be seen clearly in the writings of such *moderni* as Ockham,[108] Robert Holcot,[109] Marsilius of Inghen,[110] Pierre d'Ailly[111] and Gabriel Biel.[112] The particular significance of the *pactum* to our study lies in relation to the interpretation of the celebrated medieval axiom, *facienti quod in se est, Deus non denegat gratiam* — 'God does not deny grace to the man who does his best.' For the *moderni*, this meant that God had ordained that his gift of justifying grace was conditional upon a particular response on man's part — and once that condition was met, the bestowal of grace followed as a matter of necessity (although it is a *conditional*, not an *absolute*, necessity). As we shall show in the following chapter, the leading themes of this federal theology found their way into the young Luther's discussion of what man must do if he is to be justified before God.

A point which arises from this relates to the Christology of the *via moderna*. The theology of the *via moderna* is most emphatically *not*

---

[108] *In III Sent.* q. 8 S: 'Deus ordinavit, quod aliquando aliquis diligit eum super omnia, quod tunc mereatur habere caritatem infusam et deus sibi infundit.'

[109] *(Lecciones) Super Libros Sapientiae* (Hagenau, 1494), lect. 145B: 'Sed statuta lege necessario dat gratiam necessitate consequentiae.' See H. A. Oberman, '*Facientibus quod in se est Deus non denegat gratiam*: Robert Holcot O.P. and the Beginnings of Luther's Theology', *Harvard Theological Review* 55 (1962), pp. 317-42.

[110] *In II Sent.* q. 18 a.3 concl. 2: 'Quamvis homo in statu integrae non potuerit gratiam mereri de condigno, potuit tamen ex dispositione dei mereri hanc de congruo.'

[111] Courtenay, *Covenant and Causality*, pp. 102-10.

[112] Oberman, *Harvest of Medieval Theology*, pp. 131-45; 160-83.

Christocentric. As we have argued elsewhere,[113] the entire discussion of man's justification before God on the part of the theologians of the *via moderna* proceeds without reference to the incarnation and death of the Son of God.

The theologies of justification associated with the *via moderna* have frequently been stigmatised as 'Pelagian' or 'semi-Pelagian'. This possibility can only be maintained with some difficulty.[114] The *pactum* effectively expresses the general medieval conviction that man has a positive, although strictly limited, part to play in his own justification, and places this conviction on a firmer theological foundation by safeguarding God from the charge of capriciousness. It does not express anything new, but uses the dialectic between the two powers of God to emphasise the total reliability of God in this respect, even if the present dispensation must be regarded as radically contingent. The existence of the *pactum* itself embodies the principle that it is God, and God alone, who takes the initiative in man's salvation, by providing him with a reliable framework within which his justification and ultimate salvation become a real possibility.

The following points should be noted in assessing the alleged 'Pelagianism' of the doctrines of justification associated with the *via moderna*, such as that of Gabriel Biel:

First, the western theological tradition as a whole insisted upon the necessity for a human response to the divine initiative in justification. The only essential distinction between the earlier Franciscan tradition and the *via moderna* lies in the use of the *pactum* as the conceptual foundation for this common teaching on justification.

Second, Biel does not allow a man to remit his own sin by doing *quod in se est*. Man is required to desist from consenting to sin, and as a consequence of this, God will remit his sin — which God, and God alone, can do. The link between the human act of declining to consent to sin and the divine act of remission of sin is provided by the *pactum*, by which God has graciously ordained that such an act on the part of man will be met with a corresponding act on his part.

Third, neither the Pelagian nor the Massilian controversies operated

---

[113] Alister E. McGrath, '*Homo Assumptus?* A Study in the Christology of the *Via Moderna*, with Particular Reference to William of Ockham', *Ephemerides Theologicae Lovanienses* 60 (1984), pp. 283-97.

[114] We have argued this point *contra* Oberman *inter alia*: A. E. McGrath, 'The Anti-Pelagian Structure of "Nominalist" Doctrines of Justification', *Ephemerides Theologicae Lovanienses* 57 (1981), pp. 107-19.

within the context of a federal theology such as that of the *via moderna*. As such, it is historically incorrect to style such a theology 'Pelagian', 'semi-Pelagian', etc.

Fourth, Biel's understanding of Pelagianism was based upon the canons of the Council of Carthage (417-418). As we noted in the previous chapter, the decrees of Orange II were unknown during the medieval period. *By the known standards of the time*, Biel's theology of justification was not Pelagian. Furthermore, Biel's respect for the *determinationes ecclesiae* was such that, had he known of the substance of Orange II, he would undoubtedly have incorporated it into his theology of justification. If orthodoxy is determined in terms of *known* pronouncements of the teaching office of the church, Biel's doctrine of justification must be regarded as orthodox.

Those who regard Biel's doctrine of justification as being essentially Pelagian, or who find his teaching on justification contradictory, because it is 'at once *sola gratia* and *solis operibus*',[115] must be challenged concerning their conclusions. *Any* theology of justification which permits man to have a limited role in his own justification is open to precisely the same criticism — and yet exactly this understanding of justification is characteristic of the western church! God's gift of grace to the man who does *quod in se est* is due to an act of generosity on God's part: God bestows his grace *sola liberalitate*, in that it is given under the terms of a covenant which itself originates from and expresses an act of divine compassion. By his *grace*, God has ordained that the man who does *quod in se est* may be granted the gift of justifying grace. There is nothing 'remarkable' or 'Pelagian' about this. In practice, the charge of Pelagianism levelled against the *moderni* stands or falls with the definition of 'Pelagianism' employed.[116] We therefore wish to reiterate the following points: *by the generally accepted standards of the time* (that is, in terms of the canons of the Council of Carthage) and *by his own definition of Pelagianism*, Biel's doctrine of justification is not only not Pelagian, but is actually strongly anti-Pelagian.[117]

---

[115] Oberman, *Harvest of Medieval Theology*, pp. 176-7: 'It is clear that Biel has a remarkable doctrine of justification: seen from different vantage-points, justification is at once *sola gratia* and *solis operibus*. . . *It is therefore evident that Biel's doctrine of justification is essentially Pelagian*'.
[116] For the understandings of Pelagianism current at the time of the Reformation, see A. T. Jörgensen, 'Was verstand man in der Reformationszeit unter Pelagianismus?', *Theologische Studien und Kritiken* 83 (1910), pp. 63-82.
[117] McGrath, *The Anti-Pelagian Structure*, pp. 115-19. Similar criticisms were made

As will become clear in the following chapter, many aspects of the theology of the *via moderna* can be shown to be present in the young Luther's theology of justification, with the conspicuous exception of the dialectic of the two powers of God. This does not, however, necessarily mean that Luther's thinking on these matters is directly due to the *via moderna*: as we shall indicate in the following section, similar ideas were current within the Augustinian Order during the later medieval period. It is therefore necessary to consider the nature of such theological trends within that order before turning to examine Luther's early theology of justification. In the following section, we are particularly concerned with such trends as they converged on the Augustinian Cloister at Wittenberg, and to a lesser extent, at Erfurt, at the opening of the sixteenth century.

SCHOLA AUGUSTINIANA MODERNA

In the first decades of the present century, A. V. Müller argued that Luther stood within a school of thought which existed within the Augustinian Order of his day, and whose theology was more 'Augustinian' than that of their contemporaries. [118] According to Müller, there existed *una differenza di forma, non di sostanza*, between the theology of the young Luther and that of this school within the Augustinian Order, whose representatives included Simon Fidati of Cassia (†1348), Hugolino of Orvieto (†1374), Agostino Favaroni of Rome (†1443) and Jacobus Perez of Valencia (†1470). Although Eduard Stakemeier rejected Müller's original thesis as untenable, [119] he modified the thesis somewhat by arguing that the doctrine of double justification associated

---

by Francis Clark, 'A New Appraisal of Late Medieval Nominalism', *Gregorianum* 46 (1965), pp. 733-65. It may also be pointed out that Oberman confuses the issue by following Carl Feckes in using terms such as predestination *ante praevisa merita* and *post praevisa merita*, both of which date from a later period, and carry with them overtones quite absent from Biel's own thinking: McGrath, *The Anti-Pelagian Structure*, pp. 108-11. Cf. C. Feckes, *Die Rechtfertigungslehre des Gabriel Biel* (Münster, 1925), p. 88, n. 268; Oberman, *The Harvest of Medieval Theology*, pp. 192-3; 205; 211; 213.
[118] A. V. Müller, *Luthers theologische Quellen: Seine Verteidigung gegen Denifle und Grisar* (Gießen, 1912); 'Agostino Favaroni e la teologia di Lutero', *Bilychnis* 3 (1914), pp. 373-87; 'Giacomo Perez di Valenza, Vescovo di Chrysopoli e la teologia di Lutero', *Bilychnis* 9 (1920), pp. 391-403, etc.
[119] E. Stakemeier, *Der Kampf um Augustin: Augustinus und die Augustiner auf dem Tridentinum* (Paderborn, 1937), p. 21.

with Giralmo Seripando during the Tridentine proceedings *de iustificatione* could only be properly understood in the light of this late medieval Augustinian school.[120] This thesis has not stood up to critical examination.[121] Since then, considerable scholarly attention has been directed towards the theologians of the Augustinian Order of the later medieval period,[122] with primary sources being edited and collated, largely through the efforts of members of the Augustinian Order itself. As a result, we are now in a much better position to attempt an evaluation of the thesis of an Augustinian school of theology during the later Middle Ages.

Before beginning such an evaluation, however, it must be pointed

---

[120] Stakemeier, *Der Kampf um Augustin*, p. 22.

[121] It was subjected to a devastating review on its appearance by Hubert Jedin: *Theologische Revue* 36 (1937), pp. 425-30. Cf. his *History of the Council of Trent* (2 vols: Edinburgh, 1957-61), Vol. II, p. 258.

[122] A. V. La Valle, *La giustizia di Adamo e il peccato originale secondo Egidio Romano* (Palermo, 1939) is useful as a pre-war contribution. For the modern discussion, see: A. Zumkeller, 'Hugolino von Orvieto über Urstand und Erbsünde', *Augustiniana* 3 (1953), pp. 35-62; 165-93; 4 (1954), pp. 25-46; 'Hugolino von Orvieto über Prädestination, Rechtfertigung und Verdienst', *Augustiniana* 4 (1954), pp. 109-56; 5 (1955), pp. 5-51; N. Toner, 'The Doctrine of Original Sin according to Augustine of Rome (Favaroni)', *Augustiniana* 7 (1957), pp. 100-17; 349-66; 515-30; 'The Doctrine of Justification according to Augustine of Rome (Favaroni)', *Augustiniana* 8 (1958), pp. 164-89; 299-327; 497-515; W. Werbeck, *Jacobus Perez von Valencia. Untersuchungen zu seinem Psalmenkommentar* (Tübingen, 1959); A. Zumkeller, *Schriftum und Lehre des Hermann von Schildesche* (Rom/Würzburg, 1959); M. Ferdigg, 'De vita et operibus et doctrina Joannis de Paltz', *Analecta Augustiniana* 30 (1967), pp. 210-321; 31 (1968), pp. 155-318; D. C. Steinmetz, *Misericordia Dei: The Theology of Johannes von Stauptiz in its Late Medieval Setting* (Leiden, 1968); A. Zumkeller, 'Der Wiener Theologieprofessor Johannes von Retz und seine Lehre von Urstand, Erbsünde, Gnade und Verdienst', *Augustiniana* 22 (1972), pp. 118-84; 540-82; W. Eckermann, *Wort und Wirklichkeit: Das Sprachverständnis in der Theologie Gregors von Rimini und sein Weiterwirken in der Augustinerschule* (Würzburg, 1978); A. Zumkeller, 'Johannes Klenkok O.S.A. im Kampf gegen den "Pelagianismus" seiner Zeit: Seine Lehre über Gnade, Rechtfertigung und Verdienst', *Recherches Augustiniennes* 13 (1978), pp. 231-333; 'Die Lehre des Erfurter Augustinertheologen Johannes von Dorsten über Gnade, Rechtfertigung und Verdienst', *Theologie und Philosophie* 53 (1978), pp. 27-64; 127-219; 'Der Augustinertheologe Johannes Hiltalingen von Basel über Urstand, Erbsünde, Gnade und Verdienst', *Analecta Augustiniana* 43 (1980), pp. 57-162; 'Erbsünde, Gnade und Rechtfertigung im Verständnis der Erfurter Augustinertheologen des Spätmittelalters', *Zeitschrift für Kirchengeschichte* 92 (1981), pp. 39-59; 'Der Augustiner Angelus Dobelinus, erster Theologieprofessor der Erfurter Universität, über Gnade, Rechtfertigung und Verdienst', *Analecta Augustiniana* 44 (1981), pp. 69-147. The findings of these works, as they relate to the question of a 'medieval Augustinian school on justification', are summarised and analysed in our *Iustitia Dei*, Volume I, pp. 172-9.

out that an astonishing variety of interpretations have been placed upon the term 'Augustinian' by historians, with an equally great degree of confusion arising as a result. [123] It is therefore necessary to make it clear that we are dealing with the specific question of whether there existed a distinctive, well-defined school of theology within the Augustinian Order itself, and with the theological characteristics of this putative school, whether or not these happen to correspond to the teachings of St Augustine himself. Several studies of importance have dealt with this question, and we propose to consider their findings.

We have already noted the emergence of the *via moderna* in the German universities of the fourteenth century, characterised by its epistemological nominalism and its logical-critical attitude. In an important study, Damasus Trapp argued that precisely such a polarisation between the *via antiqua* and the *via moderna* developed within the Augustinian Order during the fourteenth century. [124] While both *moderni* and *antiqui* placed increasing emphasis upon the importance of accurate citation of St Augustine, the *antiqui* regarded the *moderni* as being eclectic and unduly logico-critical, while the *moderni* considered that they were under obligation to correct the errors of the past, using 'modern' conceptual tools such as the dialectic between the two powers of God. Trapp thus divides Augustinian theology into two periods: the first, which encompasses the period between Giles of Rome and Thomas of Strassburg; and the second, which began with Gregory of Rimini. The earlier period is heavily influenced by Giles of Rome, and includes such theologians as James of Viterbo, Alexander of San Elpido, Robert Cowton and William of Ware. [125] As Trapp has shown, Giles of Rome was cited with sufficient frequency by his fellow-Augustinians during this period to indicate that he was regarded as a theological authority, thus justifying those who dubbed this earlier period of Augustinian theology as the *schola Aegidiana*. Giles, it may be noted, is generally regarded as a student of St Augustine who

---

[123] Steinmetz distinguishes *five* meanings of the term 'Augustinian', and comments on the danger of confusing them: *Luther and Staupitz*, pp. 13-16.
[124] D. Trapp, 'Augustinian Theology of the Fourteenth Century: Notes on Editions, Marginalia, Opinions and Book-Lore', *Augustiniana* 6 (1956), pp. 147-265. Trapp makes the important point (p. 151) that no Augustinian theologians can be called logico-critical extremists. In their use of the dialectic between the two powers of God, these theologians avoided the unorthodox speculation associated with John of Mirecourt and Nicholas of Autrecourt, as well as of the English theologians Nicholas of Aston and Ulcredus of Durham.
[125] Trapp, *Augustinian Theology*, p. 265.

displays Thomist tendencies at points, rather than as a Thomist with an unusual interest in the theology of St Augustine. [126] The stamp of the authentic theology of St Augustine, particularly in relation to the theology of grace, [127] may therefore be regarded as having been placed upon the early Augustinian school.

Adolar Zumkeller argued that the early Augustinian school was characterised by its Aristotelian-Thomist foundations (such as the important distinction between *essentia* and *existentia*), coupled with certain distinctively Augustinian elements. [128] It is significant that Zumkeller locates most of these elements in areas which fall within the scope of the doctrine of justification — for example, the emphasis upon the primacy of love and the primacy of grace, both authentic elements of St Augustine's own teaching on justification. Zumkeller points out that these elements, already present in the early Augustinian school, are intensified in the period after Gregory of Rimini, with an increasing emphasis upon the personal presence of the Holy Spirit in believers. Furthermore, Zumkeller points out that the later Augustinians appear to depend upon St Augustine rather than upon Giles of Rome, reflecting the intense source studies carried out within the Order. [129] There are thus excellent grounds for suggesting that a characteristic theology of justification, approximating to that of St Augustine himself, became current within sections of the Augustinian Order during the early fifteenth century.

In a study of the doctrines of justification associated with the theologians of the Augustinian Order during the later medieval period, we showed that there was considerable diversity of opinion within the Order on the question of the formal (that is, immediate) cause of justification. [130] The earlier theologians of the *schola Aegidiana* followed

[126] See J. Beumer, 'Augustinismus und Thomismus in der theologischen Prinzipien-lehre des Aegidius Romanus', *Scholastik* 32 (1957), pp. 542-60.

[127] For the influence of St Augustine upon Giles in this respect, see A. Trapè, *Il concorso divino nel pensiero di Egidio Romano* (Tolentino, 1942).

[128] A. Zumkeller, 'Die Augustinerschule des Mittelalters: Vertreter und philosophisch-theologische Lehre', *Analecta Augustiniana* 27 (1964), pp. 167-262, especially pp. 193-5. For an excellent register of the major theologians of the Augustinian Order during the period, see pp. 174-6.

[129] This point was developed and confirmed with particular reference to Gregory of Rimini by Oberman, *Werden und Wertung der Reformation*, pp. 82-140.

[130] A. E. McGrath, ' "Augustinianism"? A Critical Assessment of the So-called "Medieval Augustinian Tradition" on Justification', *Augustiniana* 31 (1981) pp. 247-67. This article is supplemented in our *Iustitia Dei*, Volume I, 172-9.

St Thomas Aquinas and Giles of Rome in teaching that the formal cause of justification was a created habit of grace within the soul. This opinion can be shown to be prevalent within the Order up to the time of Thomas of Strassburg, although some later theologians of the Order, such as Johannes von Retz, continued this teaching after it had been abandoned elsewhere. However, beginning with Gregory of Rimini, an increasing emphasis came to be placed upon the role of uncreated grace — the personal presence of the Holy Spirit within the believer — in justification. This move towards a more personalist concept of grace began with Gregory of Rimini, Hugolino of Orvieto and Dionysius of Montina, and was developed by later theologians of the Order, such as Alphonsus of Toledo, Johannes Klenkok and Johannes Hiltalingen of Basel. The particular emphasis placed by Johannes von Staupitz on the role of uncreated grace in justification thus appears to reflect a well-established theological tradition within the Augustinian Order of the later Middle Ages.[131] In this, and in other respects, there appears to have been a move on the part of the theologians of the Augustinian Order away from the theology of the early Dominican school towards that of the later Franciscan school.[132] For example, the earlier Augustinian theologians followed Giles of Rome and St Thomas Aquinas in rejecting the doctrine of the immaculate conception, whereas its later theologians followed Duns Scotus in adopting a strongly immaculist position.[133]

The essential point which we wish to make is that, by the time of Luther, a theology of justification had developed within certain sections of the Augustinian Order which can only be regarded as a hybrid species, incorporating much of the authentic theology of St Augustine (for instance, the emphasis upon the depravity of man, the priority of grace and love, and the necessity of grace for morally good acts), whilst simultaneously including the results of the application of logico-critical methods, such as the dialectic of the two powers of God, associated with the *via moderna* (for example, the critique of the role of supernatural habits in justification, and the concepts of *necessitas consequentis* and *necessitas consequentiae*, as expressed in the

[131] See Steinmetz, *Misericordia Dei*, pp. 105-8.
[132] For characterisation of these schools, see our *Iustitia Dei*, Volume I, pp. 158-60 and pp. 163-6.
[133] McGrath, *Augustinianism*, p. 259. It is interesting to note that Gregory of Rimini, who was otherwise instrumental in effecting most of the changes associated with the later Augustinian school, was implacably opposed to the immaculist position.

pactum-theology). The importance of this observation to the theological
development of the young Luther will be evident. Certain aspects of the
characteristic theologies of justification associated with the *via moderna*
came to be associated with the theologians of the Augustinian Order
during the later Middle Ages — and yet were linked to other teachings
on justification (such as man's total depravity) which set them apart
from the *via moderna*. Verbal similarities between the theologians of
the *via moderna* and of the Augustinian Order must therefore be treated
with the greatest caution, as they frequently mask profound conceptual
differences. [134] This point also serves to emphasise the total futility
of attempting to draw a sharp distinction between 'Nominalism' and
'Augustinianism' during the later medieval period. Not only did many
'Augustinian' theologians adopt a nominalist epistemology (for
example, Gregory of Rimini, Hugolino of Orvieto): they also incorporated aspects of 'Nominalist' teaching into their doctrines of
justification. Indeed, it is precisely this variation between individual
'Augustinian' theologians in respect to the extent to which they
adopted elements of 'Nominalism' which caused so much of the
confusion currently surrounding the characteristics of a putative
'Augustinian' school of theology.

What was the influence of this 'modern Augustinian school' at
Wittenberg? Before considering this point, it must be made clear that
the term 'school' must be understood in a somewhat loose sense: Trapp
reminds us that, when dealing with the theologians of the Augustinian
Order, one should speak 'cautiously of attitudes, not schools'. [135] It
is clear, however, that a distinctive attitude towards theological sources
and methods came to be associated with many theologians of the Order
during the period, even if it is not appropriate to speak of a 'school'
in the strictest of senses.

In an important essay, [136] Heiko Oberman argued that the statutes
of the University of Wittenberg established the presence of the *schola
Augustiniana moderna* within the faculty of arts. We have already noted
how the revised statutes of 1508 permitted members of that faculty

---

[134] For example Johannes von Staupitz uses the concept of the *pactum* between God
and man in the course of his doctrine of justification: see the cautionary comments
by Steinmetz, *Misericordia Dei*, p. 55.

[135] Trapp, *Augustinian Theology*, p. 150.

[136] H. A. Oberman, 'Headwaters of the Reformation: *Initia Lutheri — Initia Reformationis*', in *Luther and the Dawn of the Modern Era*, ed. H. A. Oberman (Leiden, 1974),
pp. 40-88.

to teach *secundum viam Gregorii*, and have stated our reasons for asserting that the *via Gregorii* is synonymous with the *via moderna*. Oberman, however, regards the *via Gregorii* as synonymous with the *schola Augustiniana moderna*, which he takes to have been initiated by Gregory of Rimini. [137] This is an extremely interesting suggestion, and it is a matter for regret that the evidence which Oberman presents in support of his contention is, by his own admission, circumstantial. It seems to us that the evidence in favour of the *via moderna* being thus designated far outweighs that in favour of Oberman's interesting suggestion. Viewed in terms of the *mens auctoris* (that is, Christoph Scheurl), there is every reason to suppose that the statutes refer to the *via* then associated with Jodocus Trutvetter — the *via moderna*. There are thus no substantial grounds for concluding that the *schola Augustiniana moderna* was represented at the University of Wittenberg in the early sixteenth century. But what of the Augustinian Cloisters at Erfurt and Wittenberg?

Unfortunately, we do not have sufficient evidence to draw reliable conclusions on this question. We can, however, draw such conclusions concerning those theologians of the Augustinian Order who exerted significant influence upon the young Luther — which is more significant from the standpoint of the present study. We have already pointed out the general tendency of the later theologians of the Order to adopt elements of the doctrines of justification associated with the *via moderna*, and the tendency on the part of monastic theologians to align themselves with the *via* (*via antiqua* or *via moderna*) prevalent at their local university. It is therefore perhaps not surprising that the two Erfurt Augustinians who exerted the greatest influence over the young Luther appear to have been followers of the *via moderna*, rather than members of the *schola Augustiniana moderna*. Johannes Nathin and Bartholomäus Arnoldi of Usingen were both noted *moderni*, and

[137] Oberman, 'Headwaters', pp. 77; 79-82. See also his *Werden und Wertung*, pp. 131-2, where he points to the influence of Gregory on Wendelin Steinbach as evidence for his suggestion. Oberman's thesis is defended in the study of M. Schulze, '"Via Gregorii" in Forschung und Quellen', in *Gregor von Rimini*, pp. 1-126, especially pp. 25-64. While Schulze's arguments go some way towards confirming that there was a loose school of *theological* opinion, of basically Augustinian provenance, associated with Gregory of Rimini in the later Middle Ages, the fact remains that we are not dealing with the statutes of the faculty of *theology*, but with those of the faculty of *arts*. In terms of the disciplines associated with this latter faculty at Wittenberg, the positions of Gregory of Rimini and other *moderni* (such as Buridan, Ockham and Biel) are essentially the same, as recent studies have confirmed.

Arnoldi's doctrine of justification in particular is practically indistinguishable from that of Gabriel Biel.[138] The fact that Luther began his theological studies under the auspices of the Augustinian Order cannot, therefore, be assumed to imply that he was taught according to the *schola Augustiniana moderna*, originating from Gregory of Rimini. Indeed, the fact that Luther does not appear to have come across Gregory of Rimini until 1519,[139] linked with his frequently repeated praise of Ockham, suggests that Luther, during his Erfurt days, belonged to that school of thought within the Augustinian Order which approximated most closely to the *via moderna*. The Erfurt priory may well have been exceptional in its affinity with the *via moderna*, but the fact remains that it was at this priory that Luther began his study of theology.[140]

There are therefore excellent reasons for suggesting that Luther's relationship to the *schola Augustiniana moderna* is considerably more complex than might at first be thought. If Zumkeller is correct in his statement that a distinctive school of thought existed within the Augustinian Order during the later medieval period, whose adherents followed Augustine in stressing the primacy of grace and love, it would appear that Luther did not encounter such a school during his time at Erfurt. It is much more plausible that Luther encountered such a school of thought at the Augustinian Cloister at Wittenberg, at least during his conversations with Johannes von Staupitz. Nevertheless, a critical examination of the sources which Staupitz employs suggests that he cannot be regarded as a member of the *schola Augustiniana moderna*. Staupitz does not refer to any theologians usually held to be associated with this school — such as its founding member, Gregory of Rimini.[141] Indeed, where he does refer to Augustinian theologians,

---

[138] See Oberman, *The Harvest of Medieval Theology*, pp. 178-81. It may also be pointed out that Johannes de Paltz, who was then at the Erfurt priory, was also no follower of Gregory of Rimini: Oberman, *Werden und Wertung*, p. 131, n. 172. It may be pointed out that Oberman does not consider the '*via Gregorii*' (in his sense) to represent the theology of the Augustinian Order *as a whole*.

[139] L. Grane, 'Gregor von Rimini und Luthers Leipziger Disputation', *Studia Theologica* 22 (1968), pp. 29-49.

[140] It is not without significance that the theologians of religious orders tended to follow the school of thought then prevalent in the university in which their religous house was situated. Erfurt was a centre for the *via moderna* by 1500. See n. 12.

[141] See the excellent analysis of these sources presented by Ernst Wolf, *Staupitz und Luther. Ein Beitrag zur Theologie des Johannes von Staupitz und deren Bedeutung für Luthers theologischen Werdegang* (Leipzig, 1929), pp. 23-5.

it is clear that he regards himself as a representative of the *schola Aegidiana*, rather than the *schola Augustiniana moderna*.[142] It is therefore very difficult to agree with Oberman when he concludes:

> We can point to the *schola Augustiniana moderna*, initiated by Gregory of Rimini, reflected by Hugolin of Orvieto, apparently spiritually alive in the Erfurt Augustinian monastery, and transformed into a pastoral reform-theology by Staupitz, as the *occasio proxima* — not the *causa!* — for the inception of the *vera theologia* at Wittenberg.[143]

Oberman's evidence for this conclusion is purely circumstantial, and fails to take account of the fact that the three Augustinian theologians who exercised the greatest influence over Luther (Nathin, Arnoldi and Staupitz) cannot be regarded as representatives of the school to which Oberman refers. There can be no doubt that Luther was influenced by theological currents and methods associated with his Order — but he appears to have encountered these in the form of specific personalities within that Order, both at Erfurt and Wittenberg, and there appear to be excellent grounds for suggesting that these personalities were simply not typical of the school of thought which some scholars have identified within the Order during the later Middle Ages.

---

[142] See Steinmetz, *Misericordia Dei*, pp. 22-8; idem., *Luther and Staupitz*, pp. 27-31.
[143] Oberman, 'Headwaters of the Reformation', p. 82. For a more general critique of this conclusion, see Alister E. McGrath, 'Forerunners of the Reformation: A Critical Examination of the Evidence for Precursors of the Reformation Doctrines of Justification', *Harvard Theological Review* (1982), pp. 219-42, especially pp. 236-41.

3

Luther as a Late Medieval Theologian

IN the previous chapter, we indicated that there were excellent reasons for suggesting that Luther's early theological opinions were moulded by theological currents then prevalent at Erfurt and Wittenberg, and that these currents were typical of the later Middle Ages. In the present chapter we propose to demonstrate that, between 1509 and early 1514, Luther's theology in general, and his theology of justification in particular, was typical of the later medieval period. This suggestion is not, of course, new. In his celebrated critique of the reformer, Heinrich Denifle argued that Luther's rejection of catholic theology was ultimately a reflection upon the particular type of 'catholic' theology with which Luther was familiar. For Denifle, Luther was only familiar with the 'unsound' theology of the later medieval period,[1] such as that of Gabriel Biel, and not with the catholic theology of St Thomas Aquinas or Bonaventure. Perhaps surprisingly, modern Luther scholarship has tended to endorse Denifle's judgement: whereas Luther frequently demonstrates first-hand knowledge of the writings of the leading theologians of the fourteenth and fifteenth centuries, such as Pierre d'Ailly and Gabriel Biel, such knowledge is

---

[1] H. Denifle, *Luther und Luthertum* (Mainz, 2nd edn, 1906) Vol I, 2 pp. 535-6. The substance of Denifle's argument is that Luther's knowledge of medieval theology is mediated through the historical sections of Biel's *Collectorium*. As Biel gave a totally distorted version of the theology of the earlier medieval period, frequently citing its representatives at second or third hand, it was inevitable that this perverted impression would prejudice Luther's attitude towards 'catholic' theology as a whole. Scheel also draws our attention to the perverted 'Geschichtsbild seiner Erfurter Lehrer' in evaluating Luther's relationship to the theology of the Middle Ages as a whole: O. Scheel, *Martin Luther: Vom Katholizismus zur Reformation* (2 vols: Tübingen, 1921), Volume II, p. 163. For a similar estimation of Biel, see C. Feckes, *Die Rechtfertigungslehre des Gabriel Biel und ihre Stellung innerhalb der nominalistischen Schule* (Münster, 1925), pp. 25-6; 86.

conspicuously absent in the case of earlier medieval theologians, such as St Thomas Aquinas. It must, of course, be pointed out that this is precisely what is to be expected, if Luther was educated within the *via moderna*, characterised by its logico-critical attitudes and an epistemological nominalism: the great theologians of the thirteenth century belonged to the *via antiqua*, characterised by an epistemological realism, from which Luther would have been taught to distance himself by his mentors at Erfurt. Nevertheless, when Luther's knowledge of *spiritual* writings is analysed, it again becomes clear that he is most familiar with those of the later medieval period:[2] indeed, if the influence of earlier spiritual writings, such as those of Bernard of Clairvaux, can be demonstrated, it is possible to argue that this influence is mediated directly through those later medieval spiritual treatises with which Luther can be shown to have been familiar.[3]

Luther began his theological career at Wittenberg in 1512 steeped in both the methods and the presuppositions of late medieval theology and, as we shall see, acutely aware of at least some of its problems. It must therefore be regarded as methodologically unacceptable to attempt to study Luther's theological development in isolation from, or with purely incidental reference to, this context. Although there is undoubtedly some truth in the frequently encountered statement that the whole of Luther's later theology is present in the *Dictata super Psalterium*, there is even greater truth in the much less frequently encountered observation that the entire late medieval theological tradition is also present. It is the precise relationship between the received tradition and Luther's own developing theological insights which must form the subject of any study of Luther's theological development over the period 1509-19.[4] The present chapter is therefore concerned

---

[2] See the excellent study of M. Elze, 'Züge spätmittelalterlicher Frömmigkeit in Luthers Theologie', *Zeitschrift für Theologie und Kirche* (1965), pp. 381-402. This study adopts a significantly different standpoint from the earlier study of H. Preuss, 'Das Frömmigkeitsmotiv von Luthers Tessaradeks und seine mittelalterlichen Wurzeln', *Neue kirchliche Zeitschrift* 26 (1915), pp. 217-43. For an excellent study of the spiritual tradition at the Erfurt Augustinian Cloister, as exemplified by Johannes de Paltz, see B. Hamm, *Frömmigkeitstheologie am Anfang des 16. Jahrhunderts: Studien zu Johannes von Paltz und seinem Umkreis* (Tübingen, 1982).
[3] e.g., his *Sermo in Cant.* 43,4 is cited frequently in later medieval spiritual writings: see Elze, 'Züge spätmittelalterlicher Frömmigkeit', p. 396, n. 55. See further pp. 394-7.
[4] Hendrix's comment on the development of Luther's ecclesiology is illuminating: 'We cannot be content with maintaining that there are both traditional and new elements in Luther's ecclesiology in the *Dictata* . . . Luther's new ecclesiology in its

with establishing the *terminus a quo*, and demonstrating its late medieval provenance.

The most important source for our study of Luther's early theological development is his first course of lectures on the Psalter, the *Dictata super Psalterium*.[5] On 8 July 1513 Johannes Grünenberg published an edition of the Psalter with particularly wide margins, suitable for both marginal and interlinear glossing. Luther had this edition reprinted for the use of his students, and in his own copy entered his comments (usually of a grammatical or philological nature) in the ample space available. It is these notes which are referred to as *glosses*. The glossing of a biblical text was standard practice in the medieval period, the most familiar examples being the *Glossa ordinaria* and the *Glossa interlinearis*.[6] In addition to these brief notes, Luther prepared much more detailed and wider treatments of the overall text of each psalm, relating it to matters of spiritual or theological interest. These more extended notes are referred to as *scholia*.[7] The original manuscript copies of both the glosses and scholia are preserved, and the original Weimar edition of the *Dictata* has recently been corrected from them.[8] Luther would retain the practice of providing glosses and scholia in his Romans lectures of 1515-16.

The chief difficulty in using the *Dictata* as a source for the study of Luther's early theology relates to the dating of Luther's comments on individual psalms. The following points are of particular importance in this respect:

---

essence is already present in his first lectures on the Psalms. The new elements which make up this essence remain individual rivulets in the *Dictata*; they have not yet merged into the navigable stream of Luther's mature ecclesiology.' S. Hendrix, *Ecclesia in via: Ecclesiological Developments in the Medieval Psalms Exegesis and the Dictata super Psalterium of Martin Luther* (Leiden, 1974), p. 286.

[5] For an excellent introduction, see G. Ebeling, 'Luthers Psalterdrück vom Jahre 1513', in *Lutherstudien I* (Tübingen, 1971), pp. 69-131. Boehmer suggests that Luther began to lecture on the Psalter for the first time at 6 a.m. on 16 August 1513, and ended on 20 October 1515: H. Boehmer, *Luthers erste Vorlesung* (Berichte über die Verhandlungen der Sächsischen Akademie der Wissenschaften zu Leipzig, philologisch-historisch Klasse 75/1: Leipzig, 1924), p. 5.

[6] See B. Smalley *The Study of the Bible in the Middle Ages* (Notre Dame, Ind., 1970), pp. 46-66.

[7] The singular *Scholion* or *Scholium* is hardly ever encountered.

[8] The original edition is contained in volumes 3 and 4; the later edition in volume 55. At the time of writing, this last volume is incomplete. K. A. Meissinger reported finding more than 1400 important textual misreadings in volume 3 alone. The policy adopted in the present study is to refer to volume 55 where this is possible, with the corresponding reference to the earlier edition in parentheses.

First, Luther appears to have glossed psalms in advance, so that there is a discrepancy between the dates of the gloss and the scholion on most of the psalms. The practice of the editors of the first Weimar editions of the *Dictata* in printing the gloss and scholion together, as if they were written consecutively, to yield a complete commentary upon each psalm must therefore be regarded as potentially misleading, implying a closer chronological connection between the two than is probably the case.

Secondly, Luther revised his material for publication, probably between 1515 and 1516. His practice of leaving ample space at the end of each Psalm for further comments at a later date doubtless facilitated this process, and certainly adds to the confusion surrounding the dating of Luther's comments. On the basis of a careful study of paper and ink types, it is possible to show that Luther's comments on the first four psalms, while containing much material which may be dated from 1513, also contain material which can only be dated from 1516.[9]

Thirdly, at several points, including one of significance, the Dresdener Psalter, containing the scholia, appears to include leaves which were bound into the work at a later date.[10]

In the present chapter, we shall examine certain key aspects of Luther's early understanding of the doctrine of justification, and indicate how they are characteristic of the theology of the later medieval period. Before doing this, however, it is necessary to consider Luther's biblical hermeneutic. Luther's theological breakthrough took place during the course of a prolonged series of lectures on biblical material, and is clearly intimately associated with the substance of this material. In the previous chapter, we indicated the importance of humanist biblical scholarship in making these texts available in their original languages, along with the necessary apparatus to translate them more

---

[9] Boehmer, *Luthers erste Vorlesung*, passim.

[10] H. Wendorf, 'Der Durchbruch der neuen Erkenntnis Luthers im Lichte der hand-schriftlichen Überlieferung', *Historische Vierteljahrschrift* 27 (1932), pp. 124-44; 285-324; pp. 134-42; The most serious difficulty relates to folio 103 of the handwritten manuscript, which appears to have been bound the wrong way round — i.e., fol. 103a is actually fol. 103b, and *vice-versa* — as well as having been added later. Thus WA 3.461.20 — 463.37 appears to be a later addition, which interposes between Luther's exposition of Psalm 71 (= Psalm 72, Vulgate) on fol. 102 and 104. On this vexed problem, see H. Bornkamm, 'Iustitia Dei beim jungen Luther', in *Der Durchbruch der reformatorischen Erkenntnis bei Luther*, ed. B. Lohse (Darmstadt, 1968), pp. 289-383; pp. 292-9.

accurately. It must be emphasised, however, that the problem of the proper interpretation of scripture concerns far more than the mere accurate translation of the original texts. If scripture is to be the foundation of theology, a valid and universally recognised means of interpreting it must be established, thus bringing the question of biblical hermeneutics to the forefront of our study,[11] in that a theologian's hermeneutical presuppositions inevitably dictate his theological conclusions. Indeed, the *'sola scriptura'* principle[12] is quite meaningless unless linked to the question of how scripture should be interpreted, once its authority is conceded. It is therefore of enormous interest to observe that Luther's biblical hermeneutic up to 1515 is characteristic of the later medieval period, although containing a Christological emphasis which foreshadows much of his later theology.

The early controversies within the Christian church, particularly those concerning Gnosticism, made it necessary to distinguish between the *literal* and the *spiritual* sense of scripture. Although this device was originally polemical, it soon became clear that it was capable of being exploited by theologians to expose a deeper spiritual significance to an otherwise unedifying text. Thus St Augustine, finding himself quite unable to detect anything particularly edifying or illuminating in the literal sense of Exodus 23.19 ('You shall not boil a kid in its mother's milk'), chose to interpret it allegorically, in terms of a prophecy that Christ should not himself perish in the slaughter of the innocents.[13] By the thirteenth century, three quite distinct spiritual senses of scripture had been established in addition to the literal sense: the allegorical, the tropological or moral, and the anagogical. This four-fold scheme for establishing the sense of scripture became known as the *Quadriga*,[14] and was summarised in the famous verse due to the Dominican, Augustine of Denmark (†1285):[15]

[11] See the invaluable study of H. Feld, *Die Anfänge der modernen biblischen Hermenutik in der spätmittelalterlichen Theologie* (Wiesbaden, 1977).
[12] On this, see E. Egli, 'Zur Einführung des Schriftprinzips in der Schweiz', *Zwingliana* 1 (1903), pp. 332-9.
[13] Augustine, *Quaestiones in Heptateuchum* ii, 90. See Smalley, *Study of the Bible*, pp. 281-308.
[14] H. de Lubac, *Histoire et Esprit: l'intelligence de l'Ecriture d'après Origène* (Paris, 1950) provides an excellent introduction. For the best study, see his later work, *Exégèse médiévale: les quatres sens de l'Ecriture* (4 vols: Paris, 1959-64).
[15] See S. A. Walz, 'Des Aage von Dänemark "Rotulus pugillaris" im Lichte der dominikanischen Kontroverstheologie', *Classica et Mediaevalia* (Copenhagen) 15 (1954), pp. 198-252; 16 (1955) pp. 136-194.

Littera gesta docet; quid credas allegoria,
Moralis quid agas; quo tendis, anagoria.

The application of this four-fold scheme may be illustrated from one of the most important works on theological method from the period of High Scholasticism, the *Breviloquium* of Bonaventure:

The depth of scripture consists in a multiplicity of mystical interpretations. Besides the literal sense, some passages have to be interpreted in three different manners, namely allegorically, morally and tropologically. There is *allegory*, when one fact points to another, by reference to which one should believe. There is *tropology* or *morality*, when facts make us understand rules of conduct. There is *anagogy* or elevation of the mind towards the eternal felicity of the saints.[16]

It was, of course, evident that a considerable degree of restriction had to be placed upon the use of the spiritual senses of scripture, if biblical exegesis was to avoid becoming mere flights of fancy. The fundamental principle established during the earlier medieval period to avoid this development was the following: *the literal sense of scripture must always be regarded as the most fundamental, and nothing may be believed on the basis of a spiritual sense of scripture unless it has first been established on the basis of the literal sense.* This principle can be illustrated from medieval theologians as diverse as St Thomas Aquinas,[17] Jean Gerson,[18] and

---

[16] *Breviloquium* prol. 4, 1. Cf. *Collationes in Hexaemeron* xiii, 11: 'Allegory concerns what is to be believed; anagogy concerns what is to be hoped for; tropology concerns what is to be done'. See G. H. Tavard, *Transiency and Permanence: The Nature of Theology according to St Bonaventure* (New York/Louvain, 1954), pp. 31-55, for an excellent discussion.

[17] *In I Sent.* Prol. q.1 a.5: 'Ad destructionem autem errorum non proceditur nisi per sensum litteralem, eo quod sensus sint per similitudines accepti, et ex similitudinaris locutionibus non potest sumi argumentatio.' Cf. *In I Sent.* Prol. q.1 a.7: 'Ad secundum de occasione errorus, dicendum quod ex multiplicitate sensuum nulla datur errandi occasio: quia ut Augustinus dicit in libro de doctrina christiana: "Nihil secundum spiritualem sensum est in scriptura exponendum, quod alibi secundum sensum litteralem manifeste non exprimatur." Unde et sensus spiritualis non est idoneus ad aliquid confirmandum, nisi sensu litterali fulciatur.' See A. Reyero, *Thomas von Aquin als Exeget* (Einsiedeln, 1971); A. Haufnagel, 'Wort Gottes: Sinn und Bedeutung nach Thomas von Aquin', in *Wort Gottes in der Zeit*, ed. H. Feld and J. Nolte (Düsseldorf, 1973), pp. 236-56.

[18] See F. Hahn, 'Zur Hermeneutik Gersons', *Zeitschrift für Theologie und Kirche* 51 (1954), pp. 34-50.

Wendelin Steinbach.[19] Furthermore, there was general agreement
that the exegesis of scripture was a public event — in other words,
the individual's personal exegesis of particular biblical passages was
subject to the corporate exegesis of the church as a whole.[20]

At the same time as Luther began to lecture on the Psalter for the
first time, Wendelin Steinbach began to lecture at Tübingen on
Galatians.[21] These lectures are of particular interest, as they exemplify
the methods of biblical exegesis as the end of an era drew near,[22] and,
when studied in conjunction with his Hebrews lectures of 1517, the
lectures give invaluable insight into the tensions arising when a
theologian of the *via moderna* encounters the thought of St Paul.[23]
Steinbach does not use the *Quadriga* extensively, preferring to concentrate upon the literal sense.[24] Of particular interest in this respect is
his leading hermeneutical principle: that the Old Testament, *in its
literal sense*, must be regarded as referring to Christ and his church.[25]
Oberman has drawn attention to a feature of Steinbach's exegesis
which is of significance in relation to the *via moderna* — the need to
contextualise the *modus loquendi* of the New Testament writers, and
particularly St Paul. Thus, for example, the Pauline emphasis upon
the priority of faith — which Steinbach, interestingly, summarises
in terms of the slogan *sola fides sufficiat* — must be understood in terms
of the apostle's polemic against those who maintained that human
nature, given proper instruction, could attain salvation unaided.[26]
Steinbach allows that *sola fides sufficiat* — but insists that this is an

---

[19] See Feld, *Anfänge der modernen biblischen Hermeneutik*, pp. 70-83.

[20] This point is made by most theologians of the period, but is stated with particular
force by Gerson — cf. *De sensu literali sacrae scripturae*, cited Feld, *Anfänge der modernen
biblischen Hermeneutik*, p. 57, n. 117: 'Sensus scripturae literalis judicandus est prout
Ecclesia Spiritu Sancto inspirata et gubernata determinavit et non ad cuiuslibet
arbitrium et interpretationem.'

[21] The edition we have used is that edited by H. Feld, *Wendelini Steinbach Opera
Exegetica quae supersunt omnia I* (Wiesbaden, 1976).

[22] We refer not merely to the end of the Middle Ages, but to the end of the Bielian
ascendancy at Tübingen: in 1517, after he finished his lectures on Hebrews, Steinbach
was evicted from his lodgings, along with other members of the Brethern of the
Common Life: see H. Feld, *Martin Luthers und Wendelin Steinbachs Vorlesungen über den
Hebräerbrief* (Wiesbaden, 1971), pp. 4-18.

[23] For an excellent discussion, see H. A. Oberman, *Werden und Wertung der Reformation*
(Tübingen, 1977), pp. 118-40.

[24] Feld, *Vorlesungen über den Hebräerbrief*, 145-52.

[25] Feld, *Vorlesungen über den Hebräerbrief*, pp. 146-7.

[26] *Opera exegetica I* (see n.21) lect. III cap. 17; 132.19-133.1.

appropriate *modus loquendi* only for those who have just begun the Christian life: those who are more versed in its principles know that faith cannot save unless it is accompanied and informed by a habit of charity.[27] Indeed, Steinbach interprets Abraham's response of faith as an illustration of the general maxim 'God will not deny his grace to those who do *quod in se est.*'[28] Even though Steinbach is commenting upon the very epistle which Luther would later indicate to be his particular favourite, and even though he concedes that Paul speaks of justification *sola fide*, the Tübingen exegete is still able to derive and support the leading features of the doctrine of justification associated with the *via moderna* from his text. This fact serves to emphasise the point which we made earlier: the hermeneutical presuppositions with which the exegete approaches scripture effectively determine his conclusions. With this point in mind, we now turn to consider Luther's hermeneutical presuppositions implicit in his exposition of the Psalter, 1513-15.

Luther's *Dictata super Psalterium* are an outstanding example of late medieval biblical exegesis, illustrating brilliantly the features which we have identified as characteristic of the period. Luther employs the *Quadriga* with an enthusiasm and brilliance which must have captivated his audience. Even as late as 1519, Luther conceded that, provided it was not abused, the *Quadriga* was a valuable exegetical aid.[29] The four-fold exegetical scheme dominates Luther's exposition of the Psalter.[30] Luther is careful, following the standard guidelines, to subordinate the three spiritual senses of scripture to the literal (or historical) sense, expressly stating that nothing can be held on the basis of the allegorical, tropological or anagogical senses unless it can first be shown to be explicitly stated in the literal sense.[31] It is the literal sense of scripture which is the most fundamental, and to which the other three are subordinate.[32]

[27] *Opera exegetica I* lect. III cap. 17; 134.12-17; lect. III cap. 16; 131.11-18; lect. III cap. 17; 136.22-137.2. Cf. Oberman, *Werden und Wertung*, p. 127.

[28] *Opera exegetica I* lect. III cap. 19; 152.7-9; lect. II cap. 12; 97.1-4.

[29] See his comments on Galatians 2.14: WA 2.511.

[30] K. Holl, 'Luthers Bedeutung für den Fortschritt der Auslegungskunft', in *Gesammelte Aufsätze zur Kirchengeschichte I: Luther* (Tübingen, 1948), pp. 544-82, especially pp. 545-50; H. Bornkamm, *Luther und das Alte Testament* (Tübingen, 1948).

[31] WA 55 I.4.20-22 (= 3.11.33-5): 'In Scripturis . . . nulla valet allegoria, tropologia, anagoge, nisi alibi hystorice idem expresse dicatur. Alioquin ludibrium fieret Scriptura.'

[32] WA 4.305.6-8: 'Quod inde puto venire, quia propheticum, id est literalem, primo non quesierunt: qui est fundamentum ceterorum, magister et lux et author et fons atque origo.'

Luther makes an important distinction between the *literal-historical* meaning of his Old Testament text (that is, the literal meaning of the text, as determined by its historical context), and its *literal-prophetic* sense (that is, the meaning of the text, as interpreted as referring to the coming of Christ and the establishment of his church). The Christological concentration, which is so characteristic a feature of the *Dictata*, is achieved by placing emphasis upon the *literal-prophetic*, rather than the *literal-historic*, sense of scripture. In this manner, Luther is able to maintain that Christ is the *sensus principalis* of scripture.[33] Once this Christological hermeneutical principle is conceded, the four senses of scripture form a common confluence, testifying to the coming of Christ and the benefits which this confers upon believers.[34] In an important essay, Ebeling pointed out how Luther appears to combine the traditional *Quadriga* with Lefèvre d'Etaples' Christological exegesis of the Psalter, referring the literal sense of scripture to Christ and his church, rather than the historical situation of Israel at the time.[35] It seems to us that the publication of Steinbach's lectures on Galatians and Hebrews, dating from precisely the same time as Luther's *Dictata*, permits us to call the novelty of this approach into question, as it appears to have been a commonplace for later medieval exegetes to refer the literal sense of the Old Testament to Christ, so that the Old Testament *histories* — and not just the prophecies — must be seen as statements concerning Christ and his church. As is well known, Luther's biblical hermeneutic underwent a decisive change in the period immediately following the *Dictata*,[36] although elements of this

[33] G. Ebeling, 'Die Anfänge von Luthers Hermeneutik', in *Lutherstudien I* (Tübingen, 1971), pp. 1-68; p. 61.

[34] WA 55 II.63.10-11 (= 3.46.28-9): 'Et hoc modo omnes quatuor sensus Scripture in unum confluunt amplissimum flumen'; WA 3.369.6: 'Hec omnia Christus simul.'

[35] Ebeling, *Anfänge von Luthers Hermeneutik*, pp. 54-61.

[36] As noted by Holl, *Luthers Bedeutung*; E. Hirsch, 'Initium theologiae Lutheri', in *Der Durchbruch der reformatorischen Erkenntnis bei Luther*, pp. 64-95, especially pp. 93-5; E. Vogelsang, *Die Anfänge von Luthers Christologie nach der ersten Psalmenvorlesung* (Berlin/Leipzig, 1929), pp. 16-30; 40-61; E. Seeberg, 'Die Anfänge der Theologie Luthers', *Zeitschrift für Kirchengeschichte* 53 (1934), pp. 229-41. The suggestion by K. Bauer (*Die Wittenberger Universitätstheologie und die Anfänge der deutschen Reformation* [Tübingen, 1928], pp. 145-7), that Luther's later hermeneutic is due to the influence of Johannes von Staupitz has been adequately refuted: see D. C. Steinmetz, *Luther and Staupitz: An Essay in the Intellectual Origins of the Protestant Reformation* (Durham, N.C., 1980), pp. 35-67, especially pp. 65-7.

shift can be argued to be latent within the *Dictata*.[37] Nevertheless, it seems to us that the Christological concentration, so characteristic a feature of the *Dictata*, and so significant in relation to Luther's theological breakthrough, cannot be regarded as constituting an *innovation* on Luther's part. Even on this point, Luther must be regarded as standing within a late medieval hermeneutical tradition. The totally medieval character of the hermeneutic employed within the *Dictata* is confirmed by the observation that Luther insists that the interpretation of scripture is a public event, which takes place within the body of the church.[38] The church is the portal of salvation,[39] outside of which there is no true knowledge of God.[40] Furthermore, following Gerson, Luther explicitly states that the church's rule of faith must be regarded as a hermeneutical canon, which defines the area within which the exegesis of scripture may be legitimately pursued.[41] Those familiar only with the later Luther may find this assertion astonishing — but the fact remains that the young Luther was, in this respect as in so many others, thoroughly medieval.

The medieval character of Luther's theology is, of course, at its most evident in the *Randbemerkungen* of 1509-10. Following the medieval Augustinian emphasis upon the priority of *caritas* over faith,[42] Luther insists that faith alone cannot justify: although faith may be regarded as directing the individual believer towards invisible realities, it is incapable of justifying that individual unless it is informed by *caritas*.[43] The most significant point of contact with the theology of justification of the later medieval period relates to his critique of the role of created habits in justification. Although an earlier generation of scholars

[37] Particular attention is usually directed towards the increasing importance which Luther came to attach to the tropological sense of scripture. The theory of J. S. Preus, *From Shadow to Promise: Old Testament Interpretation from Augustine to the Young Luther* (Cambridge, Mass., 1969) — that this *hindered* rather than *assisted* Luther's breakthrough — is quite untenable: see E. G. Rupp's review of this work in *Journal of Theological Studies* 23 (1972), pp. 276-8; Hendrix, *Ecclesia in via*, pp. 263-87.
[38] This is not to say that Scripture is totally subject to the church: WA 3.516.40 — 517.4; 4.318.3-6.
[39] WA 4.25.12-17.
[40] WA 3.268.37-38: 'Extra enim Ecclesiam non est cognitio vera Dei.'
[41] WA 3.517.33-40.
[42] On this, see our *Iustitia Dei: A History of the Christian Doctrine of Justification* (2 vols. Cambridge, 1986), Volume I, pp. 29-34.
[43] WA 9.72.4: '*fides enim qua iustificatus es*: Talis fides non est sine charitate'; WA 9.72.11-12: 'hic non simpliciter fides dicitur, sed per dilectionem operatur vel qua iustificati sumus'; WA 9.90.32: 'charitas facit totam personam gratam.'

regarded this as marking a complete break with the medieval tradition, it is becoming increasingly clear that this is simply not the case.

During the thirteenth century the concept of a created habit of grace or charity had become inextricably linked with the discussion of the mode of man's justification before God. The concept appeared to provide a solution to a dilemma which the theological renaissance of the twelfth century had highlighted: in what manner can God be said to dwell in the souls of the justified?[44] It was clearly necessary to distinguish the mode of the human and divine union in this instance from the unique case of the hypostatic union, and yet the conceptual framework through which this might be achieved was not then available. Peter Lombard attempted to resolve the problem by directly equating the *caritas* which is infused into the human soul in justification with the person of the Holy Spirit.[45] This solution, however, was regarded with suspicion by his successors. For St Thomas Aquinas, the union of the uncreated Holy Spirit with the created human soul was quite incompatible with the ontological distinction it was necessary to maintain between them. St Thomas therefore located the solution to the problem as lying in the concept of a created habit which, although essentially indistinguishable from God, nevertheless remains an entity created within the human soul by him.[46] The created habit was thus understood as a hybrid species, interposed as a created intermediate between God and man, whose presence determines whether or not a man is justified.

Underlying the implication of a created habit of grace in justification is a particular concept of causality. For St Thomas, Peter Aureole and others,[47] the nature of grace, sin and divine acceptation were such that a created habit of grace was necessary in justification by the very nature of things (*ex natura rei*). When this concept of causality was called into question by Duns Scotus, the role of created habits in justification appeared increasingly uncertain. For Scotus, the relationship between

[44] For this question, see our *Iustitia Dei*, Volume I, I.1.5. See also: Z. Alszeghy, *Nova Creatura: la nozione della grazia nei commentari medievali di S. Paolo* (Roma, 1956); B. Gillon, 'La grâce incréée chez quelques théologiens du XIVe siècle', *Divinitas* 11 (1967), pp. 671-680; B. Stoeckle, *"Gratia supponit naturam"*. *Geschichte und Analyse eines theologischen Axioms* (Rom, 1962).
[45] *I Sent.* dist. xvii. For an extremely helpful survey of the points at issue in the medieval discussion of this distinction, see W. Dettloff, *Die Entwicklung der Akzeptations- und Verdienstlehre von Duns Skotus bis Luther* (Münster, 1963).
[46] *In I Sent.* dist. xvii q.1 a.1.
[47] See our *Iustitia Dei*, Volume I, pp. 145-54 for further details.

grace, sin and divine acceptation was purely contingent, depending upon divine ordination rather than the nature of the entities themselves.[48] It is this concept of causality, usually referred to as *covenantal* or *sine qua non* causality, and discussed at length in the previous chapter, which is characteristic of the *via moderna*. During the later fourteenth century, it also became highly influential within certain sections of the Augustinian Order.

Although the theologians of the Augustinian Order were initially faithful to the teaching of Giles of Rome on the necessity of created habits in justification, the role of such habits was increasingly called into question from the time of Gregory of Rimini onwards. For Thomas of Strassburg, the last theologian of the earlier Augustinian school, the axiom which determined the necessity of created habits in justification was *nullus potest esse formaliter Deo gratus nisi sit informatus gratia a Deo creata*;[49] for Gregory of Rimini, usually regarded as the first representative of the *schola Augustiniana moderna*, the axiom which called the necessity of such habits into question was Scotus' maxim *nihil creatum potest esse ratio actus divini*.[50] As we have shown elsewhere, there was a substantial body of opinion within the Augustinian Order during the later Middle Ages which shared the misgivings of the *via moderna* concerning the logical necessity of created habits in justification. Beginning with Gregory of Rimini, criticism of the role of created habits in justification became a commonplace within the Order, being associated with such theologians as Hugolino of Orvieto, Dionysius of Montina, Alphonsus of Toledo, Johannes Klenkok and Johannes Hiltalingen of Basel.[51] Although the *de facto* necessity of such habits was not actually denied, justification came to be seen as a direct, personal act of God himself, which need not involve any created intermediates *ex natura rei*.

By the end of the medieval period, two factors had combined to make created habits unnecessary hypotheses in justification. The first of these was the conclusive demonstration by the theologians of the

---

[48] W. Dettloff, *Die Lehre von der Acceptatio Dei bei Johannes Duns Skotus* (Werl, 1954).
[49] *In II Sent.* dist. xxvi, xxvii, a.1 q.1.
[50] e.g., as used by Gabriel Biel, among countless others of the period: *In I Sent.* dist. xvii q.3 a.3 dub. 2.
[51] A. E. McGrath, ' "Augustinianism?" A Critical Assessment of the so-called "Medieval Augustinian Tradition" on Justification', *Augustiniana* 31 (1981), pp. 247-67; *Iustitia Dei*, Volume I, pp. 172-9. For references, see note 122 of previous chapter.

via moderna that there was no logical necessity for such habits in justification. Applying the general principle of Ockham's Razor — *Quia frustra fit per plura quod potest equaliter fieri per pauciora*[52] — their existence was deemed irrelevant, if they existed at all. Secondly, the tendency within the modern Augustinian school to emphasise the personal nature of the divine action within man inevitably led to emphasis being shifted from the concept of *created* grace to that of *uncreated* grace — away from the concept of the habit, towards the Holy Spirit himself. The interpretation of the Holy Spirit as the bond of love which unites Father and Son, the Godhead and the believer, which is ultimately due to St Augustine himself, thus came to assume a new significance. This emphasis upon the primacy of *gratia increata* over *gratia creata* can be particularly well illustrated from Staupitz' Tübingen sermons of 1497-98.[53] In view of this consensus within the theological traditions which the young Luther encountered during his years at Erfurt (1505-8) and his first Wittenberg period (1508-9), it would not be surprising if he incorporated the substance of this consensus into his marginal comments to Peter Lombard's *Sentences*. An examination of these comments indicates that this is the case.

In his marginal comments to the *Sentences*, we find Luther expressing precisely the same sentiments concerning created habits as those we noted above, although it is not clear which of the two considerations we noted above was the more influential upon his deliberations.[54] Luther's study of Augustine's *de Trinitate*, which dates from this period, clearly made a deep impression upon him, particularly in connection with the relationship between *dilectio* (or *caritas*) and the Holy Spirit. For Luther, the concept of a created habit caused more problems than it solved, and he therefore attempts to resolve the dilemma on the basis of the lines indicated by St Augustine himself. Setting aside hypothetical speculation *de potentia Dei absoluta* — the traditional method of demonstrating the radical contingency of the role of created habits — Luther argues that *de facto* it is impossible to separate the gifts of *caritas* and the Holy Spirit:

[52] Ockham, *In II Sent.* qq. 14-15; O.

[53] D. C. Steinmetz, *Misericordia Dei: The Theology of Johannes von Staupitz in its Late Medieval Setting* (Leiden, 1968), pp. 106-7.

[54] For an excellent, although now somewhat dated, discussion, see P. Vignaux, *Luther Commentateur des Sentences (Livre I, Distinction XVII)* (Paris, 1935), pp. 5-44. Vignaux relates Luther's *habitus*-critique to the prevailing theology of the *via moderna*; modern Augustinian scholarship has indicated the necessity to modify this thesis somewhat in the light of newly published sources.

both are given simultaneously and in conjunction with one another.[55] To illustrate the essential relationship between the concepts, Luther alludes to I Corinthians 1.30: 'Christ is our faith, righteousness, grace and our sanctification.' Although Luther's discussion of this point is intensely compressed, the point which he is making is clear: the relationship between *caritas* and the Holy Spirit is to be regarded as analogous to that between *iustitia* and Christ. Although the seeds of Luther's mature thought of the nature of justification are contained within these terse statements, they are not developed further. Luther confines himself to arguing that the Holy Spirit is *caritas*,[56] just as he would later argue that Christ is the righteousness of faith.[57] For Luther, the concept of the *habitus* is quite unhelpful and unnecessary: if the term must be used, it should be used in an Augustinian, and not in an Aristotelian, sense, referring to the bond of love which unites man to God, rather than a created intermediate interposed between them. Luther's meditation upon Augustine's *de Trinitate*, with its characteristic emphasis upon the Holy Spirit as the bond of love which unites Father and Son, the Godhead and the believer, has evidently found its expression in a criticism of the *habitus*-doctrine which is as penetrating as it is condensed. If Augustine's soteriology is understood to underlie Peter Lombard's remarks on the relationship between the Holy Spirit and *caritas* or *dilectio*, Luther observes that the Master of the Sentences came close to the truth: *habitus autem adhuc est spiritus sanctus*.[58] Luther here reproduces an authentically Augustinian theme which had assumed increasing importance in later medieval theology — the conviction that justification involves a direct personal encounter between the Holy Spirit and man. Although Luther explicitly rejects one medieval tradition on the nature of the grace of justification, it is only to adopt another. Far from breaking free from the medieval tradition at this point, Luther merely shifts his position within it.

The most characteristic feature of the late medieval discussion of the doctrine of justification to be found in the *Dictata super Psalterium* is that

[55] WA 9.42.35-38. On Augustine's soteriology, see A. Capanága, 'La deificacíon en la soteriología agustiniana', in *Augustinus Magister* (Paris, 1954), Volume II, pp. 745-54.
[56] WA 9.42.39 — 43.6.
[57] WA 40 I.229.28.
[58] WA 9.44.1-4: 'Ad hanc authoritatem quae expressa nimis est: quia deo conjungi per charitatem est quasi per medium ad objectum, diceret Magister, quod Augustinus hic loquitur de actu charitatis qui nos deo jungit, habitus autem est spiritus sanctus.' The same conclusion is implicit earlier: WA 9.43.2-8.

of a *pactum* between God and man, on the basis of which God is able
to justify the sinner. This theme is particularly associated with the *via
moderna*, and has been discussed in the previous chapter, to which the
reader is referred. As medieval theological scholarship has now established,[59] the idea of a self-imposed limitation upon the divine activity was
a commonplace from the twelfth century onwards. Broadly speaking,
God was understood to have committed himself to justify man, provided
man first fulfilled a certain minimum requirement on his part. It is this
fundamental principle which underlies the celebrated scholastic maxim *facienti quod in se est Deus non denegat gratiam.*[60] The basic principle expressed here is that when man fulfils his obligations to God (by doing
'what lies within him', *quod in se est*), God will respond by bestowing the
gift of justifying grace. The use of this principle is as characteristic of
the early Dominican and Franciscan schools as it is of the later Franciscan school and the *via moderna.*[61] There was, of course, considerable
divergence of opinion within the schools concerning the precise *nature*
of man's obligations to God, and whether man could fulfil these unaided
(*ex puris naturalibus*) or whether he required the assistance of prevenient
grace, and concerning whether this 'preparation' or 'disposition' for
justification could be considered to be meritorious *de congruo*. Nevertheless, practically the entire medieval theological tradition from the
end of the twelfth century to the beginning of the sixteenth assumed that
justification proceeded upon this basis.

The particular development of this principle associated with the *via
moderna* lies in the conceptual elaboration of the foundation upon which
justification takes place. The earlier medieval tradition had insisted that
God was under a self-imposed obligation to bestow grace upon the man
who did *quod in se est*, and had no qualms about employing terms such
as *obligatio* or *debitum* to refer to this obligation upon the part of God.
The theologians of the *via moderna* correlated this idea of a divine obligation with the newly-emerging economic and political ideas of covenants
or contracts, and thus came to speak of a covenant or contract (*pactum*)
between God and man, on the basis of which God had promised to

---

[59] The best study is the richly documented investigation of B. Hamm, *Promissio,
Pactum, Ordinatio: Freiheit und Selbstbindung in der scholastischen Gnadenlehre* (Tübingen,
1977). The reader who is not familiar with this concept should read this work before
proceeding further.
[60] See our *Iustitia Dei*, Volume I, pp. 83-91 for an analysis of the various interpretations placed upon this maxim in the period.
[61] See our *Iustitia Dei*, Volume I, pp. 158-72 for discussion.

bestow grace upon man, provided he fulfilled certain basic conditions. [62] This conceptual device served to emphasise the divine reliability: once man had fulfilled his part of the covenant, he could rest assured that God would fulfil his. It must be emphasised that the introduction of the *pactum*-motif does not represent an *alteration* of the common medieval teaching on the divine obligation to justify man, but merely a technical refinement. The conditions under which God will bestow his grace are defined by the terms of the *pactum*, and once man has fulfilled those conditions, God is under obligation (by a *necessitas coactionis* or *necessitas consequentiae*) to fulfil his part of the covenant. While other late medieval theologians, such as Staupitz, might wish to avoid using the concept of the *pactum*, and might have their reservations about the interpretation placed upon the conditions for justification by the *moderni*, they still worked within the same conceptual framework. [63]

Precisely this general principle, and also the same technical vocabulary, is employed by Luther in the *Dictata*. Luther uses the terms *pactum* and *testamentum* interchangeably, although at a later date he would begin to distinguish between them. [64] The following passage illustrates this point particularly clearly:

> God has made himself a debtor to us through the promise of he who is merciful, not through the dignity of the human nature of he who merits. He required nothing except preparation, in order that we might be capable of receiving this gift, just as if a prince or king of the earth would promise a robber or a murderer one hundred florins, providing he awaited him at a specified time and place. Thus it is clear that the king would be a debtor through his gratuitous promise and mercy without that man's merit; nor would the king deny what he had promised on account of that man's demerit. [65]

This passage brilliantly summarises the characteristic teaching of the medieval period on the necessity of a human preparation for

---

[62] See note 106 of previous chapter for references.

[63] Steinmetz, *Misericordia Dei*, pp. 93-7.

[64] e.g. in the Galatians lectures of 1517 (WA 57 II.82.1-15) and the Galatians commentary of 1519 (WA 2.521.25-37). For an excellent discussion of the *pactum*-motif in the young Luther, see O. Bayer, *Promissio. Geschichte der reformatorischen Wende in Luthers Theologie* (Göttingen, 1971), pp. 119-23; 313-17; Hamm, *Promissio, Pactum, Ordinatio*, pp. 377-90. Luther later tended to associate *pactum* with life, and *testamentum* with death: cf. WA 6.514.7-10: 'Deus testatus est, ideo necesse fuit eum mori: mori autem non potuit, nisi esset homo: ita in eodem testamenti vocabulo compendiosissime et incarnatio et mors Christi comprehensa est.'

[65] WA 4.261.32-39.

justification, as well as demonstrating the general principle of a self-imposed divine obligation to bestow grace, upon the fulfilment of certain minimum conditions (in this case, turning up to receive the gift at a specified time and place). The following points of contact with the teaching of the *via moderna* may be noted:

(1) The emphasis that the gift is bestowed through the divine liberality, and not through human merit: the play on the words *miserentis* and *merentis* is significant.
(2) The specification of a minimum condition for justification (that is, defining precisely what is meant by *quod in se est*).
(3) The invocation of the principle that God is under an obligation to bestow grace once this minimum condition is met, irrespective of the merit or demerit of the *viator*.
(4) The use of the image of a king, which was commonly used by the *moderni* to illustrate the principle of covenantal causality, which underlies this analogy.[66]
(5) The use of the principle of covenantal causality itself, characteristic of the *via moderna*: what determines the relationship between the robber's receiving one hundred florins and his turning up at a specified time and place is not any inherent ontological connection between the two, but merely the king's promise that these two are thus correlated. The *sine qua non* character of this covenantal causality is well illustrated by this analogy: turning up at the specified time and place is the *conditio sine qua non* for receiving the gift.

The principle of covenantal causality lies at the centre of Luther's doctrine of justification, as expounded in the *Dictata*. As Luther makes it clear, the implication of grace and faith in justification is itself a consequence of the divine covenant (*pactum*) and not a consequence of their essential natures:

Even grace and faith, through which we are justified today, would not justify us of themselves (*ex seipsis*), without God's covenant. It is precisely for this reason, that we are saved: God has made a testament (*testamentum*) and

---

[66] See W. J. Courtenay, 'The King and the Leaden Coin: The Economic Background to Sine Qua Non Causality', *Traditio* 28 (1971), pp. 185-209.

covenant (*pactum*) with us, so that whoever believes and is baptised shall be saved. In this covenant God is truthful and faithful, and is bound by what he has promised.[67]

This important passage not merely illustrates the concept of covenantal causality with some brilliance: it also allows us to understand Luther's early appeal to his being baptised in his spiritual struggles. *Ego baptisatus sum!* — and as Luther *was* baptised, the above passage demonstrates how the concept of covenantal causality would have enabled him to rely upon the divine faithfulness in his time of distress. Furthermore, the similarity between Luther and Steinbach on *fides* as man's doing *quod in se est* will be evident.

Once it has been established that Luther operates with a covenantal concept of causality in respect to justification, the question of the minimum condition required for man's justification becomes important. *Homini facienti quod in se est Deus infallibiliter dat gratiam*, as Luther reminds his hearers. But what is to be understood by '*quod in se est*'? For Luther, the basic condition which man must meet in order to be justified appears to be a recognition of one's need for grace, and an appeal to God, in his mercy, to bestow it. This is indicated by Luther's discussion of faith and humility, to which we shall shortly return, but also by his frequent use of verbs such as 'cry out',[68] 'ask', 'seek', and 'knock', as in the following crucial passage:

'Ask, and you will receive; seek, and you will find; knock, and it shall be opened to you. For everyone who asks receives, etc.' (Matthew 7.7-8). Hence the doctors rightly say that God gives grace without fail to the man who does what lies within him (*homini facienti quod in se est Deus infallibiliter dat gratiam*), and though he could not prepare himself for grace in a manner which is meritorious *de condigno*, he may do so in a manner which is meritorious *de congruo* on account of this promise of God and the covenant of mercy (*pactum misericordiae*).[69]

---

[67] WA 3.289.1-5. Bayer points out how Luther uses the terminology associated with the *pactum*-motif frequently elsewhere in the *Dictata* (e.g. *dispositio, facere quod in se est, paratus esse, meritum de congruo, capax esse*): Bayer, *Promissio*, p. 140. The suggestion that there is a fundamental semantic difference between Luther and the later medieval tradition here cannot be sustained: Hamm, *Promissio, Pactum, Ordinatio*, p. 384.

[68] WA 4.375.16-30.

[69] WA 4.262.2-7. Luther abbreviates phrases such as 'mereri de congruo' to 'de congruo'.

As Bayer points out, God gives his grace *per definitionem* only to those who ask for it.[70] More significantly, Luther here reproduces the substance of Lection 59 of Gabriel Biel's commentary on the text of the Mass,[71] a textbook which he himself studied as a student, thus confirming that the origins of his opinions lie with the *via moderna*.

In 1958, Ernst Bizer caused a storm by arguing that Luther's theological breakthrough must have taken place in the winter of 1517-18,[72] so that Luther's doctrine of justification in the *Dictata* must be regarded as thoroughly medieval. One of the factors which led him to this conclusion was his analysis of Luther's teaching in the *Dictata* on the proper disposition for justification: God gives his grace to the humble.[73] While we do not agree with Bizer's conclusions concerning the dating of Luther's theological breakthrough, it nevertheless seems to us that he has made a telling point concerning Luther's attitude to the relationship between justification and humility, at least in the years 1513-14. Luther's use of terms such as *accusatio sui* and *iudicium* is usually, although not invariably, related to man's awareness of his own spiritual poverty and emptiness *coram Deo*, which motivates him to cry out to God for grace. This conclusion is suggested by a number of converging themes in the *Dictata*.

(1) *Iudicium* is sometimes used to refer to the judgement of God himself.[74] When this sense is employed, the judgement which God pronounces upon man through his Word is that he is a sinner. If the sinner rejects this judgement, he makes God out to be a liar.[75]

(2) *Iudicium* is usually the sinner's admission that he is indeed a sinner, worthy of punishment and death.[76] Once he admits this, he is prepared to receive the gift of justifying grace, and thus avoid final judgement.[77]

---

[70] Bayer, *Promissio*, p. 128.
[71] Bayer, *Promissio*, pp. 129-32, with documentation from the original sources. In the Romans lectures of 1515-16, Luther again reproduces this characteristic feature of the later medieval theological tradition, when commenting on Romans 4.7: see Bayer, *Promissio*, pp. 137-43.
[72] E. Bizer, *Fides ex auditu. Eine Untersuchung über die Entdeckung der Gerechtigkeit Gottes durch Martin Luther* (Neukirchen, 3rd edn, 1966), p. 165.
[73] Bizer, *Fides ex auditu*, p. 19.
[74] e.g., WA 3.368.3-5.
[75] e.g., WA 3.288.8-12.
[76] e.g., WA 55 II.32.18-20.
[77] e.g., WA 4.198.19-21.

(3) Luther frequently states that humility is the precondition for the reception of grace. Once man is forced to recognise the reality of his situation, he is moved to confess his sin and praise God for his mercy.[78] By this *duplex confessio*, he demonstrates that he has fully appreciated his hopelessness before God.

(4) Luther excludes the possibility that man can be justified by works of the law,[79] essentially because of the pride this engenders, similar to that encountered in the parable of the Pharisee and the Publican (Luke 18.9-14).[80] The righteousness of God excludes human righteousness,[81] so that God, in effect, justifies the humble and not the proud.[82]

These themes are clearly convergent. Luther's basic theme is that the Word of God forces man, despite his outward morality, to recognise his sin and emptiness, and thus to turn to God, crying out for the gift of grace which he now recognises he needs. The Christian, in other words, is a spiritual beggar, who can do nothing except cry out for the salvation which is his in Christ.[83] Once he does this, he has fulfilled the condition necessary for the bestowal of grace by the terms of the divine *pactum*, and the gift of grace follows as a matter of course. While Luther's understanding of what man must do in order to receive grace differs from Biel's in its emphasis, the theological framework within which both operate is essentially the same — that of a covenant, which imposes obligations upon God and man alike, which both must meet if justification is to take place. Even if Luther grafted an essentially Augustinian emphasis upon humility on to the covenant theology of the *via moderna*,

[78] e.g., WA 4.91.4-5; 4.111.33-37; 3.124.12-14. For *accusatio sui* as that precondition, see WA 3.288.30-32; 3.370.18. On the *duplex confessio*, see WA 4.239.1-3.

[79] WA 3.170.33-34; 3.172.30-36; 55 II.92.17-19.

[80] Luther's discussion of this parable in the *Dictata* is thoroughly medieval. On the late medieval interpretation of this parable, see A. Zumkeller, 'Das Ungenügen der menschlichen Werke bei den deutschen Predigern des Spätmittelalters', *Zeitschrift für katholische Theologie* 81 (1959), pp. 265-305. The Gospel set for the Eleventh Sunday after Pentecost is the Parable in question. Zumkeller's comments on Luther's relationship to this tradition may be noted: Zumkeller, *Das Ungenügen der menschlichen Werke*, p. 305.

[81] e.g., WA 3.154.32-4.

[82] e.g., WA 4.344.24-7.

[83] For an extremely helpful analysis, see H. A. Oberman, 'Wir sind Pettler. Hoc est verum. Bunde und Gnade in der Theologie des Mittelalters und der Reformation', *Zeitschrift für Kirchengeschichte* 78 (1967) pp. 232-52. Oberman conclusively rejects the opinion that the *humilitas* in question was understood by Luther to be a monastic virtue.

he would still remain thoroughly medieval in respect of his doctrine of justification in the *Dictata*. It is, however, clear that changes in Luther's thought took place even within the *Dictata*, and we therefore propose to limit the scope of our investigation to the end of the year 1514, when we conclude that the Luther of the early *Dictata* is unquestionably a medieval theologian, and displays considerable affinity at points with the theology of the *via moderna*.[84]

In 1514 Luther held a doctrine of justification which was firmly set within a well-established medieval theological tradition. All that was required of man was that he humbled himself before God, in order that he might receive the gift of grace which God would then bestow upon him. If Luther's early theology of justification is approached from the standpoint of the later medieval period, rather than from that of the later Luther himself, this theology fits naturally into place within the overall development of the doctrine within this period. The fact that Luther displays such a continuity with this later medieval tradition serves to emphasise the significance of his break from it, rather than to detract from it. It is the nature and development of this break, which finally led to the formulation of the *theologia crucis*, that forms the subject of the second part of this study. That break appears to have come about through Luther's prolonged meditation upon a concept which he had frequently encountered during his exegesis of the Psalter — that of *iustitia Dei*, 'the righteousness of God'. The origins of the theology of the cross lie in Luther's initial difficulty in seeing how the idea of a righteous God could conceivably be good news for sinful man. It is to the question of the nature and date of Luther's discovery of the righteousness of God, probably one of the most tantalising aspects of modern Luther scholarship, that we now turn.

---

[84] Grane concludes: 'daß hier ein Theologe der via moderna spricht': L. Grane, *Contra Gabrielem: Luthers Auseinandersetzung mit Gabriel Biel in der Disputatio contra scholasticam theologiam* (Gyldendal, 1962) p. 309; Hamm, *Promissio, Pactum, Ordinatio*, p. 377.

PART II

THE BREAKTHROUGH

Luther in Transition 1514-19

4

Mira et nova diffinitio Iusticiae: Luther's Discovery of the Righteousness of God

IN 1545, the year before Luther's death, an edition of his works was published at Wittenberg. Luther, then an old man, contributed a preface to the first volume of this edition, taking the opportunity to reflect upon his early career at Wittenberg. While the reminiscences of old men are notoriously unreliable, Luther's account of his early years appears to be remarkably accurate.[1] The historical accuracy of this account is of particular significance to our study, as it lends considerable support to the accuracy of the section of the preface in which Luther, in a remarkable piece of sustained theological analysis, reflects upon the theological problem which had, he alleges, been troubling him for some considerable period of time — the 'righteousness of God'. After describing the origins and development of the indulgences controversy and the mission of Miltitz, he continues:

Interim eo anno iam redieram ad Psalterium denuo interpretandum, fretus eo, quod exercitatior essem, postquam S. Pauli Epistolas ad Romanos, ad Galatas, et eam, quae est ad Ebraeos, tractassem in scholis. Miro certe ardore captus fueram cognoscendi Pauli in epistola ad Rom., sed obstiterat hactenus non frigidus circum praecordia sanguis, sed unicum vocabulum, quod est

Meanwhile in that year [1519], I had returned to interpreting the Psalter again, confident that I was better equipped after I had expounded in the schools the letters of St Paul to the Romans and the Galatians, and the letter to the Hebrews. I had certainly been overcome with a great desire to understand St Paul in his letter to the Romans, but what had hindered me thus far was not any

[1]   e.g. E. Stracke, *Luthers großes Selbstzeugnis 1545 über seine Entwicklung zum Reformator historisch-kritisch untersucht* (Leipzig, 1926), pp. 112-28.

Cap. 1: Iustitia Dei revelatur in illo. Oderam enim vocabulum istud 'Iustitia Dei', quod usu et consuetudine omnium doctorum doctus eram philosophice intelligere de iustitia (ut vocant) formali seu activa, qua Deus est iustus, et peccatores iniustosque punit.

Ego autem, qui me, utcunque irreprehensibilis monachus vivebam, sentirem coram Deo esse peccatorem inquietissimae conscientiae, nec mea satisfactione placatum confidere possem, non amabam, imo odiebam iustum et punientem peccatores Deum, tacitaque si non blasphemia, certe ingenti murmuratione indignabar Deo, dicens: quasi vero non satis sit, miseros peccatores et aeternaliter perditos peccato originali omni genere calamitatis oppressos esse per legem decalogi, nisi Deus per euangelium dolorem dolori adderet, et etiam per euangelium nobis iustitiam et iram suam intentaret. Furebam ita saeva et perturbata conscientia, pulsabam tamen importunus eo loco Paulum, ardentissime sitiens scire, quid S. Paulus vellet.

Donec miserente Deo meditabundus dies et noctes connexionem verborum attenderem, nempe: Iustitia Dei revelatur in illo, sicut scriptum est: Iustus ex fide vivit, ibi iustitiam Dei coepi intelligere eam, qua iustus dono Dei vivit, nempe ex

'coldness of the blood' so much as that one phrase in the first chapter: 'The righteousness of God is revealed in it.' For I had hated that phrase 'the righteousness of God' which, according to the use and custom of all the doctors, I had been taught to understand philosophically, in the sense of the formal or active righteousness (as they termed it), by which God is righteous, and punishes unrighteous sinners.

Although I lived an irreproachable life as a monk, I felt that I was a sinner with an uneasy conscience before God; nor was I able to believe that I had pleased him with my satisfaction. I did not love — in fact, I hated — that righteous God who punished sinners, if not with silent blasphemy, then certainly with great murmuring. I was angry with God, saying 'As if it were not enough that miserable sinners should be eternally damned through original sin, with all kinds of misfortunes laid upon them by the Old Testament law, and yet God adds sorrow upon sorrow through the gospel, and even brings his wrath and righteousness to bear through it!' Thus I drove myself mad, with a desperate disturbed conscience, persistently pounding upon Paul in this passage, thirsting most ardently to know what he meant.

At last, God being merciful, as I meditated day and night on the connection of the words 'the righteousness of God is revealed in it, as it is written: the righteous shall live by faith', I began to understand that 'righteousness of God' as that by

fide, et esse hanc sententiam, revelari per euangelium iustitiam Dei, scilicet passivam, qua nos Deus misericors iustificat per fidem, sicut scriptum est: Iustus ex fide vivit. Hic me prorsus renatum esse sensi, et apertis portis in ipsam paradisum intrasse. Ibi continuo alia mihi facies totius scripturae apparuit. Discurrebam deinde per scripturas, ut habebat memoria, et colligebam etiam in aliis vocabulis analogiam, ut opus Dei, id est, quod operatur in nobis Deus, virtus Dei, qua nos potentes facit, sapientia Dei, qua nos sapientes facit, fortitudo Dei, salus Dei, gloria Dei.

Iam quanto odio vocabulum 'iustitia Dei' oderam ante, tanto amore dulcissimum mihi vocabulum extollebam, ita mihi iste locus Pauli fuit vere porta paradisi. Postea legebam Augustinum de spiritu et litera, ubi praeter spem offendi, quod et ipse iustitiam Dei similiter interpretatur: qua nos Deus induit, dum nos iustificat. Et quamquam imperfecte hoc adhuc sit dictum, ac de imputatione non clare omnia explicet, placuit tamen iustitiam Dei doceri, qua nos iustificemur.

which the righteous lives by the gift of God, namely by faith, and this sentence, 'the righteousness of God is revealed', to refer to a passive righteousness, by which the merciful God justifies us by faith, as it is written, 'The righteous lives by faith'. This immediately made me feel as though I had been born again, and as though I had entered through open gates into paradise itself. From that moment, the whole face of scripture appeared to me in a different light. Afterwards, I ran through the scriptures, as from memory, and found the same analogy in other phrases such as the 'work of God' (that which God works within us), the 'power of God' (by which he makes us strong), the 'wisdom of God' (by which he makes us wise), the 'strength of God', the 'salvation of God' and the 'glory of God'.

And now, where I had once hated the phrase 'the righteousness of God', so much I began to love and extoll it as the sweetest of words, so that this passage in Paul became the very gate of paradise for me. Afterwards, I read Augustine, *On the Spirit and the Letter*, where I found that he too, beyond my expectation, interpreted 'the righteousness of God' in the same way — as that which God bestows upon us, when he justifies us. And although this is expressed somewhat imperfectly, and he does not explain everything about imputation clearly, it was nevertheless pleasing to find that he taught that the 'righteousness of God' is that, by which we are justified.

| Istis cogitationibus armatior factus coepi Psalterium secundo interpretari. | Made more excited by these thoughts, I began to interpret the Psalter for the second time. [2] |

The passage bristles with difficulties, particularly the possibility that Luther, in his old age, may have contracted the time scale during which his reflections upon the meaning of *iustitia Dei* took place, so that insights which accumulated over a number of years are presented as if they occurred in a devastating moment of illumination. It is quite possible that Luther may have unconsciously modelled his account of his own theological breakthrough upon that of St Augustine, as it is recounted in the eighth book of the African bishop's *Confessions*: Luther frequently refers to this passage in the course of the *Dictata*, [3] indicating that he is aware of its significance in this respect. A more tantalising difficulty relates to the material upon which we are obliged to base our assessment of the theological reliability of the autobiographical fragment. As we shall indicate later, there is every reason to suppose that Luther's discovery of the 'new'meaning of the 'righteousness of God' took place at some point during the year 1515, possibly while he was still delivering his first course of lectures upon the Psalter. It is improbable, however, that we shall find sentiments similar to those of the autobiographical fragment expressed in the *Dictata*. As noted in the previous chapter, the young Luther regarded the exposition and interpretation of scripture as a *public*, rather than a *private* event, so that it is unlikely that he would incorporate accounts of his own personal doubts and anxieties into the substance of his lectures. Nevertheless, if Luther's understanding of the concept of the 'righteousness of God' underwent such a dramatic alteration during the period covered by the *Dictata*, it should be possible to detect clear evidence of this change in the substance of these lectures — as, in fact, turns out to be the case.

There has been considerable disagreement on the part of Luther scholars concerning the precise nature of Luther's theological

---

[2] WA 54.185.12-186.21. German scholars have often commented on the curious manner in which English scholars have translated this passage in the past (e.g. J. Mackinnon, *Luther and the Reformation* [London, 1925], p. 153; E. G. Rupp, *The Righteousness of God: Luther Studies* [London, 1953], pp. 121-2): G. Pfeiffer, 'Das Ringen Luthers um die Gerechtigkeit Gottes', in *Der Durchbruch der reformatorischen Erkenntnis bei Luther*, ed. B. Lohse (Darmstadt, 1968), pp. 163-202; p. 180 n. 79.

[3] e.g. WA 3.169.28-34; 3.535.20-22; 3.549.26-32. See A. Hamel, *Der junge Luther und Augustin* (2 vols: Gütersloh, 1934-5), Volume I, pp. 157-62.

breakthrough, and the date to which it may be assigned. Indeed, the date assigned to the breakthrough is itself determined by the prior decision on the part of the scholar as to the precise nature of Luther's discovery. Nevertheless, there still appears to be a clear distinction between the approach based upon an analysis of the autobiographical fragment itself, which appears to date the breakthrough in the winter of 1518-19, and that based upon an analysis of Luther's early works, particularly the *Dictata*, which places the breakthrough in the year 1514 or 1515. The force of the arguments adduced in favour of the former by Bizer,[4] and the latter by Bornkamm,[5] suggests that the nature of the discovery is actually considerably more complex than might at first appear to be the case. In the present study, we propose to argue the case for what we regard as the most satisfactory solution to the problem.

The position adopted in the present study, which will be elaborated and justified in the following chapters, is the following. Initially, Luther's understanding of *iustitia Dei* and cognate concepts is essentially that of the *via moderna*. However, over a period of time, Luther broke free from this matrix, eventually formulating his own position in the *theologia crucis* of 1518. The formulation of the *theologia crucis* took place over a period of several years, and was catalysed by Luther's initial difficulties concerning the question of what was meant by the 'righteousness of God'. As a consequence of Luther's 'new' answer to this question, the entire substance of his theology had to be reworked, leading eventually to the theology of the cross. As we shall show, the leading features of the theology of the cross are present in Luther's discovery of the true meaning of *iustitia Dei*. In other words, Luther's discovery of the righteousness of God is but one step in the process leading to the theology of the cross — but it is nevertheless the decisive catalytic step, which forced Luther to reconsider the theological matrix within which this concept was set. The old wineskins of the theology of the *via moderna* were simply incapable of containing the new wine with Luther thereby introduced. Indeed, Luther's passing reference to his rethinking of the meaning of terms such as *potentia Dei*, *sapientia Dei*, *fortitudo Dei*, and *gloria Dei* is practically a

[4] E. Bizer, *Fides ex auditu: Eine Untersuchung über die Entdeckung der Gerechtigkeit Gottes durch Martin Luther* (Neukirchen, 3rd edn, 1966).
[5] H. Bornkamm, 'Zur Frage der Iustitia Dei beim jungen Luther', in *Der Durchbruch der reformatorischen Erkenntnis*, pp. 289-383.

programmatic description of the development of the *theologia crucis*.

In the remainder of this study, we shall demonstrate how Luther's discovery of the new meaning of *iustitia Dei* necessitated a complete reexamination of his theology of justification, eventually forcing Luther to the theology of the cross. The development of Luther's theology of justification over the years 1514-19 is not a series of isolated and unrelated episodes, but is an essentially unitary process by which Luther incorporated the consequences of his theological breakthrough into his theology of justification with a logical rigour normally associated with Calvin. Before documenting and analysing this development, however, we propose to demonstrate how Luther's initial difficulties are the consequence of, and must be understood in the light of, the covenant theology of the *via moderna*.

LUTHER'S DIFFICULTIES IN THE LIGHT OF LATE MEDIEVAL THEOLOGY

If *iustitia* means rendering good for good and evil for evil, how can God justify sinful man? How can God, in his righteousness, render good for evil? Underlying the question of what is meant by the 'righteousness of God', *iustitia Dei*, is the deeper question of what is meant by *iustitia* itself. It is a well-established fact that the vocabulary of Christian theology contains a number of important concepts which originate from a Hebraic context, and whose transference to that of western Europe results in shifts of meaning which have quite unacceptable theological consequences. The Hebrew terms *sdq* and *sdqh* provide an excellent example of this phenomenon. [6] The Hebrew root-morpheme *sdq* is a theological, rather than a secular term, which frequently assumes strongly soteriological overtones which simply cannot be conveyed by the mere substitution of *iustitia* at its every occurrence — a point which is particularly evident when the difficulties faced by the Septuagint translators in dealing with *sdq* or *sdqh* are considered. [7] The most appropriate designation of the Hebrew terms

---

[6] On this whole question, see A. E. McGrath, 'Justice and Justification: Semantic and Juristic Aspects of the Christian Doctrine of Justification', *Scottish Journal of Theology* 35 (1982), pp. 403-18.

[7] McGrath, *Justice and Justification*, pp. 405-13. The problem is further discussed in our *Iustitia Dei*, Volume I, pp. 4-16.

sdq or *sdqh* is that of *iustitia salutifera*:[8] God, in his righteousness, acts to redeem and sustain his people. The Hebrew terms simply cannot bear the meaning, characteristic of western thought, of *iustitia distributiva*, as it is encapsulated in the Ciceronian definition of justice as 'giving to each man what he is entitled to': *iustitia est habitus animi, communi utilitate conservata, suam cuique tribuens dignitatem.*[9] It is for this reason that the question of Luther's knowledge of Hebrew at the time of the first course of lectures of the Psalter becomes so significant: had he such a knowledge, the strongly soteriological connotations of *iustitia Dei* would have impressed themselves upon him. However, although Luther's knowledge of Hebrew was such that, by the time of the *second* course of lectures on the Psalter (1518-21), he appears to have fully appreciated this semantic point,[10] there is no evidence whatsoever to indicate he knew of it earlier.

The influence of Roman law over the world in which the early theology of the Latin-speaking church was forged made it inevitable that Roman understandings of the *nature* of justice would be projected on to the term as and when it occurred in Holy Scripture.[11] The first significant critique of this tendency occurred during the course of the Pelagian controversy, in the exchange between Julian of Eclanum and Augustine of Hippo.[12] According to Julian, God deals with man in justice and in equity, rendering to each man that to which he is entitled as a result of his merit, without reference to his person. The Ciceronian idea of *reddens unicuique quod suum est* permeates his discussion of

[8] The term was coined at the end of the last century by Cremer: H. Cremer, *Die paulinische Rechtfertigungslehre im Zusammenhang ihrer geschichtlichen Voraussetzungen* (Gütersloh, 1899).
[9] Cicero, *Rhetoricum libri duo qui sunt de inventione rhetorica* lib. II cap. 53; cf. Justinian, *Institutiones* I, i: 'Iustitia est constans et perpetua voluntas suum unicuique ius tribuens.'
[10] S. Raeder, *Grammatica Theologica: Studien zu Luthers Operationes in Psalmos* (Tübingen, 1977), pp. 119-31 (with respect to Psalm 5.9); pp. 209-14 (with respect to Psalm 17.1). It seems to us that it is not possible to conclude that Luther's new understanding of *iustitia Dei* is influenced by his knowledge of Hebrew: cf. pp. 305-7.
[11] For the use of the Ciceronian sense of *iustitia* in the earlier western tradition, up to the thirteenth century, see O. Lottin, 'Le concept de justice chez les théologiens du Moyen Age avant l'introduction d'Aristote', *Revue Thomiste* 44 (1938), pp. 511-21. See also A. Beck, *Römisches Recht bei Tertullian und Cyprian: Eine Studie zur frühen Kirchenrechtsgeschichte* (Aalen, 1967); V. Vitton, *I Concetti giuridici nelle opere di Tertulliano* (Roma, 1972), pp. 50-4.
[12] A. E. McGrath, 'Divine Justice and Divine Equity in the Controversy between Augustine and Julian of Eclanum', *Downside Review* 101 (1983), pp. 312-19.

what it means to state that God is *iustus* and deals with man according to *iustitia*. For Augustine, however, the divine justice cannot be equated with human justice in this manner, as the Parable of the Labourers in the Vineyard illustrates. God is righteous, in that he is faithful to his promises, irrespective of the merit of those to whom the promise is made. On the basis of Julian's understanding of *iustitia Dei*, it is simply impossible for God to justify the *ungodly*. It is one of the more remarkable aspects of Augustine's theology of justification that he appears to discern intuitively, rather than analytically, the basic sense of the Hebrew term *sdqh*, despite the prevailing tendency to interpret this in a Ciceronian sense. [13]

A similar critique of the application of secular concepts of *iustitia* to characterise the divine dispensation towards mankind is due to Anselm of Canterbury. [14] Once more, the Ciceronian understanding of *iustitia* is considered as a possible means of articulating the relationship between God and man, only to be rejected. For Anselm, it is simply not possible to explain how God acted to redeem the world in Christ in terms of the Ciceronian understanding of justice as *reddens unicuique quod suum est*. A similar difficulty lies at the heart of a vernacular poem, *The Pearl*, probably written *c.*1370 by a member of the household of John of Gaunt. Here the question of the meaning of the 'righteousness of God' is explored with reference to the fate of a dead infant. How can an allegedly righteous God bestow salvation upon someone who died so young, and thus had done nothing which could be said to merit such a reward? [15] The poet's initial delight at finding his infant daughter in paradise gives way to a radical questioning of how God can justly reward her in such a manner. The dead infant, whose theological acumen belies her tender age, effectively reproduces Augustine's critique of Julian of Eclanum's understanding of the righteousness of God (which is remarkably similar to her

[13] A. E. McGrath, '"The Righteousness of God" from Augustine to Luther', *Studia Theologica* 36 (1982), pp. 63-78. This article is of particular relevance to the present section.

[14] A. E. McGrath, 'Rectitude: The Moral Foundation of Anselm of Canterbury's Soteriology', *Downside Review* 99 (1981), pp. 204-13. Our interpretation of this aspect of Anselm's theology is supported by G. Söhngen, 'Rectitudo bei Anselm von Canterbury als Oberbegriff von Wahrheit und Gerechtigkeit', in *Sola Ratione*, ed. H. Kohlenberger (Stuttgart, 1970), pp. 71-7.

[15] A. D. Horgan, 'Justice in *The Pearl*', *Review of English Studies* 33 (1981), pp. 173-80; McGrath, '*The Righteousness of God*', pp. 70-1; McGrath, *Divine Justice and Divine Equity*, pp. 317-8.

father's), before clinching her case by appealing to the Parable of the Labourers in the Vineyard.

How can the idea of a righteous God be good news for sinful man? It is this question, which had troubled other before him, which would so concern the young Luther. Numerous examples, from every period of his life from 1516 to 1545, may be given to illustrate how he frequently returns to his early hatred for the idea of a 'righteous God'.[16] Who, he asked in 1538, can love a God who wants to deal with sinners according to justice?[17] The essential point which we wish to make here before proceeding further is this: Luther's distress over the concept of *iustitia Dei* was not a difficulty of Luther's own invention, but a genuine theological *crux* involving the tension between two rival concepts of *iustitia*, which had not merely attracted the attention of the great doctors of the church before him, but which had even found its way into the vernacular religious literature. Even those who find it difficult to sympathise with Luther's difficulties at this point will concede that these difficulties represent a real theological problem which had preoccupied others before him. Although it is conceivable that Luther's troubled conscience may have exacerbated the difficulties involved, they remain real difficulties nonetheless.

It may, of course, be argued that, if Luther's difficulty represented a problem which had been adequately discussed within the earlier western theological tradition, it remains to be explained why Luther appears to have been quite unaware of the established solutions to this problem. The answer given to this objection is substantially the same as that given to the charge of Heinrich Denifle — that Luther had misrepresented the western theological tradition as a whole.[18] According to Denifle, not a single writer in the western church, from Ambrosiaster to the time of Luther himself, understood *iustitia Dei* in the sense which Luther noted. Both objections are based upon the assumption that Luther was familiar with the earlier western theological tradition — which, as we have emphasised earlier, appears

[16] e.g. WATr 4.4007; 5.5247; 5.5553. See also the study referred to in note 20.
[17] WA 40 II.445.24-9, Following the printed version of 1538: 'Porro hoc vocabulum Iusticiae magno sudore mihi consistit; sic enim fere exponebant, Iusticiam esse veritatem, qua Deus pro merito damnat seu iudicat male meritos. Et opponebant iusticiae misericordiam, qua salvantur credentes. Haec expositio periculosissima est, praeterquam quod vana est, concitat enim occultum odium contra Deum et eius iusticiam. Quis enim eum potest amare, qui secundum iusticiam cum peccatoribus vult agere?'
[18] H. Denifle, *Luther und Luthertum* (Mainz, 2nd edn, 1905) Vol. 1/2.

not to have been the case. Luther is only familiar with the theology of the *moderni*, such as William of Ockham, Pierre d'Ailly and Gabriel Biel at first hand, and shows little familiarity with other theologians. Indeed, where such familiarity can be demonstrated, there are usually grounds for suspecting that he has encountered them indirectly, at second hand. Denifle, as was quickly pointed out,[19] did not consider the writings of the *moderni* in his criticism of Luther. Furthermore, it is perfectly obvious that Luther's references in the autobiographical fragment to his having been taught, by the use and consent of all doctors, (*usu et consuetudine omnium doctorum doctus eram*) to understand *iustitia Dei* as the formal justice of God implies a reference to his early days at Erfurt, as he began his theological studies under the supervision of the various *moderni* to whom we have already referred in an earlier chapter. The question with which we are therefore concerned is this: in what sense was *iustitia Dei* understood by the theologians of the *via moderna*?[20]

As noted in the previous chapter, the soteriology of the *via moderna* is inextricably linked to the concept of covenantal causality. This has as its fundamental presupposition the axiom that God has entered into a self-imposed limitation upon his actions, in that he has committed himself to reward man with grace upon the fulfilment of certain specified conditions. God's promise of grace is thus understood to be conditional upon man meeting certain requirements; as noted earlier, the concept of covenantal or *sine qua non* causality is such that these requirements need have no inherent connection with the nature of grace or of sin — all that is necessary is that they are specified as constituting the precondition for the bestowal of grace. In the case of Gabriel Biel, this may be summarised as follows: God, in his mercy and liberality, ordained to enter into a *pactum* with man, by which he is prepared to ascribe a much greater value to human acts than they are inherently worth. Thus although a man who does *quod in se est* has done nothing of any particular inherent value, God accords it a much greater value within the terms of the *pactum*, allowing it to function as the contracted link between man's natural state and the state of grace. The present order of salvation, although the consequence

[19] e.g., E. Hirsch, 'Initium Theologiae Lutheri', in *Der Durchbruch der reformatorischen Erkenntnis*, pp. 64-95.
[20] On this, see Alister E. McGrath, 'Mira et nova diffinitio iustitiae. Luther and Scholastic Doctrines of Justification', *Archiv für Reformationsgeschichte* 74 (1983), pp. 37-60.

of radically contingent decisions upon the part of God, must now be regarded as strictly immutable[21] — and hence as utterly reliable. God, having freely determined to enter into such a *pactum* with man according to which he will reward whoever does *quod in se est* with grace, is now obliged to respect the terms of this covenant — even though it is he who imposed them in the first place. *Deus dat gratiam facienti quod in se est necessitate immutabilitatis et ex suppositione quia disposuit dare immutabiliter gratiam facienti quod in se est.*[22]

As has often been pointed out,[23] the notion of a contracted obligation, such as that defined by the *pactum*, can be expressed particularly well in terms such as those deriving from Roman or canonical law. Indeed, practically all the terms used by the theologians of the *via moderna* to express the notion of a binding self-limitation upon the part of God can be shown to have their origins in Justinian's *Corpus Iuris Civile.*[24] Of these terms, we are here particularly concerned with *iustitia*. Underlying the Ciceronian concept of justice, and hence ultimately that of canon law, is the notion of an agreement upon what rights and obligations are placed upon each member of the contracting political community — in other words, the idea of the *iuris consensus.* The difficulty facing earlier western theologians as they attempted to adapt the Ciceronian concept of *iustitia* as *reddens unicuique quod suum est* within a *theological* context was that there existed no obvious theological equivalent to this *iuris consensus.* This fundamental difficulty was overcome by the theologians of the *via moderna* who, by analogy with the economic and political covenant models of their day, were able to employ the *pactum* in precisely this manner. The *pactum* thus defines a reliable framework within which the mutual rights and obligations of God and man have their context, so that what is 'just' may be specified in each case. As used by the theologians of the *via moderna*, the phrase *iustitia Dei* thus comes to refer to the divine faithfulness within the context of the ordained order of salvation. In effect, Biel is able to apply the Ciceronian or Aristotelian concept of distributive justice directly to God, avoiding contravening Duns Scotus' principle

[21] *In I Sent.* dist. xli. q. unica a.3 dub. 3 summ.3; *Collectorium circa quattuor libros sententiarum*, ed. W. Werbeck and U. Hofmann (4 vols: Tübingen, 1973-7) 1.732.16-18.
[22] *In II Sent.* dist. xxvii q. unica a.3 dub.4 O: 2.253.7-9.
[23] e.g., B. Hamm, *Promissio, Pactum, Ordinatio: Freiheit und Selbstbindung Gottes in der scholastischen Gnadenlehre* (Tübingen, 1977), pp. 462-6.
[24] For a list, see Hamm, *Promissio, Pactum, Ordinatio*, p. 463.

of the univocity of *iustitia* and similar terms.[25] God is *iustus*, in that he gives to man what is his due (*quod suum est*) under the terms of the *pactum*. Thus the man who does *quod in se est* is rewarded with grace and eternal life; the man who does not is punished. Therefore *iustitia Dei*, the 'righteousness of God', can refer to *either* the righteousness by which God justifies sinners *or* to the righteousness by which he punishes them — as Scotus insisted, there is only one righteousness of God, and the different consequences in each case reflect differences on the part of the sinners, and not any difference within God himself. God considers only the acts and motives of the individual in determining what his reward or punishment shall be.[26] It is up to the individual, knowing the divine will, to conform to it if he wishes to be rewarded.[27] Any failure on the part of God to abide by the terms of the *pactum* would open him to the charge of injustice, which is quite unthinkable: *ita etiam quod stante sua promissione qua pollicitus est dare vitam eternam servantibus sua mandata non posset sine iniusticia subtrahere eis premia repromissa.*[28]

It is therefore evident that Biel regards *iustitia Dei* as referring to the general principle that God is faithful and equitable within the context of the *pactum*, bestowing the gift of grace upon those who have fulfilled the conditions laid down, irrespective of who they are, and punishing those who do not. This being the case, two aspects of this understanding of *iustitia Dei* may be distinguished.

The 'Righteousness of God' as God's faithfulness to his promises of mercy and grace

God is therefore righteous, in that he abides by the promises of grace which are incorporated within the *pactum*. In many respects, this understanding of *iustitia Dei* is similar to that which goes back to

[25] Scotus, *In IV sent.* dist. xlvi q.1 nn. 2-7. See especially n.7: 'In deo non est nisi unica iustitia... Nullam iustitiam habet nisi ad reddendum suae bonitati vel voluntati, quod eam condecet.' On the concept of univocity, see M. C. Menges, *The Concept of Univocity regarding the Predication of God and Creatures according to William of Ockham* (New York/Louvain, 1952).
[26] Biel, *In II Sent.* dist. xxvii q. unica a.1 nota 3 C; 2.510.4-6.
[27] *In II Sent.* dist. xxxvi q. unica a.1 nota 3 C; 2.622.5-633.10.
[28] *Sacri canonis missae expositio* (Basel, 1510) lection 59 S. See also lect. 59 N:'Meritum condigni super rationem meriti addit debitum reddendi premium secundum iusticiam.'

Ambrosiaster: *Iustitia est Dei quia quod promisit dedit.*[29] The introduction of the conceptual framework of the *pactum* allows this understanding of the 'righteousness of God' to be placed upon a firmer foundation, ensuring a contracted link between the promise and the reward. The soteriology of the *via moderna*, as we have already observed, is based upon the presupposition that God's promises of grace are *conditional*: God has promised to bestow grace upon man upon condition that he does *quod in se est*. If man fails to meet this condition, God is under no obligation to give him grace.

The young Luther faithfully reproduces this aspect of the theology of the *via moderna* during the course of the *Dictata*. As we have already noted, Luther's understanding of the condition which man must meet if he is to be justified can be defined in terms of self-abasement and crying out to God for grace. Once man fulfils this condition, God, in his righteousness, may be relied upon to be faithful to his promise of grace: *Et sic fit iustitia. Quia qui sibi iniustus est et ita coram Deo humilis, huic dat Deus gratiam suam.*[30] One can, however, observe several differences in emphasis between Luther's understanding of this aspect of *iustitia Dei* and that of the *via moderna*, as well as a major difference in substance. This latter relates to the manner in which Luther interprets *iustitia* Christologically: God's righteousness, understood as faithfulness to his promises, is demonstrated in the incarnation and death of the Son of God.[31] It is, however, the second aspect of *iustitia Dei* which is of particular significance, and to which we now turn.

The 'Righteousness of God' as God's rendering to each man his due (reddens unicuique quod suum est)

This is the most important aspect of *iustitia Dei*, as the concept is used within the context of the *pactum*-theology of the *via moderna*. We have already emphasised how the *pactum* functions as the theological equivalent of the *iuris consensus*, thus allowing the Ciceronian sense of *iustitia* as *reddens uniquique quod suum est* to be applied directly to God's

[29] Ambrosiaster, *Comm. in Rom.* 3.3; MPL 17.56B. On this, see K. Holl, 'Die iustitia Dei in der vorlutherischen Bibelauslegung des Abendlandes', in *Gesammelte Aufsätze zur Kirchengeschichte* (3 vols: Tübingen, 1928), Vol. III pp. 171-88; H. Bornkamm, 'Iustitia Dei in der Scholastik und bei Luther', *Archiv für Reformationsgeschichte* 39 (1942) pp. 1-46; McGrath, 'The Righteousness of God'.
[30] WA 3.462.37-8.
[31] See O. Bayer, *Promissio: Geschichte der reformatorische Wende in Luthers Theologie* (Göttingen, 1972), pp. 115-18. Cf. WA 4.17.33-9.

dealings with men. Luther reproduces the Bielian understanding of
iustitia Dei as he comments upon Psalm 9 (10). 9,[32] as the following
extract makes clear:

Equity (*equitas*) and justice (*iustitia*) are usually distinguished in the scriptures,
in that equity is concerned with persons, while justice deals with causes.
He who is fair (*equus*) is he who is the same towards all and conducts himself
fairly, and is not influenced in favour of one rather than another, neither
on account of hatred or love, riches or poverty. Thus God is said to be fair,
because he offers his grace to all men... He is the same for all men, of
the same severity and leniency, and for no one more or less... 'Justice',
however, is said to be rendering to each man his due (*'Iustitia' autem dicitur
redditio unicuique quod suum est*). Thus equity comes before justice, and is, as
it were, its prerequisite. Equity distinguishes merits, while justice renders
rewards. Thus the Lord 'judges the world in equity' (in that he is the same
towards all men, and wishes them all to be saved), and he 'judges in justice',
in that he gives to each man his reward (*reddit uniquique suum premium*).[33]

Before analysing the theological significance of this early passage,
we may consider the concept of *equitas* which Luther employs in this
passage. The general sense of the term 'equity', as used by the canon
lawyers, bears little, if any, resemblance to this.[34] In general, the term

[32] For those unfamiliar with this method of referring to the Psalter in Luther's *Dictata*,
the following explanation may be given. The numbering of the Hebrew and Latin
Psalters differs significantly between Psalms 9 and 147: see O. Eissfeldt, *The Old
Testament: An Introduction* (Oxford, 1974), pp. 445-6 for details. As Luther used the
Vulgate numeration, and modern readers that of the Massoretic text, it is clear that
considerable confusion could result. The universally recognised solution to this
problem is to refer to the Vulgate number, with that of the Massoretic text — if
it is different — immediately following this in parentheses. Thus a reference to Psalm
9 (10). 9 should be read as: Psalm 9.9 following the Vulgate numeration, as used
by Luther himself; Psalm 10.9, using the numeration familiar to modern readers.
[33] WA 55 II.108.15-109.11 (scholion) (= 3.91.1-14). See also the gloss to this verse,
WA 55 I.70.9-11 (= 3.84.18-20): '*Et ipse iudicabit orbem terrae in aequitate* i.e. sine
acceptione personarum, est idem et equus omnibus: *iudicabit populos in iusticia* reddens
unicuique quod suum est' Cf. WA 3.77.14-17.
[34] On this, see E. Wohlhaupter, *Aequitas Canonica: Eine Studie aus dem kanonischen
Recht* (Paderborn, 1931); H. Lange, 'Die Wörter aequitas und Iustitia auf römischen
Münzen', *Zeitschrift der Savigny-Stiftung für Rechtsgeschichte*, Romanistische Abteilung,
52 (1932), pp. 296-314; G. Zanetti, 'Iustitia, Aequitas ed Ius nell'allegoria delle
"Quaestiones de iuris subtilitatibus"', *Istituto Lombardo di Scienze e Lettere*, Classe di
Lettere 83 (1950), pp. 85-123; C. Lefebvre, 'Le rôle de l'équité en droit canonique',
Ephemerides Iuris Canonici 7 (1951), pp. 137-53. On the concept of *aequitas* in particular,
see G. Kisch, *Erasmus und die Jurisprudenz seiner Zeit* (Basel, 1960), especially pp. 14-49.
On the concept as used by Philip Melanchthon, see G. Kisch, *Melanchthons Rechts-
und Soziallehre* (Berlin, 1967), pp. 168-84.

is used to refer to the paradox that justice is impossible on the basis of the strict application of written law.[35] Luther, however, uses the term in the sense of 'absence of partiality' — if God judges in equity, he considers only a man's *deeds*, and not who the agent actually is. This is the sense of the term as it is used by Julian of Eclanum in his controversy with Augustine, where it is understood to mean *sine acceptione personarum*.[36] There are, however, several medieval texts which indicate that, in the opinion of at least some canon lawyers, *aequitas* and *aequalitas* are practically synonymous,[37] and it is possible that Luther may have encountered these during his early training as a lawyer at Erfurt.

The theological significance of this passage will be clear. God judges in equity and in righteousness. According to Luther, this means that God judges a man solely on the basis of his deeds, without respect of his person (whether he is Jew or Gentile, rich or poor). There is no partiality in the manner in which God deals with men — he shows exactly the same severity or leniency to everyone. On what basis, then, does the divine judgement take place? What criteria does God take into account in passing judgement? It will be obvious that if God rewards man with salvation in equity (*sine acceptione personarum*) and in justice (*reddens unicuique quod suum est*), it necessarily follows that there must be some quality about the sinner who is justified which permits God to justify him in the first place. In other words, justification can only be based upon merit: *Et equitas merita distinguit, iustitia premia reddit.*[38] Of course, the concept of 'merit' in question requires careful elaboration, as it is clear that Luther is referring to the concept of *congruous* merit. As we have pointed out above, the theologians of the *via moderna* recognised congruous merit as the contracted link between man's natural state and the state of grace, in that God was obliged, *ex sua iustitia*, to reward the man who did *quod in se est* with grace. As Luther points out in the above passage, God offers his grace to *all* men; he wishes *all* men to be saved. This necessarily implies that he shows the same degree of severity or leniency to all men —

---

[35] e.g. *Codex Iustinianus* III.i.8: 'Placuit in omnibus rebus praecipuam esse iustitiae aequitatisque quam stricti iuris rationem.' On this, see H. Lange, 'Ius aequum und ius strictum bei den Glossatoren', *Zeitschrift der Savigny-Stiftung für Rechtsgeschichte, Romanistische Abteilung*, 71 (1954), pp. 211-244.

[36] See McGrath, *Divine Justice and Divine Equity*, pp. 314-15.

[37] e.g., Kisch, *Erasmus und die Jurisprudenz*, pp. 31-6.

[38] WA 55 II.109.9 (= 3.91.12).

and hence that the same standard is demanded of all men if they are to be justified (namely, that they do *quod in se est*).

It will be clear that this exposition immediately leads to a question of major importance: how can a man know whether he has, in fact, done *quod in se est*? If doing this prescribed minimum constitutes the sole condition for justification, it is clearly of enormous importance for the individual to know whether he has actually fulfilled the condition for the bestowal of grace. It is here that we encounter a major difficulty in the soteriology of the *via moderna*: according to Gabriel Biel, the individual cannot know for certain whether he has done *quod in se est*.[39] In this, Biel faithfully reproduces the medieval theological tradition, which was unanimous concerning this point: man simply cannot know with certainty whether he is worthy of hate or love by God.[40] The relevance of this observation to Luther's early theology of justification will be clear: if man cannot know whether he has fulfilled the condition laid down for his justification, he cannot know whether God will justify or condemn him. The 'righteousness of God' thus remains an unknown quantity, the impersonal attribute of an utterly impartial and scrupulously just judge, which stands over and against

---

[39] *In II Sent.* dist. xxvii q. unica a.3 dub.5 O; 2.525.11-526.17. 'Homo non potest evidenter scire se facere quod in se est, quia hoc facere includit in se proponere oboedere deo propter deum tanquam ultimum et principalem finem quod exigit dilectionem dei super omnia quam ex naturalis suis homo potest elicere. Haec enim est proxima dispositio ad gratiae infusionem, qua existente, certissime infunditur gratia. Difficulum autem est scire se habere illam dilectionem quia etsi scire possumus nos diligere deum, non tamen evidenter scire possumus illam circumstantiam ''super omnia''.' This is an extremely important passage, and is immediately followed by a critique of the Scotist mode of extra-sacramental justification: see Alister E. McGrath, *Iustitia Dei: A History of the Christian Doctrine of Justification* (3 vols: Cambridge, forthcoming), Volume I, pp. 96-9.

[40] On this question in the early sixteenth century, see V. Beltran de Heredia, 'Controversia de certitudine gratiae entre Domingo de Soto y Ambrosio Catarino', *Ciencia Tomista* 62 (1941), pp. 133-62; M. Guerards des Lauriers, 'Saint Augustin et la question de la certitude de la grâce au Concile de Trente', *Augustinus Magister* (Paris, 1954), Vol. II pp. 1057-69; V. Heynck, 'A Controversy at the Council of Trent concerning the Doctrine of Duns Scotus', *Franciscan Studies* 9 (1949), pp. 181-258; idem., 'Zur Kontroverse über die Gnadengewissheit auf dem Konzil von Trient', *Franziskanische Studien* 37 (1955), pp. 1-17; 161-88; H. Huthmacher, 'La certitude de la grâce au Concile de Trente', *Nouvelle Revue Théologique* 60 (1933), pp. 213-226; M. Oltra, *Die Gewissheit des Gnadenstandes bei Andres de Vega: Ein Beitrag zum Verständnis des Trienter Rechtfertigungsdekretes* (Düsseldorf, 1941). The Council of Trent may be regarded as endorsing the earlier medieval tradition upon this point.

man, and ultimately justifies or condemns him on the basis of a totally unknown quality — and is thus the cause of much *Anfechtungen*! To someone such as Luther, who appears to have become increasingly uncertain about his own moral qualities as the *Dictata* progress, it must have seemed inevitable that God, in his righteousness, would condemn him. The theme of the 'wrath of God' is deeply embedded in the pages of the *Dictata*,[41] and is closely linked with that of the 'righteousness of God'. This point may be linked with Luther's early Christological understanding of the 'righteousness of God'.

We have already noted how Luther appeals to the fulfilment of the divine promise of the Saviour as a demonstration of the 'righteousness of God', understood in its first aspect. The theologians of the *via moderna*, however, regarded Christ as *Legislator* rather than *Salvator*,[42] as has frequently been noted. In his early years, Luther appears to have regarded Christ as the embodiment of *iustitia Dei*, an idea which is probably reflected in his exegesis of Psalm 30 (31). In later years, Luther often spoke of his early difficulties arising from his conception of Christ as the righteous judge of sinners: 'I knew Christ as a stern judge, from whose face I wished to run away, and yet could not.'[43] On the basis of passages such as these, it appears that Luther initially regarded Christ as embodying the righteousness of God, containing in his own person the terrifying standard which the Christian was required to attain. Whatever value these later passages may have, it is certainly true that the theologians of the *via moderna* were unable to fit Christ satisfactorily into their scheme of salvation. In effect, there is a Christological lacuna in the soteriology of the *via moderna*: Christ can only assist man externally, by means of his example and instruction, to perform the demands of the law. Under the Old and New dispensations alike, the demand made of man if he is to be justified remains the same: he must do *quod in se est* — an ill-defined, and ultimately an unverifiable, demand.

The concept of *iustitia* as *reddens unicuique quod suum est*, as found

---

[41] See L. Pinomaa, *Der Zorn Gottes in der Theologie Luthers* (Helsinki, 1938). His later study, *Der existentielle Charakter der Theologie Luthers* (Helsinki, 1940), takes up this theme. See also G. Rost, 'Der Zorn Gottes in Luthers Theologie', *Lutherischer Rundblick* (1961), pp. 1-32.

[42] e.g. H. A. Oberman, *The Harvest of Medieval Theology* (Cambridge, Mass., 1963), p. 117.

[43] WA 38.148.12. See also: 40 I.298.9; 40 I.326.1; 41.653.41; 45.482.16; 47.590.1.

in Aristotle's *Nicomachean Ethics*,[44] Cicero's legal and political works, and the body of canon law, was found by Luther to have the most appalling theological ramifications when applied analogically to God, in that it led to a doctrine of the justification of the godly. As Luther remarked in 1532, the idea of a righteous God was simply not gospel: who could love a God who wanted to deal with sinners on the basis of justice?[45] Throughout Luther's later criticisms of the concept of 'righteousness' he had used as a younger man, we find recurring reference to the idea of *iustitia* as *reddens unicuique quod suum est*. For example, during the course of the Galatians lectures of 27 October 1516 — 13 March 1517,[46] Luther makes his underlying criticism of the application of this concept of 'righteousness' within a *theological* context perfectly clear. When commenting on Galatians 2.16, Luther exclaims:

A wonderful new definition of righteousness! This is usually described thus: 'Righteousness is a virtue which renders to each man according to his due' (*iustitia est virtus reddens unicuique quod suum est*). But here it says: 'Righteousness is faith in Jesus Christ' (*fides Jhesu Christi*)![47]

In another passage dating from the year 1516, Luther again contrasts the Aristotelian-Ciceronian interpretation of *iustitia* with that found in scripture. Commenting upon Psalm 22 (23). 3 — 'he leads me in the paths of righteousness' — Luther remarks: *Iustitia autem ista non est ea, de qua Aristoteles 5. Ethicorum vel iurisperiti agunt, sed fides seu gratia Christi iustificans.*[48] Indeed, in the years 1515-17, Luther frequently

---

[44] *Nicomachean Ethics* V 1129[a-b]. On Aristotle's concept of justice, see W. D. Ross, *Aristotle* (London, 1930), pp. 209-13; P. Moraux, *Le Dialogue 'Sur le Justice'* (Louvain/ Paris, 1957); R. A. Gauthier, *La Morale d'Aristote* (Paris, 1963). For a helpful discussion of Cicero's use of Aristotle in this connection, see Moraux, *Le Dialogue*, pp. 65-79. See also works cited in note 34.
[45] WA 40 II.445.24, following the printed version of 1538.
[46] These *lectures* must not be confused with the Galatians *Commentary* of 1519! These lectures are preserved in the form of two students' notes, and were initially edited by Hans von Schubert, and published by the Heidelberg Academy of Sciences in 1918. These lectures have now been published as volume 57 of the Weimar edition. The commentary on Galatians may be found in WA 2.436-618, and although it is clearly based upon Luther's notes for his earlier lectures, there are significant points of difference.
[47] WA 57.69.14-16. A similar passage may be found in the Galatians commentary of 1519, WA 2.503.34-6.
[48] WA 31 I.456.36. '*3. Ethicorum*' is clearly incorrect.

refers to his intense distaste for the concept of *iustitia* which he had used earlier. For example, while commenting upon Romans 4.7 in 1515, Luther insisted upon a careful distinction between human and divine righteousness: 'Scripture uses the terms 'righteousness' and 'unrighteousness' very differently from the philosophers and lawyers'.[49] Indeed, as we shall demonstrate later, Luther's criticism of the application of Aristotle's *Ethics* in a theological context is ultimately an expression of his total rejection of the Aristotelian-Ciceronian concept of *iustitia distributiva* to characterise God's dealings with sinners.

From the beginning of Luther's lectures on Romans (1515-16) onwards, a sustained critique of *iustitia* as *virtus reddens unicuique quod suum est* is encountered. Yet, as Luther glossed Psalm 61 (62). 12 in late 1514, he was still working with precisely this concept of *iustitia*.[50] The obvious question which we must now consider is this: what happened to make Luther change his mind? In attempting to answer this question, we must turn to a consideration of the concept of *iustitia fidei*, 'the righteousness of faith', which comes to play so important a role in Luther's theology of justification.

'THE RIGHTEOUSNESS OF GOD' AND 'THE RIGHTEOUSNESS OF FAITH'

In the earlier part of the *Dictata*, Luther displays a tendency to gloss the term *iustitia* with *fidei* at certain points. For example, Psalm 35 (36). 7 refers to *iusticia tua*: Luther glosses this as follows: *Iusticia* fidei *tua* qua coram te iusti sumus.[51] (We here follow the conventional practice of printing the text of the Psalm itself in italics, and Luther's glosses in Roman type.) In every case, the reference is to a righteousness by which the individual is righteous in the face of God, as summarised in the formula: *iustitia fidei, qua coram deo iusti fiunt*. In an important study, Vogelsang argued that Luther here reproduced the essential features of Augustine of Hippo's understanding of

[49] WA 56.287.16-17.
[50] WA 3.354.5-8: '*Duo haec audivi, quia potestas Dei est* ad puniendum tanquam Domini. *Et tibi Domine misericordia*, gratia ad praemiandum tanquam patris: *quia tu reddes unicuique secundum opera sua*, pro bonis bona, pro malis mala.'
[51] WA 3.199.18. Cf. WA 3.200.18-19 (On Psalm 35 (36).11): '*Et iusticiam tuam* fidei, qua iustus fiant'; 3.269.21 (On Psalm 47 (48).11): '*Iusticia* fidei, que coram Deo facit iustos.'

iustitia Dei as a righteousness which *comes from* God, which God gives to man in order that he might be justified.[52] It is clear that Vogelsang is here dependent upon Karl Holl's essay of 1921, in which he explored the understandings of *iustitia Dei* in the pre-Lutheran works of biblical exegesis.[53] In particular, attention was drawn to three *loci* from Augustine's *De spiritu et littera*, particularly that of chapter 9: *iustitia Dei non qua deus iustus est, sed qua induit hominem.*[54] There are, however, certain difficulties attending Vogelsang's contention that Luther's concept of *iustitia fidei* is an allusion to Augustine's concept of *iustitia Dei*. First, it can be shown that Luther probably would not have encountered this work of Augustine at this stage in his career.[55] Further, the remaining *locus* in the works of St Augustine in which Holl locates a clear statement of his understanding of *iustitia Dei* is found in a work[56] which Luther hardly knew, and which is never cited in the course of the *Dictata*.[57] In addition to this, Luther's understanding of *iustitia fidei* appears to have forensic overtones which are quite absent from Augustine's concept of *iustitia Dei*. Luther generally links the phrase *iustitia fidei* with *coram Deo*,[58] suggesting that he is referring to a righteousness which is *sui generis*, valid before God but not recognised by human standards of righteousness.

Luther's use of the phrase *iustitia fidei* in the earlier parts of the *Dictata* was closely examined by Hirsch,[59] among others, and on the basis of this, three characteristic features of the concept were established. *Iustitia fidei* is:

(1) A righteousness which is a gift from God, rather than a righteousness which belongs to God.

---

[52] E. Vogelsang, *Die Anfänge von Luthers Christologie nach der ersten Psalmenvorlesung* (Berlin/Leipzig, 1929), pp. 45-6.

[53] K. Holl, *Die iustitia Dei in der vorlutherischen Bibelauslegung des Abendlandes* (see note 29).

[54] Holl, *Die iustitia Dei*, p. 175.

[55] Hamel, *Der junge Luther und Augustin*, Vol. I, pp. 9-11.

[56] *In Joh. Ev. tract.* 26,1: cf. Holl, *Die iustitia Dei*, p. 175.

[57] Hamel, *Der junge Luther und Augustin*, Vol. I, pp. 31-2.

[58] There are passages in which *iustitia fidei* is not specifically linked with the phrase *coram Deo* — e.g. WA 3.200.18-19; 3.414.23-4. It seems to us that Gordon Rupp has put his finger unerringly upon a central theme of the young Luther's theological preoccupations when he entitled the second part of his *magnum opus*, dealing with Luther's development from 1509-21, 'coram Deo': E. G. Rupp, *The Righteousness of God: Luther Studies* (London, 1953), pp. 81-256.

[59] E. Hirsch, 'Initium Theologiae Lutheri', in *Der Durchbruch der reformatorischen Erkenntnis*, pp. 64-95; pp. 87-93.

(2) A righteousness which is valid *coram Deo*, although not *coram hominibus*.

(3) A righteousness which is itself *fides Christi*.

These conclusions are unquestionably correct, although we must leave open the question of whether *iustitia fidei* is more appropriately translated as 'a righteousness which *is* faith', or 'a righteousness which *comes from* faith'. The importance of faith in this connection is well illustrated by Luther's comments upon Psalm 7. After emphasising that God judges in equity — which Luther explicitly defines as 'being the same toward all without regard for or discrimination of persons' (*equus*)[60] — Luther moves on to consider the basis of the divine judgement. Glossing verse 9, (*dominos iudicat populos*), Luther remarks: *Non enim emit in sacco nec in confuso omnia, sed iudicat et discernit. Qui crediderit salvus erit.*[61]

It seems that Luther here understands God's judgement to be universal rather than particular, based upon a general condition which must be fulfilled. The only righteousness which here pertains before God is *iustitia fidei*, the 'righteousness of faith'. This may appear to be totally inappropriate by human standards of justice, but it remains the criterion by which God will judge mankind. This point is made with particular force in Luther's comments upon Psalm 49 (50). 6: *Coeli annunciant iustitiam Dei: quoniam Deus iudex est.* Luther glosses this verse as follows: . . . *iusticiam*, fidem, scil. Dei reddentis unicuique quod suum meritum: *quaniam Deus* Ihesus Christus *iudex est.*[62] Two points may be noted here:

First, *iustitia* is identified with 'faith' — but the 'faith' in question is faith in a God who rewards according to merit, using the Ciceronian understanding of *iustitia Dei* we discussed earlier (*reddens unicuique quod suum est*).

Secondly, Christ is here understood to function *qua Deus* as the divine judge of mankind. This statement closely parallels those passages we noted above, dating from later in Luther's career, in which he referred to his early tendency to regard Christ solely as a stern judge.[63] The *novum verbum* of the gospel is that God himself will judge man in Christ

[60] WA 55 II.95.5-96.1 (= 3.77.14-16): 'Et hoc nomen Equitas illud significat. Quia scilicet sine acceptione et differentia personarum omnibus idem est, qui equus est.'
[61] WA 55 I.52.27-8 (= 3.75.30-31).
[62] WA 3.278.11-12.
[63] See note 43.

on the basis of whether he possesses *iustitia fidei*. This point is further developed in the scholion to the same verse:

The heavens declare the righteousness of God, for God is judge. The apostles have declared this new word, that God himself — and not a man in his place — will one day judge. It is therefore necessary that this judgement be universal and all-inclusive, as it is the judgement of God. . . Therefore to declare that God is judge is to declare a universal judgement, and that an individual's righteousness — which he might have in the eyes of men (*coram hominibus*) — is not sufficient; the righteousness of God is required, so that the individual might be righteous in the sight of God (*coram Deo*). And this is required because he will be judged, not by man, but by God: *for God is judge.* [64]

Luther's basic intention is perfectly clear: God intends to judge the world in Christ, and the criterion upon which this judgement will be based is the 'righteousness of faith'. As this judgement is universal, and as God will judge *in equity* (that is, without respect of persons, treating everyone equally) and *in justice* (*reddens unicuique quod suum est*), the only basis upon which judgement can proceed is the universal norm encapsulated in the concept of *iustitia fidei*. But how are we to make sense of this concept?

One solution which has been suggested is that Luther understands *iustitia fidei* to be the divine gift of faith, given to the sinner irrespective of his merit or demerit, on the basis of which he can be accounted righteous before God. Attractive though this possibility may appear, there is every reason to suppose that Luther's intention here is totally different. His vocabulary and theological framework reflect the *pactum*-theology of the *via moderna*. For example, in his exposition of the psalm immediately following that cited above, Luther indicates how faith can be said to justify man *coram Deo*:

Even grace and faith, through which we are justified today, would not justify us of themselves, without God's covenant. It is precisely for this reason that we are saved: God has made a testament and covenant with us, so that whoever believes and is baptised shall be saved. In this covenant God is truthful and faithful and is bound by what he has promised. [65]

[64] WA 3.283.31-9.
[65] WA 3.289.1-5; See note 67 of previous chapter.

We have already indicated in the prevous chapter how the *pactum*-theology of the *via moderna* permeates the bulk of the *Dictata*, and how the concept of covenantal or *sine qua non* causality underlies Luther's early discussion of justification. It is within this theological context that Luther's discussion of *iustitia fidei* must be set. Once this point is conceded, the relationship between *iustitia Dei* and *iustitia fidei* becomes clear. In the previous chapter, we pointed out how Luther tended to interpret the minimal precondition for justification, as required by the soteriology of the *via moderna* (specifically, *facere quod in se est*) in terms of *humility*. One of the most controverted areas of Luther scholarship relates to the question of how the young Luther, at the time of the Romans lectures (1515-16), understood the relationship between *fides* and *humilitas*. The difficulty is that they are clearly closely associated — but which is, so to speak, prior to the other? The intense controversy between Bizer and Bornkamm over this issue[66] has served to demonstrate how intimately the two concepts are linked, rather than to resolve the question. Faith and humility are inseparable: indeed, they may even be linked as the *humilitas fidei*.[67] In the case of the *Dictata*, Bizer argues, this relationship is even more intimate: '*Fides* is merely another expression for *humilitas*.'[68] While we take Bornkamm's criticism of Bizer with the utmost seriousness, it nevertheless seems to us that Bizer's assertion of the near-identity of *humilitas* and *fides* is undeniable. Bizer may well have been corrected by later studies in some respects, but he most emphatically has not been refuted, at least on this specific point. All the evidence suggests that, at least during the course of the *Dictata*, Luther regards humility as the necessary consequence of faith, and the equally necessary precondition for justification. It is therefore clear that, linking Luther's statements concerning the role of *humility* in justification with those concerning *faith*, *iustitia fidei* is nothing more and nothing less than the necessary precondition for justification on the basis of the *pactum*-theology which underlies Luther's theology at this point. Whether justification is understood to be effected by grace, faith or humility, the ultimate cause is the divine *pactum* which underlies the established

[66] Bizer, *Fides ex auditu*, pp. 29-39; 193-203; Bornkamm, *Iustitia Dei beim jungen Luther*, pp. 306-45.
[67] WA 56.282.9-13. The phrase occurs frequently in the *Dictata*: e.g. WA 3.588.8; 4.127.10; 4.231.7. Note also the statement at WA 56.449.8 'Universalis ergo iustitia est humilitas'. Cf. WA 56.199.30.
[68] Bizer, *Fides ex auditu*, pp. 19-21. Cf. WA 56.471.17.

order of salvation. *Homini facienti quod in se est Deus infallibiliter dat gratiam.* [69] For Luther, *iustitia fidei* is that righteousness which arises through doing *quod in se est.*

It may be objected at this point that our interpretation of Luther's statements concerning *iustitia fidei* does not account for Luther's insistence that the righteousness in question originates from God. This is, in fact, not the case. On the basis of the *pactum*-theology of the *via moderna*, which Luther expounds so ably in the *Dictata*, there exists a radical discrepancy between the inherent value of human moral acts and their much greater ascribed value within the terms of the *pactum*: this point has already been emphasised in the previous chapter. How can God, in his righteousness, accept so trivial a thing as faith as worthy of man's justification? The answer is elementary: viewed *coram hominibus*, it cannot, as the inherent value of faith is so little; viewed *coram Deo*, however, it has a much greater contracted value, in that God is prepared to accept it *ex pacto suo* as worthy of justification, not because of its inherent value, but simply because he has decided that this will be the case. The radical dichotomy between human and divine estimations of righteousness is a frequent theme in the *Dictata*, and it is entirely understandable that most commentators should concentrate their attention of Luther's rejection of the worth of human righteousness *coram Deo*. Nevertheless, it must be emphasised that Luther is equally insistent that men are unable to discern the worth of *divine* concepts of righteousness. The radical dichotomy between the moral and meritorious realms is one of the most characteristic features of the theology of the *via moderna*. To unbelievers, it may appear ridiculous to assert: *iustitia est credere deo.* [70] Nevertheless, within the *pactum*-theology this assertion is valid. As the *pactum* is itself a divine gift to man, and is ultimately an expression of the divine generosity and liberality, the fact that faith may thus be reckoned as *iustitia* must be regarded as a consequence of, and also an expression of, this divine gift. *Iustitia fidei* is only *iustitia* on account of the prior gift of God. *Credere Deo* represents the inherent value of faith, while *iustitia* represents its ascribed value, within the context of the *pactum*. *Iustitia fidei* is therefore a righteousness which originates from God, in that *fides* would not be *iustitia coram Deo* were it not for the divine *pactum* which

---

[69] For this quotation from Luther in its proper context, see the previous chapter (p. 89).

[70] WA 3.331.3.

transforms its *bonitas intrinseca* (= *credere Deo*) into its *valor impositus* (= *iustitia fidei*). In that God has provided the sole means by which this transformation may take place, *iustitia fidei* must be recognised as (1) being a divine gift to man, and (2) originating from God. Nevertheless, it must be emphasised that it is a general gift to all men, rather than a specific gift to an individual, and that it originates indirectly, rather than directly, from God. The significance of this observation will become clear in a later section of the present chapter.

If it is accepted that the *pactum*-theology of the *via moderna* underlies Luther's discussion of both *iustitia Dei* and *iustitia fidei* in the earlier parts of the *Dictata*, the precise relationship between *iustitia Dei* and *iustitia fidei* becomes clear. *Iustitia fidei* is the precondition of justification. In other words, for a man to become righteous *coram Deo*, 'the righteousness of God' demands that he possess 'the righteousness of faith'. The two concepts are not identical, [71] but they are clearly closely related, in that their common denominator is the *pactum*. By virtue of that covenant, God accepts man's faith as the righteousness required for his justification *coram Deo*.

Some scholars have argued that Luther's understanding of the nature and relationship of *iustitia Dei* and *iustitia fidei* underwent a dramatic alteration during the course of his exposition of Psalms 70 (71) and 71 (72), thus placing the date of Luther's discovery of the new meaning of the 'righteousness of God' in the winter of 1514. In view of the importance of this theory, we propose to examine it in some detail.

LUTHER'S EXPOSITION OF PSALMS 70 (71) AND 71 (72)

'When I became a doctor, I did not yet know that we cannot make satisfaction for our sins.' [72] The historical accuracy of this statement is generally conceded, and it has therefore been generally assumed, particularly by an earlier generation of Luther scholars, that Luther's theological discovery must have taken place at some time during the course of the *Dictata*. Initially, Hirsch argued that a 'new' understanding of *iustitia Dei* was apparent in Luther's exposition of

---

[71] e.g., Hirsch, *Initium theologiae Lutheri*, pp. 88-9: 'Die iustitia fidei qua iustificati sumus, das ist die iustitia dei.'
[72] WA 45.86.18.

Psalms 30 (31) and 31 (32). [73] This conclusion was, however, challenged by Erich Vogelsang, in one of the most seminal essays of modern Luther scholarship. [74] In this essay, Vogelsang argued that Luther's discovery of the 'new' meaning of *iustitia Dei* must have taken place shortly before, or possibly even during, his exposition of Psalms 70 (71) and 71 (72). This thesis has proved to be of continuing significance today, particularly in the light of Regin Prenter's careful examination of the exegesis of Psalm 70 (71). 2 in the *Dictata*. [75] Before we can even begin to consider the theological issues involved, it is necessary to return to a difficulty with the source material which we noted briefly in the previous chapter, arising from the manner in which the Dresdener Psalter, containing the scholia, is bound.

The text of the scholia to Psalms 70 (71) and 71 (72) includes page 103 of the Dresdener Psalter. Not only was this page bound into that Psalter at a later date — it also appears to have been bound the wrong way round. The second side of the page (103b) was clearly written before the first (103a). It is not easy to see how this mistake arose, although Wendorf has some helpful suggestions to make. [76] But what are the consequences of this mistake?

The text on page 103 gives little indication of whether the material which it contains may be assigned to Luther's comments upon Psalm 70 (71) or Psalm 71 (72). The simplest means of reconstructing the text is that favoured by Prenter, and proceeds as follows. The Weimar edition, it is argued, assumes that the correct sequence of sides is 102b-103a-103b-104a, whereas the correct sequence is 102b-103b-103a-104a. After making the necessary contextual adjustments, the text of the Weimar edition can then be rearranged as follows: after 3.458.7 (the end of 102b), insert 462.15-463.37 (103b), followed by 458.8-11 and 461.20-462.14 (103a). This assumes that the material found on page 103 is a continuation of the comments on the themes of *iudicium* and *iustitia* found in the scholion to Psalm 70 (71), and which therefore prepares the ground for the scholion to Psalm 71 (72).

---

[73] Hirsch, *Initium Theologiae Lutheri*.

[74] Vogelsang, *Die Anfänge von Luthers Christologie*.

[75] R. Prenter, *Der barmherzige Richter: Iustitia Dei passiva in Luthers Dictata super Psalterium* (Kóbenhavn, 1961), pp. 94-121.

[76] H. Wendorf, 'Der Durchbruch der neuen Erkenntnis Luthers im Lichte der handschriftlichen Überlieferung', *Historische Vierteljahrschrift* 27 (1932), pp. 124-44; 285-327; especially pp. 134-42.

Vogelsang, however, has a rather different understanding of how the necessary rearrangement of the text should be carried out, upon which his theory of the nature and date of Luther's discovery of the new meaning of *iustitia Dei* ultimately depends. Vogelsang argues that the material contained on page 103 is part of the scholion on Psalm 71 (72), taking page 103b to be a continuation of the marginal gloss of page 104a (that is, WA 3.464.20-37). [77] In this, he is followed by Bornkamm, [78] who points out that the arguments on page 104 (that is, 464.1-467.4) prepare the ground for those on page 103. Nevertheless, the force of Prenter's arguments against this construction [79] must serve to warn us that we simply do not know for certain which of the two possible contexts for the comments of page 103 is correct.

In a previous chapter, we considered Luther's hermeneutics, and particularly his use of the *Quadriga*, in the *Dictata*. The distinction between the literal and the spiritual senses of scripture is of particular importance in relation to the question of the date and nature of Luther's discovery of the righteousness of God. When Luther refers to the literal sense of Scripture, he intends us to understand the sense of the text, as it refers to Jesus Christ. [80] In its allegorical sense, scripture refers to Christ's aid to his church; in its tropological sense, it refers to the work of Christ as it benefits the Church and individual believers; in its anagogical sense, it refers to the completion of that work in the future. [81] Luther's increasing emphasis upon the *tropological* sense of scripture is one of the characteristic features of the later parts of the *Dictata*, and is of particular significance in relation to the two psalms under consideration. Luther ends his comments on Psalm 70 (71) with the following words:

And your righteousness, O God, even unto the highest. In this verse the correct distinction between divine and human righteousness is described at last. For the righteousness of God reaches up to the highest of heavens, and causes us to reach there. It is righteousness even to the highest, namely, of reaching the highest: human righteousness, however, is not so, but rather reaches down to the depths. And this is so, because he who exalts himself will be humbled, and he who humbles himself will be exalted. But now the entire

[77] Vogelsang, *Die Anfänge von Luthers Christologie*, p. 49 n.2.
[78] Bornkamm, *Die Iustitia Dei beim jungen Luther*, pp. 292-4.
[79] Prenter, *Der barmherzige Richter*, pp. 97-104.
[80] e.g. WA 4.305.6-12. Cf. WA 55 I.8.8-11.
[81] For this distinction, the reader is referred to the discussion and references in the previous chapter.

righteousness of God is this (*iustitia Dei est tota haec*): viz., to humble oneself into the depth. The man who does this comes to the highest, because he first went down into the lowest depth. And here he rightly refers to Christ, who is the power of God and the righteousness of God through the greatest and deepest humility. Therefore he is now in the highest through supreme glory.

The Weimar edition then continues with the following final paragraph:

Therefore, whoever wants to understand the apostle and other Scriptures wisely must understand everything tropologically: truth, wisdom, strength, salvation, righteousness, namely, that by which he makes us strong, safe, righteous, wise, etc. So it is with all the works of God and the ways of God: every one of them is Christ literally, and faith in him (*fides eius*) morally. [82]

As noted in the previous chapter, the *moral* sense of scripture is merely a synonym for the *tropological* sense. It is therefore clear that Luther singles out the literal and tropological senses of scripture as being of paramount importance: the first sense refers to Christ, and the second to his reception and appropriation by faith. Nevertheless, the textual problem noted above is of relevance here, as it is almost certain that the second paragraph quoted above has its place in the scholion on Psalm 71 (72), so that Luther's comments upon Psalm 70 (71) should be understood to end with '. . . through supreme glory'. [83] This being the case, it is important to appreciate precisely what Luther is saying in this final paragraph.

It is clear that Luther is stating nothing more than the *humilitas-*theology we noted earlier. What Luther is stating is that the righteousness which is valid *coram Deo* (that is, *iustitia ad altissima*) can only be attained through the total humiliation of the individual, following the example set him in Christ. [84] By the *pactum*, God has ordained to accept *humilitas* or *humiliatio* as *iustitia fidei*, the covenantal righteousness which alone is valid in his sight, despite being insignificant *coram hominibus*. *Et sic fit iustitia. Quia qui sibi iniustus est et ita coram Deo humilis, huic dat Deus gratiam suam.* [85] Luther here appears to construct his statement as a parallel to the celebrated maxim of the

[82] WA 3.457.38-458.11.
[83] See the arrangement of the text in *Der Durchbruch der reformatorischen Erkenntnis bei Luther*, pp. 506-12.
[84] The implicit reference to Philippians 2.8-9 should not be overlooked.
[85] WA 3.462.37-8.

via moderna: Facienti quod in se est dat Deus gratiam suam. [86] What must a man do if he is to receive the grace of God? What is to be understood by doing *quod in se est?* Luther's reply to this question is stated with the utmost clarity in the earlier part of this citation: *facere quod in se est = esse sibi iniustus et ita coram Deo humilis.* The covenantal framework of Luther's theology of justification makes it clear that Luther here states precisely the same relationship between *iustitia Dei* and *iustitia fidei* as we noted earlier in the *Dictata.* But does it remain thus in the course of the exposition of the following Psalm?

Luther begins his exposition of Psalm 71 (72) by drawing attention to the contrast between the judgement (*iudicium*) of men and of God. After noting the anagogical and allegorical senses of *iudicium Dei*, Luther passes on to consider its tropological sense:

This is its most frequent use in Scripture. This is that by which God himself condemns, and also causes us to condemn, whatever we have of ourselves, the whole old man (*totum veterem hominem*) with his deeds. This is properly humility and even humiliation. For it is not the man who reckons himself humble who is righteous, but he who considers himself to be detestable and damnable in his own eyes.... Scripture uses this word 'Judgement' to express the true nature of humility, which is the vilification and contempt and complete damnation of oneself.... This is called the 'Judgement of God' (*Iudicium Dei*), like the righteousness or the strength or the wisdom of God. It is that by which we are wise, strong, righteous and humble, or by which we are judged. [87]

In its tropological sense, we are concerned with the concept of *iudicium Dei* as it relates to the individual believer. Rather than considering the concept in isolation, Luther expounds its relevance to the individual — and this relevance lies in the evocation of total humility. It is only by being forced into recognising one's total unworthiness — even to the point of total contempt and hatred of oneself — that justification comes about. For Luther, a prayer to God for judgement is a prayer for total humiliation, that by plunging into the depths one might be raised, through the merciful promises of God in his covenant, into the highest of heavens. [88] It is by lowering oneself into the depths that

---

[86] The maxim can, of course, be stated in a number of forms, including that noted here. For Luther's own statement of the maxim, see WA 4.262.2-7.

[87] WA 3.465.1-35.

[88] e.g. WA 3.466.36-7: '...ut sit sensus, Iudica me Domine, id est, da mihi veram humilitatem et carnis meae mortificationem meiipsius damnationem, ut sic per te

one is raised by God into the heights, just as Christ's self-humiliation led to his glorification. Luther's phrase *iusti et humiles vel iudicati sumus* brings out the close connection between righteousness, humility and judgement: by the terms of the ordained order of salvation (the *pactum* or *testamentum dei*), *humilitas* is reckoned as *iustitia coram Deo*. It is clear that there is a close link between *humilitas* and *fides* which is paralleled by that between *iudicium* and *iustitia Dei*: God's *iudicium* forces man to recognise his *humilitas*, which God recognises, in his righteousness, as the *iustitia fidei*.

Luther's interpretation of *iustitia Dei* reaches a crucial stage in the exposition of Psalm 71 (72). The passage which follows is generally regarded as a *crux interpretativum*:

Figurativly

In the same way, the 'righteousness of God' is also threefold. Tropologically it is faith in Christ (*fides Christi*). Romans 1.17: 'For the righteousness of God is revealed in the gospel from faith to faith.' And this is its most frequent use in scripture. [89]

But is Luther actually saying anything new here? It seems to us that Prenter is correct when he states that this scholion does not contain any ideas not already present in the scholion to the previous psalm. [90] Luther draws attention to the fact that the terms *iudicium* and *iustitia* have negative and positive overtones, in that the former relates to damnation, the latter to salvation: *quia iudicium in damnationem, sicut iustitia in salvationem sonat.* [91] Yet, as he points out, it is by damning *ourselves* that we are saved *by God*. Luther appears to use the terms *fides* and *humilitas* interchangeably at points as he attempts to spell out the nature of the righteousness of believers:

Any word of God whatever is judgement. He judges, however, in a threefold manner. First, tropologically, for he condemns the works of the flesh and the world. He shows that everything in us and in the world is abominable and damnable in the sight of God (*coram Deo*). Therefore whoever clings to

salver in spiritu'; WA 3.462.29-31: 'Et ita qui ei per fidem adhaeret, necessario sibi vilis et nihil, abominabilis et damnabilis efficitur. Quae est vera humilitas. Unde et isto vocabulo aptissime natura et proprietas humilitatis exprimitur.' Cf. A. Gyllenkrok, *Rechtfertigung und Heiligung in der frühen evangelischen Theologie Luthers* (Uppsala, 1952), pp. 20-31.
[89] WA 3.466.26-8.
[90] Prenter, *Der barmherzige Richter*, pp. 120-1, n. 107.
[91] WA 3.466.31-2.

him by faith necessarily becomes vile and nothing to himself, abominable and damnable. And that is true humility. . . . Consequently, the scourging and the crucifixion of the flesh and the condemnation of all that is in the world are the judgements of God; he carries out these things through judgement with his own, that is, through the gospel and grace. And so righteousness comes about. For to the man who is unrighteous to himself and is thus humble before God, God gives his grace. And in this way it is most frequently accepted in Scripture. Thus 'righteousness' in its tropological sense is faith in Christ (*fides Christi*).[92]

Considered tropologically, *iustitia Dei* refers to that righteousness which has a direct bearing upon individual believers — the righteousness by which they are accepted *coram Deo*, which is *iustitia fidei*. There is, however, nothing new here concerning the relationship between *iustitia fidei* and *iustitia dei*, nor are there any new statements concerning their relationship to *iudicium dei* or *humilitas*. God gives his grace to the humble. A new term has indeed been introduced (*iustitia tropologice*) — but its content is substantially identical to that of *iustitia fidei*. It may be that we have some breakthrough here — but this can only be maintained if it can be shown that the concept of *fides Christi* is something which is radically different from *humilitas*. As the preceding extract indicates, there is every reason to suppose that *fides Christi = sibi iniustus esse et ita coram Deo humilis*.

By the end of the scholion on Psalm 71 (72), it is clear that Luther has identified the tropological aspect of *iustitia Dei* as *fides Christi*. While there may have been a certain degree of conceptual clarification involved in this identification, it is not clear that any significant theological advance has been made. Vogelsang summarises the theological substance of the scholion as follows: '*Opus dei: iustitia dei, iudicium dei etc. est Christus (literaliter), id est fides Christi (tropologice), qua — iudicati — iustificamur, per quam in nobis regnat.*'[93] Nevertheless, all that Luther has done is to clarify the nature of the various *iustitiae* implicated in the justification of man: there is no shift in their fundamental point of reference. The basic question which remains to be answered is this: how does *fides Christi* arise in the individual? We may concede immediately that Christ cannot justify unless he is

[92] WA 3.462.25-463.1.
[93] Vogelsang, *Die Anfänge von Luthers Christologie*, p. 55.

effective within man — but how is this effectiveness achieved?[94] Does
humility arise through man's self-humiliation — or is it effected within
man by God, as a divine work effected without human cooperation?
It is this problem which remains to be resolved.

Later in the *Dictata*, Luther indicated that the basic condition which
man was required to meet in order to be justified was by doing *quod
in se est*. Man, having humbled himself, is driven to ask God for the
gift which he now recognises he needs:

'Ask and you shall receive; seek and you will find; knock, and it shall be
opened to you. For everyone who asks receives, etc.' (Matthew 7. 7-8).
Hence the doctors rightly say that God gives grace without fail to the man
who does *quod in se est*, and though he could not prepare himself for grace
in a manner which is meritorious *de condigno*, he may do so in a manner
which is meritorious *de congruo* on account of this promise of God and the
covenant of mercy.[95]

We have already pointed out how the theology expressed within this
gobbet is precisely that of the *via moderna*. This evidently raises the
question of the nature of man's response to the *pactum*, in that the
moderni understood the *pactum* to provide the contractual basis by which
the transition from the moral to the meritorious, from the realm of
nature to that of grace, might be effected. Is Luther therefore stating
that man's disposition for grace (whether this is defined as *humilitas*
or *fides*) is a natural human act? Luther certainly taught — even at
this late stage in the *Dictata* — that man had a free choice in his salvation,[96] and that man's free will was implicated in his justification.
For example, in a sermon of 26 December 1514, Luther argued that
man is free to place an obstacle in the path of grace, or to resist it
in some other way.[97] Although there has been no definitive analysis
of the concept of grace in the *Dictata*, it seems to us that Luther operates
within the theological framework established by the theologians of the

---

[94] WA 4.19.37-9: 'Quocirca Christus non dicitur iustitia, pax, misericordia, salus
nostra in persona sua nisi effective. Sed fides Christi, qua iustificamur, pacificamur,
per quam in nobis regnat.'
[95] WA 4.262.2-7.
[96] WA 4.295.19-35: '*Anima mea in manibus meis semper*... Anima mea est in potestate
mea et in libertate arbitrii possum eam perdere vel salvare eligendo vel reprobando
legem tuam, q.d. licet ego sim liber ad utrunque, tamen legam tuam non sum oblitus.
Et hec glosa melior est...'. Cf. WA 3.331.17-25.
[97] WA 1.32.

via moderna at this point — namely, that the proper disposition for justification must be considered to be a natural work of man, unaided by any special grace, save the external graces of public utility which are generally defined as *actual grace*. Luther's insistence upon the divine equity, which is so characteristic of the *Dictata*, precludes the implication of special grace in the salvation of mankind. God takes the initiative in man's salvation by means of the *pactum*, which offers him grace upon condition that he humble himself to receive it — but he receives no such grace until he fulfils this condition.

While some have seen in Luther's statements at this point 'a complete break' with the theology of the *via moderna*,[98] it is clear that this conclusion cannot be sustained on the basis of the evidence available. Once more, it is necessary to point out that it is not acceptable to approach the Luther of the *Dictata* from the standpoint of his mature theology, attempting to detect traces of this later theology in his earlier work. Rather, one must approach the *Dictata* from the standpoint of later medieval theology in general, with all its presuppositions and limitations, and from that of the *via moderna* in particular. When this latter approach is adopted, Luther's use of terms such as *facere quod in se est, meritum de congruo* etc., are found to fit easily into a well-established theological context. It is not merely the theological vocabulary of the *via moderna* which we encounter in the *Dictata*, but also the theological framework within which they were traditionally employed — that of the *pactum*.

However, there is evidence that Luther was preparing to make a decisive break with this theological framework. As we have stressed, the covenant-theology of the *via moderna* is based upon the presupposition that man is capable of doing *quod in se est* without the special assistance of grace. *Fides Christi = humilitas* is understood as a human disposition towards grace. But what happens to this theological framework if *fides Christi* is understood as a divine gift to man, something which man cannot effect for himself? As we shall demonstrate, Luther appears to have moved towards this latter position, which is characteristic of his later theology, at some point during the final months of his exposition of the Psalter. It is a development

---

[98] e.g. L. Grane, *Contra Gabrielem: Luthers Auseinandersetztung mit Gabriel Biel in der Disputatio contra scholasticam theologiam 1517* (Gyldendal, 1962), pp. 299-302. Cf. A. Brandenburg. *Gericht und Evangelium: Zur Worttheologie in Luthers erste Psalmenvorlesung* (Paderborn, 1960), pp. 59-69.

of decisive importance to his theology of justification, as will become clear in the section that follows.

LUTHER'S BREAK WITH THE SOTERIOLOGY
OF THE *VIA MODERNA* (1515)

At several points during the final parts of the *Dictata*, Luther appears to suggest that man's preparation or disposition for the reception of grace is itself a work of grace.[99] For example, while commenting on Psalm 118 (119). 11, Luther states:

I have hidden your words in my heart, that I may not sin against you. This means: 'I have decided to serve you with my whole heart. Therefore I have written your words on my heart, in order that I may no longer sin against them, as I did formerly.' Therefore he rightly asks for the assistance of grace before he proposes. First he says, 'Do not drive me away', and then, 'because I have hidden and set forth your words'. For what we propose is nothing, unless the grace of God disposes it.[100]

It is, however, impossible to conclude that Luther has decisively altered his mind on this matter at this stage. Nevertheless, there are indications that, by the end of his lectures on the Psalter, Luther had come to reject the presupposition upon which the soteriology of the *via moderna* was based. Whereas Luther initially understood *humilitas* to be man's response to the divine judgement passed against him, he now appears to hold that it is God, *and God alone*, who moves man to repentance and to a humble acknowledgement of the divine judgement. The evidence within the *Dictata* is not, we must emphasise, decisive: it is therefore important to appreciate that we have corroboration of this conclusion from other sources.

In 1514, a new edition of the works of Gabriel Biel was published at Lyons. A copy of this edition found its way to Wittenberg, where it attracted the attention of Luther. From the marginal comments which Luther entered in this edition, it is clear that he no longer accepts

[99] See H. Bandt, *Luthers Lehre vom verborgenen Gott: Eine Untersuchung zu dem offenbarungsgeschichtlichen Ansatz seiner Theologie* (Berlin, 1958), pp. 62-3.
[100] WA 4.309.6-11. For the theocentricity which begins to become apparent in Luther's understanding of *humilitas* at this point, see M. Kroeger, *Rechtfertigung und Gesetz: Studien zur Entwicklung der Rechtfertigungslehre beim jungen Luther* (Göttingen, 1968), p. 33, n.39.

the basic presupposition of the soteriology of the *via moderna* — that man can do *quod in se est* without the assistance of special grace. For example, commenting upon Biel's statement that man can love God above everything else by his natural unaided powers, Luther remarks:

> As a result the will is neither sick, nor does it need the grace of God. All of this is based upon the stupid principle of free will — as if the free will could, by its own power, choose to follow opposite paths, when it is prone only to evil.[101]

In other words, Luther's emerging conviction that man is naturally prone to evil calls into question whether he is naturally able to make the necessary response to the divine initiative, expressed in the *pactum*. Luther no longer believes that man is capable of the true humility required of him in order that he may receive the gift of grace — he requires grace in order to achieve this true humility in the first place. We shall develop the consequences of this insight later. The question of when Luther achieved this insight now claims our attention.

It is not clear when Luther entered his marginal comments in the Lyons edition of Biel's *Collectorium*. Although there is some evidence to suggest that they date from the beginning of 1515 to May 1516, it seems that a more probable dating is from the end of 1516 to the summer of 1517.[102] If this later date is accepted, we are brought very close to the date of the *Disputatio contra scholasticam theologiam* — by which time Luther has indeed broken totally with the *via moderna*.[103] Nevertheless, there are excellent reasons for supposing that this insight dates from 1515, in that the Romans lectures of 1515-16 are permeated with a sustained critique of the soteriology of the *via moderna* on precisely this point. Three significant changes in Luther's teaching on this matter can be detected as having taken place during or before the Romans lectures:

[101] Text as established by Grane, *Contra Gabrielem*, p. 359, based on that of Degering. For an excellent study of the development of Luther's views on the relationship of the free will and grace over the period 1513-17, see H. J. McSorley, *Luther, Right or Wrong? An Ecumenical-Theological Study of Luther's Major Work, The Bondage of the Will* (New York/Minneapolis, 1969), pp. 218-43.
[102] See H. Volz, 'Luthers Randbemerkungen zu zwei Schriften Gabriel Biels: Kritische Anmerkungen zu Hermann Degerings Publikation', *Zeitschrift für Kirchengeschichte* 81 (1970), pp. 207-19. Cf. Grane, *Contra Gabrielem*, pp. 299-300, n. 43; 348-9; 368. McSorley, *Luther*, pp. 224-5, assumes they date from 1515.
[103] See Grane, *Contra Gabrielem*, pp. 369-85.

(1) *Man is now understood to be passive towards justification.* Luther adopts the Augustinian concept of operative grace,[104] and states that man is passive towards the first grace, just as a woman is when she conceives.[105] When grace is given to man, his role is not that of action, but rather of keeping still.[106] It is clear that Luther does not exclude all human activity from justification, returning instead to the essentially Augustinian understanding of the respective human and divine roles in justification.[107] Nevertheless, this marks a considerable departure from the teaching of the *via moderna* on the matter.

(2) *Luther states that man's will is held captive by sin, and is incapable of attaining righteousness unaided by grace.* It is at this point that he first makes reference to the idea of the *servum arbitrium*, an idea which dominates his anti-Erasmian polemic of 1525.

Free will apart from the influence of grace has no capacity whatsoever to attain righteousness, but is necessarily in sin. Hence Augustine is right when, in his book against Julian, he calls it 'the *enslaved* rather than the *free* will' (*servum potius quam liberum arbitrium*)... since it is held captive in sin and thus cannot choose the good according to God.[108]

(3) *The idea that man can do 'quod in se est' is denounced as Pelagian.* This development is of particular significance, in view of the fact that Luther himself based his earlier soteriology upon the presupposition that man could do *quod in se est*, as noted above. The following passage is of particular importance:

They know that man cannot do anything from himself (*ex se*). Hence it is totally absurd (and also strongly Pelagian!) to hold the view summed up in the well-known statement: 'God infallibly infuses grace in the one who does *quod in se est* (*facienti quod in se est, infallibiliter Deus infundit gratiam*) if the phrase *facere quod in se est* is to be understood as meaning 'to do or to be capable of doing something' (*aliquid facere vel posse*). Hence it is not a matter for surprise that practically the whole church is subverted on account of the confidence that this statement expresses.[109]

[104] WA 56.379.13-15.
[105] WA 56.379.1-2: 'Ad primam gratiam sicut et ad gloriam semper nos habemus passive sicut mulier ad conceptum.'
[106] WA 56.379.2-6.
[107] See W. Joest, *Gesetz und Freiheit: Das Problem des tertius usus legis bei Luther* (Göttingen, 3rd edn, 1961), pp. 218-19; McSorley, *Luther*, p. 238.
[108] WA 56.385.15-22. On *de servo arbitrio*, see McSorley, *Luther*, pp. 297-353.
[109] WA 56.502.32-503.5.

Luther explicitly rejects the opinion that salvation is dependent upon a decision of the human will, adding that he once held this opinion himself.[110]

It is clear that Luther's definitive teaching on faith as a divine gift is expressed within the pages of the Romans lectures of 1515-16.[111] It is God, and God alone, who moves man to repentance and to the humble acknowledgement of the divine judgement which finds its proper expression in faith. Although Luther continues to understand *fides* in terms of *humilitas* for some time to come,[112] it is clear that a decisive break with his earlier understanding of the concept has taken place. It is impossible to read Luther's lectures on Romans, and particularly his comments on Romans 3.22, 4.7, 7.17, 7.25 and 10.6[113] without appreciating that Luther has had some new insight into the nature of justifying faith. That insight, as we have argued above, relates not so much to the *character* of faith as to the *mode by which* it *comes about*. What, then, are the consequences of this insight for Luther's understanding of the 'righteousness of God'?

As we noted earlier, Luther came to regard the 'righteousness of God', when understood tropologically, to refer to *fides Christi*. This, as we have emphasised, did not represent a breakthrough of any sort, but was essentially a conceptual clarification. The individual, when confronted with the judgement of God upon him, is moved to repentance and humility — and this response is the precondition which is necessary in order for him to be justified. In other words, *fides Christi* was initially understood as the *quod in se est* required of man within the terms of the *pactum*-theology upon which Luther's early soteriology was so clearly based. At this stage, *fides Christi* is still understood as a human act, performed by man with his own natural abilities, and without the special assistance of grace. Once man is moved to repent and believe, God is able to bestow upon him the gift of grace — a

---

[110] WA 56.382.26-27: '...quod nostro arbitrio fiat vel non fiat salus. Sic enim ego aliquando intellexi.'
[111] Frey argued that Luther's concept of faith involved a tension between faith, understood as a work of God within man, and faith, understood as a work of man which lies within his own ability: F. Frey, *Luthers Glaubensbegriff. Gottesgabe und Menschentat in ihrer Polarität* (Leipzig, 1939). This view has been refuted by M. Schloenbach, *Glaube als Geschenk Gottes* (Stuttgart, 1962), pp. 46-54. Cf. WA 10 III.286.7-10: WADB 7.8.30-39. This latter text was that which, in English translation, 'strangely warmed' the heart of John Wesley.
[112] As pointed out by Bizer, *Fides ex auditu*, pp. 29-39.
[113] As pointed out by Bornkamm, *Die iustitia Dei beim jungen Luther*, pp. 306-37.

gift which can only be bestowed at this point. Such was Luther's understanding of the 'righteousness of God' up to the beginning of 1515.

By the end of 1515, all this has changed. *Fides Christi* is now understood as the work of God within man, and most emphatically *not* as a response which man is capable of making to God by means of his purely natural capacities. Whereas Luther had earlier regarded *fides Christi* as an *indirect* gift of God, in that God was understood to have established the theological framework within which man's faith could be reckoned as worthy of justification, it is now regarded as a *direct* gift of God to the believer. Earlier, *fides Christi* had been understood as a *general* gift of God, in that, the general framework having been established, it was up to the individual to make the necessary response to the divine initiative in the *pactum*; now it is understood as the *specific* gift of God to the individual. It is therefore clear that Luther's exposition of *iustitia Dei* as *fides Christi* at Psalms 70 (71) and 71 (72), while not in itself constituting a theological breakthrough, nevertheless prepared the way for that breakthrough when it finally came. The righteousness which God required of man if he were to be justified was no longer to be understood as something which sinful man was incapable of attaining, but as a divine gift which God himself bestowed upon man.

The intense personal distress which Luther recorded in 1545 over his earlier wrestling with the meaning of *iustitia Dei* is readily understood in the light of our observations. Any attempt to interpret *iustitia Dei* in terms of *reddens unicuique quod suum est* could only lead to such distress upon the part of the sinner as he realised how there was nothing within him which could lead to his justification on this basis. Not only that: if it were possible for man to do *quod in se est*, he could never know for certain whether he had, in fact, achieved this, due to the rejection of certainty on this point by the theologians of the *via moderna*. Luther's personal dilemma would therefore have been abundantly and happily resolved by the 'wonderful new definition of righteousness' at which he arrived at some point during the year 1515. It may also be pointed out that Luther was certainly familiar with Augustine's *de spiritu et littera* by late 1515,[114] so that this date is

[114] C. Boyer, 'Luther et le "De spiritu et littera" de Saint Augustin', *Doctor Communis* 21 (1968), pp. 167-87; L. Grane, *Modus loquendi theologicus: Luthers Kampf um die Erneuerung der Theologie (1515-1518)* (Leiden, 1975), pp. 65-6. Cf. WA 56.36.11; 172.5.

compatible with the autobiographical fragment of 1545 on this point. It is, of course, clear that we shall have to return to a reexamination of that fragment later in the present study. However, another question claims our attention first.

As we have indicated, Luther can be shown to have decisively broken with the soteriology of the *via moderna* by the end of 1515. But what position did he assume as a consequence? Did he merely revert to an Augustinian theology of justification, similar to that of his mentor Johannes von Staupitz? There are two reasons for suggesting that he did not, developing instead a theology of justification which can only be described as Luther's own creation. The first of these reasons relates to Luther's espousal of the *servum arbitrium*, which goes far beyond Augustine's statements on the incapacitation of the human free will by sin.[115] The second, and more significant, relates to the development of the concept of *iustitia Christi aliena*, unquestionably one of the most original and creative aspects of Luther's mature doctrine of justification. This concept first makes its appearance in the Romans lectures of 1515-16, and we turn now to consider its significance.

The origins of Luther's concept of the 'alien righteousness of Christ' must be considered to lie in his holistic understanding of man. In particular, Luther argues that 'flesh' (*caro*) and 'spirit' (*spiritus*) are not to be regarded as man's lower and higher faculties respectively, but rather as descriptions of the whole person considered under different aspects. Thus *caro* is not man's lower nature, but the entire man (*totus homo*), considered as turned in upon itself (*homo incurvatus in se*) in its irrepressible egoism and its radical alienation from God.[116] Similarly, *spiritus* is to be understood as referring to the entire man in his openness to God and the divine promises. For Luther, justification relates to the entire person, both flesh and spirit: although the individual comes to put his trust in the promises of God, he nevertheless remains a sinner.[117] Thus the *totus homo* is *iustus et peccator simul* — a sinner inwardly, and yet righteous in the sight of God.[118] In effect,

---

[115] On this, see McSorley, *Luther*, pp. 224-73; 297-353.
[116] WA 56.342.33-343.2; 356.4-6. See E. Schott, *Fleisch und Geist nach Luthers Lehre, unter besonderer Berücksichtigung des Begriffs 'Totus Homo'* (Leipzig, 1930). For his later anthropology, se W. Joest, *Ontologie der Person bei Luther* (Göttingen, 1967); H. -M. Barth, 'Martin Luther disputiert über den Menschen: Ein Beitrag zu Luthers Anthropologie', *Kerygma und Dogma* 27 (1981), pp. 154-66.
[117] WA 56.351.23-352.7.
[118] WA 56.270.9-11; 343.16-23; 351.23-352.7. See further R. Hermann, *Luthers These 'Gerecht und Sünder zugleich'* (Gütersloh, 1930).

this tension arises from Luther's dialectic between the *totus homo*, viewed *coram Deo* and *coram hominibus*. The believer is righteous *coram Deo*, even though this righteousness cannot be detected empirically: indeed, those whose righteousness can be detected empirically are those who are righteous *coram hominibus*, and yet unrighteous *coram Deo* — the hypocrites.[119] The Christian is a sinner *in re*, and yet righteous *in spe*:[120] his righteousness is hidden, known only to God.

As the *totus homo* cannot be partially righteous *coram Deo*, his righteousness must be alien and extrinsic to him — it is a righteousness which is in no sense part of his person, or which can in any way be said to belong to him. It is this consideration which appears to underlie the concept of *iustitia Christi aliena*. As Oberman points out,[121] the concept is of decisive importance in distinguishing Luther's theology of justification from that of Staupitz: for the latter, justifying righteousness is a righteousness which is inherent to man, *iustitia in nobis*, which, although originating from God, may be regarded as part of the person of the believer; for the former, justifying righteousness is a righteousness which is alien to man, *iustitia extra nos*, which can never be said to belong to the person of the believer. Luther uses images such as Boaz covering Ruth with his cloak, or a mother hen covering her chicks with her wing, to illustrate how God clothes the sinner with the alien righteousness of Christ. Extrinsically, the believer is righteous, through the alien righteousness of Christ; intrinsically, he is — and will remain — a sinner. This concept of justifying righteousness is, of course, totally different from that of St Augustine, as Luther himself fully appreciates.[122] This element of Luther's thought would be developed by Melanchthon into a doctrine of forensic justification, which would become normative for Protestant understandings of justification.[123] Luther does not develop such a doctrine here, although it is clear that he lays the foundation for anyone who might care to undertake such a development.[124]

[119] WA 56.268.27-269.19. Cf. WA 56.50.16; 58.15; 173.24; 174.2.
[120] WA 56.269.27-30; 272.17-21.
[121] H. A. Oberman, *Werden und Wertung der Reformation* (Tübingen, 1977), pp. 110-112.
[122] For a full discussion of this point, see McGrath, *Iustitia Dei*, Volume II, pp. 10-20.
[123] See Alister E. McGrath, 'Forerunners of the Reformation? A Critical Examination of the Evidence for Precursors of the Reformation Doctrines of Justification', *Harvard Theological Review* 75 (1982), pp. 219-42.
[124] See A. E. McGrath, 'Humanist Elements in the Early Reformed Doctrine of

It is clear that Luther understands there to be a radical dichotomy between human and divine concepts of *iustitia*. For Augustine, the verb *iustificare* was equivalent to *iustum facere*,[125] so that man could be said to 'become righteous' as a consequence of the operation of grace within him. Luther, however, refused to allow that man could be said to *become* righteous in justification: if anything, he merely became increasingly aware of his *unrighteousness*, and was thus driven back to the cross to seek forgiveness. The believer is *semper peccator, semper penitens, semper iustus*.[126] Whereas Augustine saw the *vestigiae supernae iustitiae* in human laws,[127] Luther saw nothing in human concepts of *iustitia* which corresponded to *iustitia Dei*. The righteousness which God demands is faith, and that righteousness is only known to faith. In effect, Luther's understanding of *iustitia Dei* involves a hermeneutical circle — a circle outside of which Luther himself once stood. For Luther, St Paul's letter to the Romans represented a programmatic critique of human preconceptions of righteousness,[128] in order that man might become conscious of his need for another, strange righteousness — the *iustitia Christi aliena* — and thus turn to God in the humility of faith to receive this righteousness, which alone is valid *coram Deo*. Man must learn to distinguish human and divine concepts of *iustitia*, as it is only when this distinction is fully appreciated that his justification becomes a real possibility:

Scripture uses the term 'righteousness' and 'unrighteousness' very differently from the philosophers and lawyers. For they consider them to be a quality of the soul, but in the scriptures 'righteousness' (*iustitia*) depends more upon the imputation of God than upon the essence of the thing itself. For he who has only a quality does not have righteousness — indeed, he is actually a sinner and unrighteous. The only one who is righteous is the man who God, in his mercy, regards as righteous before him, on account of his confession of his own unrighteousness and his prayer for the righteousness of God.

Justification', *Archiv für Reformationsgeschichte* 73 (1982), pp. 5-20, *in fine*, for a discussion of the origins of the concept of forensic justification.
[125] e.g. *Exp. quar. prop. ex Ep. ad Rom.* 22; *Ad Simplicianum* I, ii, 3; *Serm.* CCXCII, 6; CXXXI, 9; *Epist.* CXL, xxi, 52; *de grat. et lib. arb.* vi, 13.
[126] WA 56.442.17.
[127] On this whole question, see P. S. Schubert, *Augustins Lex-Aeterna-Lehre nach Inhalt und Quellen* (Münster, 1924). Cf. W. von Loewenich, 'Zur Gnadenlehre bei Augustin und Luther', in *Von Augustin zu Luther* (Witten, 1959), pp. 75-87; p. 83.
[128] WA 56.3.6-7: 'Summa et intentio Apostoli in ista Epistola est omnem iustitiam et sapientiam propriam destruere.'

Thus we are all born and die in iniquity, that is, in unrighteousness, and we are righteous only by the reckoning of a merciful God through faith in his word (*sola autem reputatione miserentis Dei per fidem verbi eius iusti sumus*).[129]

In effect, Luther is here mounting a sustained polemic against human preconceptions of what precisely is entailed by the 'righteousness of God'. For Luther, there is an ever-present danger that *iustitia Dei* will be interpreted in terms of *reddens unicuique quod suum est* — an interpretation which he himself had earlier adopted, and which stood in the way of his theological breakthrough. If *iustitia Dei* is interpreted on the basis of the Aristotelian-Ciceronian concept of *iustitia*, the sinner will be tempted to think that he can attain justification by his moral efforts, on the basis of a righteousness which lies within his own grasp. As Luther emphasises throughout his lectures on Romans, it is only when the total inadequacy of human concepts of righteousness *coram Deo* is recognised that man is driven to look for the one righteousness which has any value *coram Deo* — the alien righteousness of Christ. It is on the basis of this insight that we may understand Luther's critique of Aristotle, which has frequently been misunderstood. In the following section, we propose to demonstrate that Luther's revolt against reason in general, and Aristotle in particular, is a direct consequence of his discovery of the true meaning of the 'righteousness of God'.

THE NATURE AND SIGNIFICANCE OF LUTHER'S CRITIQUE OF ARISTOTLE

On 20 May 1505 Luther began his study of law. He would have become familiar with the *Codex Iuris Civilis*, with its underlying concept of *iustitia*. In 1508, as professor appointed by the Augustinian Order, he lectured on Aristotle's *Ethics* at Wittenberg. The text of these lectures, unfortunately, has not survived. We have already noted the concept of *iustitia* associated with the *Codex* and with Book V of the *Ethics*. Furthermore, precisely this concept of *iustitia* is that demanded by reason — that of an impartial judge who dispenses justice according to the merits of the individual. When Julian of Eclanum defended this understanding of *iustitia Dei*, he concluded his argument

---

[129] WA 56.287.16-21. The verb *reputare* does not possess the forensic overtones which would later be associasted with *imputare*.

thus: *non ego, sed ratio concludit.*[130] As Karl Holl pointed out, the God who answered to reason could never be anything other than the God of a 'works-righteousness' (*Werkgerechtigkeit*), who rewarded man on a *quid pro quo* basis.[131] For Luther, however, justification is totally contrary to reason, in that God justifies *sinners.*[132] As the justification of sinful man is so evidently contrary to reason, Luther argued that the role of reason in matters of theology must be called into question. Carlson correctly pointed out that there was a general consensus among Scandinavian Luther scholars to the effect that the context in which Luther's critique of reason must be set is *soteriological*, applying 'primarily, if not exclusively, to the matter of justification'.[133] In this respect, Luther's affirmation of faith in the face of reason is quite distinct from that of William of Ockham, despite the similarities often noted between their positions.[134] The relation between Luther's doctrine of justification and his critique of reason has been further studied by Gerrish,[135] who pointed out that Luther made a careful distinction between two realms of human existence in his discussion of the capacity of human reason: man's reason is self-sufficient in relation to *das irdische Reich*, the *regnum rationis*, but fails him totally in relation to the *regnum Christi*, particularly in connection with the justification of the sinner.

In the present section, we wish to develop these observations further, particularly in the light of later medieval theology. Much confusion has been occasioned by the fact that Luther was intensely critical of Aristotle from 1509 onwards, so that his criticism of the Stagarite has not been regarded as specifically linked with his theological breakthrough. What has not been fully appreciated, however, is that Luther's reasons for criticising Aristotle underwent a radical change in late 1515, and that the nature of this change is immediately explicable in the light of this breakthrough.

[130] *Opus imperfectum contra Iulianum* I, 60.
[131] K. Holl, 'Was verstand Luther unter Religion?', in *Gesammelte Aufsätze* (3 vols: Tübingen, 1928), Volume I, pp. 1-110: p. 37.
[132] Holl, *Was verstand Luther unter Religion?*, p. 77.
[133] E. M. Carlson, *The Reinterpretation of Luther* (Philadelphia, 1948), p. 127.
[134] Cf. H. A. Oberman, 'Facientibus quod in se est Deus non denegat gratiam: Robert Holcot O. P. and the Beginnings of Luther's Theology', *Harvard Theological Review* 55 (1962), pp. 317-42. We confess ourselves unconvinced by Oberman's thesis.
[135] B. A. Gerrish, *Grace and Reason: A Study in the Theology of Martin Luther* (Oxford, 1962). See also B. Lohse, *Ratio und Fides: Eine Untersuchung über die Ratio in der Theologie Luthers* (Göttingen, 1958) pp. 82-6.

Since the period of High Scholasticism, Aristotelian categories had been employed in theological discourse, with results which were often valuable. The use of Aristotle in this respect, however, was regarded with intense distrust by several theologians of the later medieval period, such as Luther's fellow-Augustinian Hugolino of Orvieto. Hugolino mounted what is probably the most ferocious attack on the intrusion of Aristotle into theology ever to be encountered in the Middle Ages, being particularly critical of the use made of Aristotle's *Ethics* on the part of certain unnamed theologians.[136] In particular, Hugolino drew attention to the false concept of God which resulted from this practice. As Zumkeller pointed out, it is quite probable that Luther encountered Hugolino's criticisms of Aristotle by 1514 at the latest,[137] a fact which may well be reflected in several comments he makes in his earlier works.[138] Luther's criticism of Aristotle, as encountered in the 1509-10 *Randbemerkungen*, is directed against the incompatibility of theology and philosophy.[139] Theology is concerned with the affairs of heaven and philosophy with those of earth: for theologians to become philosophers is comparable to the birds of the air becoming the fishes of the sea.[140] In other words, the two disciplines are to be distinguished on the basis of their subject matter: while Aristotle is singled out for particular criticism, Luther's comments are directed against philosophy in general.[141] By 1517, however, all this has changed: Luther's wrath is now directed against Aristotle's *Ethics*, along with certain other entities. Luther's attacks on the 'enemies of the gospel' frequently involve the linking together of *ratio*, *lex*, Aristotle and the Jurists in what seems, at first sight, to be an improbable alliance of forces

---

[136] *Commentarius in Quattuor libros Sententiarum*, ed. W. Eckermann (Würzburg, 1980), Volume I. *In I Sent.* prol. q.5 a.1; 140.191-2: 'Similiter ethica Aristotelis et tota philosophia moralis superflueret'. *In I Sent.* prol. q.5 a.3; 151.72-152.73: 'Hoc totum ignorat ethica Aristotelis.'

[137] A. Zumkeller, 'Die Augustinertheologen Simon Fidati von Cascia und Hugolin von Orvieto und Martin Luthers Kritik an Aristoteles', *Archiv für Reformationsgeschichte* 54 (1963), pp. 15-37; pp. 27-8.

[138] WA 9.23.7; 43.5. See F. Nitzsch, *Luther und Aristoteles* (Kiel, 1883). WA 1.28.19-20 should also be noted in this respect.

[139] See W. Link, *Das Ringen Luthers um die Freiheit der Theologie von Philosophie* (München, 2nd edn, 1955), pp. 160-3.

[140] WA 9.65.12-19.

[141] e.g. his castigation of the 'faex philosophiae' (WA 9.43.42) or the 'larvae philosophorum' (WA 9.74.10). Note also the manner in which 'philosophers' and 'lawyers' are linked together at WA 56.287.16-17.

against the gospel. [142] Nevertheless, upon closer examination, all these have one factor in common which is immediately significant in the light of our earlier discussion of the nature of Luther's theological breakthrough: all define *iustitia* as *reddens unicuique quod suum est*. It was precisely this definition of *iustitia* which so appalled the young Luther as he struggled to make sense of how the idea of a 'righteous God' could conceivably be gospel. Furthermore, Aristotle's equation of *ho dikaios* and *ho nominos* [143] inevitably means that the righteous man is understood to be the man who keeps the law — an opinion which Luther later attributes to reason: *ratio. . . docet; si vis vivere Deo, oportet te legem servare*. [144] Similarly, the Aristotelian *dictum* that a man becomes righteous by performing righteous deeds is rejected by Luther: it is only when a man is justified (*iustus coram Deo*) that he is capable of performing good deeds. [145] Underlying this criticism of Aristotle is Luther's basic conviction that man is naturally incapable of performing anything which is good *coram Deo*, and which could be regarded as effecting his justification.

For Luther, *ratio* and its associated concept of *iustitia* (as used by Aristotle and the jurists) had its proper place in the ordering of civil affairs. Luther's rejection of *ratio* relates to his soteriology, particularly to the definition of *iustitia Dei*, which is of central importance to his theology as a whole. The concept of *iustitia* which Luther rejected in this context is none other than that of Aristotle's *Ethics*, which had been taken up by the medieval canonists and jurists, which had found its way into the soteriology of the *via moderna*, and which corresponded to a secular, common-sense understanding of justice in terms of a *quid pro quo* morality, whose validity was immediately apparent to reason. Julian of Eclanum had insisted that God judged man *rationabiliter*, which he took to be equivalent to *iuste*, [146] and had therefore applied a common-sense concept of *iustitia* by a process of analogical predication to God. God rewards each man according to his merit, which may be defined in terms of whether he has lived well by the standards set him in the law: *non ego, sed ratio concludit*. [147] A similar

---

[142]   e.g. WA 40 I.204.11; 31.456.36.
[143]   *Nicomachean Ethics* V 1129^{a-b}.
[144]   WA 40 I.268.13.
[145]   See the excellent study of E. Jüngel, 'Die Welt as Wirklichkeit und Möglichkeit', in *Unterwegs zur Sache* (München, 1972), pp. 206-31.
[146]   *Opus imperfectum contra Iulianum* III, 6.
[147]   *Opus imperfectum contra Iulianum* I, 60.

interpretation of *iustitia Dei* can be derived by direct analogical predication of the Aristotelian understanding of *iustitia*, linked with the associated interpretation of the relationship between *iustita* and *lex*, to God. The young Luther appears to have adopted precisely such a concept of *iustitia* in his early attempt to expound the Psalter: indeed, it is of particular significance that Luther should choose Psalm 9 (10). 9 to expound the relationship between *iustitia* and *equitas* in the divine judgement, as Julian of Eclanum had earlier used exactly the same passage to demonstrate the divine equity in dealing with man according to his merit![148] It was against this understanding of *iustitia*, as applied to God (but not as applied to civil affairs), that Luther rebelled when he discovered the *mira et nova diffinitio iustitiae*, with such momentous results for his theology. Luther's revolt against reason is indeed occasioned by his soteriology — but in a far more specific manner than appears to have been generally realised. Whilst it cannot be proved that Luther appreciated the theological ramifications of everything he read in Book V of the *Nichomachean Ethics*, it is beyond dispute that he recognised that the concept of *iustitia* developed therein, applied to God, had appalling theological consequences for sinners: *Tota fere Aristotelis Ethica pessima est gratiae inimica.*[149] Luther's joy at his discovery of the new definition of *iustitia* reflects his realisation that God loves and forgives sinners, and that the *iustitia* of *iustitia Dei* is not to be understood *qua philosophi et iuriste accipiunt*, but *qua in scriptura accipitur*. Luther's vitriolic attacks against Aristotle, reason, the jurists, the law, and the *Sautheologen* of the *via moderna* reflects his basic conviction that all these employed a concept of *iustitia* which, when applied to God, destroyed the gospel message of the free forgiveness of sinners. Luther's 'evangelical irrationalism' is closely correlated with his discovery of the righteousness of God: if reason and its allies were unable to comprehend the mystery of the justification of the ungodly, then so much the worse for them. Reason has its role to play in the civil affairs of men, as in so many other spheres — but when faced with the justification of sinners, the central feature of the gospel proclamation, it collapses, unable to comprehend the mystery with which it is confronted. For Luther, the word of the gospel, upon which all theological speculation was ultimately based, was that of a righteous God who justified those worthy of death: if reason was unable to comprehend this fundamental aspect of the gospel, it had forfeited its right to have any say in theology as a whole. In Luther's opinion, reason was not neutral in this matter: according to reason, God should only justify those whose deeds made them worthy of such a reward: *itaque caro est ipsa iustitia, sapientia carnis ac cogitatio rationis, quae per legem vult iustificari.* [150] Human wisdom and human concepts of righteousness are inextricably linked — and, as Luther emphasised, both were called into question by the fact that a righteous God could justify sinners. It is clear that this critique of human wisdom, which is ultimately based upon Luther's deliberations upon the concept of the 'righteousness of God', foreshadows the *theologia crucis* of 1518 in a number of respects. Before moving on to consider the nature of the theology of the cross, however, it may be helpful to summarise our conclusions concerning the nature and the date of Luther's theological breakthrough.

THE NATURE AND DATE OF LUTHER'S THEOLOGICAL BREAKTHROUGH

In a fragment of the *Table-Talk* dating from 1532, Luther refers to his theological insight concerning the true meaning of the 'righteousness of God' as having taken place 'in this tower and heated room' (*in hac turri et hypocausto*). [151] On the basis of this account, Grisar referred to Luther's breakthrough as the 'Tower Experience' (*Turmerlebnis*), thus coining a term which has become a commonplace

---

[150] WA 40 I.347.27. In view of Luther's misgivings concerning the use of Aristotle in matters theological in general, and in relation to the doctrine of justification in particular, it is somewhat ironical that later Lutheran theologians employed Aristotelian metaphysics extensively in precisely such contexts: see R. Schröder, *Johann Gerhards lutherische Christologie und die aristotelische Metaphysik* (Tübingen, 1983), pp. 69-97. The revival of Aristotelian metaphysics in this connection is particularly asociated with Christoph Scheibler's *Opus Metaphysicum* (Gießen, 1617). For the use of Aristotle in Lutheran Orthodoxy, see E. Weber, *Orthodoxie und Rationalismus* (2 vols: Gütersloh, 1937-51); C. H. Ratschow, *Lutherische Dogmatik zwischen Reformation und Aufklärung* (2 vols: Gütersloh, 1964-6). In fairness, of course, it may be pointed out that Reformed dogmatics were also influenced by Aristotle in the seventeenth century: see P. Petersen, *Geschichte der aristotelischen Philosophie im protestantischen Deutschland* (Leipzig, 1921); P. Althaus, *Die Prinzipien der deutschen reformierten Dogmatik im Zeitalter der aristotelischen Scholastik* (Darmstadt, 2nd edn, 1967).
[151] On this, see A. Peters, 'Luthers Turmerlebnis', in *Der Durchbruch der reformatorischen Erkenntnis*, pp. 243-88, esp. p. 243 n. 2.

in modern Luther scholarship.[152] More generally, Luther's theological breakthrough is often referred to by German-speaking scholars as his *reformatorische Entdeckung*, or *reformatorische Erkenntnis*.[153] It seems to us that both these practices are unjustifiable. The manuscript evidence used to support the term *Turmerlebnis* is far from unequivocal, some texts omitting reference to a 'tower' altogether.[154] Furthermore, it is questionable whether Luther's insight concerning the 'righteousness of God' can in any sense be designated as his 'reformation discovery', in that it is not specifically linked to the Reformation as a whole. As we indicated in chapter 1, the Reformation must be regarded as having been initiated by the Wittenberg theological faculty as a whole, rather than by Luther as an individual, so that a careful distinction must be drawn between the *initia Reformationis* and the *initia theologiae Lutheri*. The two cannot be considered to be equivalent, although it is clear that they are somehow related. By referring to 'Luthers reformatorische Entdeckung', a closer relationship is implied between Luther's insight concerning the meaning of the 'righteousness of God' and the dawn of his own vocation as a Reformer — not to mention that of the Reformation as a whole! — than the present state of Luther scholarship permits us to recognise as legitimate. For this reason, we prefer to refer merely to 'Luther's theological breakthrough', and leave open the greater question of the precise relationship between the *initium theologiae Lutheri* and the *initium Reformationis*.

The dating of Luther's theological breakthrough has proved to be a matter of some controversy.[155] Practically every date, from 1505 to 1519, has been suggested at some point during the past century as marking the point at which Luther's thought underwent decisive alteration. The older view, that Luther's theological breakthrough dates from his Erfurt or first Wittenberg period of 1508-9,[156] was

---

[152]   e.g. see H. Jedin, 'Luthers Turmerlebnis in neuer Sicht', *Catholica* 12 (1958), pp. 203-36.
[153]   e.g. the title of the collection of essays to which we have frequently referred: *Der Durchbruch der reformatorischen Erkenntnis bei Luther*.
[154]   e.g. WATr 2.1681, where Aurifaber's printed version of the conversation in question omits any reference to a 'Tower'.
[155]   The most significant modern study is that of Otto Pesch, 'Zur Frage nach Luthers reformatorischer Wende', in *Der Durchbruch der reformatorischen Erkenntnis*, pp. 445-505. Cf. R. Schäfer, 'Zur Datierung von Luthers reformatorischer Erkenntnis', *Zeitschrift für Theologie und Kirche* 66 (1969), pp. 151-70.
[156]   e.g. K. Benrath, *Luther im Kloster* (Halle, 1905), p. 57; H. Boehmer, *Luther im Licht der neueren Forschung* (Leipzig, 1906), p. 32.

generally discredited through the publication of numerous studies dealing with the newly published lectures on Romans and the *Dictata*. This led to increased interest in the period 1513-16. Loofs argued that the breakthrough must have taken place before the *Dictata*, perhaps in the winter of 1512-13,[157] while an increasing number of scholars pointed to the year 1513 itself as marking the transition from Luther's 'pre-reformation' to 'reformation' thought.[158] Hirsch saw the transition as taking place during the course of the *Dictata*, during the course of the exposition of Psalm 30 (31),[159] while Vogelsang saw it as taking place, or already having taken place, at the exposition of Psalm 70 (71).[160] Although Bornkamm's argument that the transition must be dated from the beginning of the lectures on Romans (1515) won some support,[161] Vogelsang's thesis appears to have gained general acceptance until 1958.

The challenge to this prevailing consensus on the dating of Luther's breakthrough dates from 1951, when Saarnivaara argued that Luther did not develop the distinctive features of his doctrine of justification until as late as 1518-19.[162] Although this conclusion rested upon questionable presuppositions concerning the nature of Luther's mature doctrine of justification,[163] it posed a very real challenge to the received view. Unaware of this study, Bizer argued for the later date of 1518-19, not only on the basis of the dating indicated by the autobiographical fragment of 1545, but also on the basis of a careful examination on

[157] F. Loofs, 'Der articulus stantis et cadentis ecclesiae', *Theologische Studien und Kritiken* 90 (1917), pp. 323-400; p. 352.
[158] e.g. Stracke, *Luthers großes Selbstzeugnis*, p. 125; Wendorf, *Der Durchbruch der neuen Erkenntnis Luthers*, pp. 316-17. The distinction between 'reformation' and 'pre-reformation' elements in Luther's thought must be treated with the utmost caution: see Grane, *Modus loquendi theologicus*, pp. 11-12.
[159] Hirsch, *Initium Theologiae Lutheri*, passim.
[160] Vogelsang, *Die Anfänge von Luthers Christologie*, p. 59. Cf. Rupp, *The Righteousness of God*, pp. 136-7.
[161] H. Bornkamm, 'Luthers Bericht über seine Entdeckung der Iustitia Dei', *Archiv für Reformationsgeschichte* 37 (1940), pp. 117-28; p. 127. In his later study, 'Iustitia Dei in der Scholastik und bei Luther', *Archiv für Reformationsgeschichte* 39 (1942), pp. 1-46, Bornkamm advanced the date of the discovery to coincide with that advocated by Vogelsang. Although this thesis is modified in a later study, his overall agreement with Vogelsang is still evident: Bornkamm, *Iustitia Dei beim jungen Luther*, p. 299.
[162] U. Saarnivaara, *Luther Discovers the Gospel: New Light upon Luther's Way from Medieval Catholicism to Evangelical Faith* (St Louis, 1951), pp. 74-87. The Finnish original dates from 1947.
[163] Cf. Bornkamm, *Iustitia Dei beim jungen Luther*, pp. 369-70.

the role of *humilitas* in Luther's theology of justification over the period
1513-19.[164] It is therefore clear that there is a real division of opinion
on this matter within contemporary Luther scholarship, with two
distinct datings being advocated for the breakthrough: 1513-15 and
1518-19. Only if the remarkably clumsy solution of *two* moments of
illumination, which later coalesced in Luther's memory, is adopted
can these two positions be reconciled.[165]

It is, of course, possible to argue that both Saarnivaara and Bizer
base their case upon mistaken dogmatic presuppositions. This,
however, does not explain the apparent reference to 1519 as the year
of Luther's discovery in the autobiographical fragment itself. If
Luther's words are taken at their face value, the chronology of the
fragment clearly implies that his breakthrough took place in 1519.
It has been suggested, nevertheless, that the unusual use of the so-
called '*double*' *pluperfect* tense at the beginning of the text (*captus fueram*
where *captus eram* would be expected) indicates that the passage should
be regarded as a digression from the main course of the narrative,
so that an earlier period in Luther's career is being referred to.[166]
This is somewhat more convincing than the suggestion that Luther
confused his second course of lectures on the Psalter (the *Operationes
in Psalmos*) with his first (the *Dictata super Psalterium*),[167] although it
cannot be regarded as totally persuading. Nevertheless, Luther's
sudden use of this tense is clearly laden with chronological significance,
and the simplest explanation of the use of the tense is unquestionably
to imply a chronological discontinuity within an otherwise continuous
narrative.

It is almost certain that the autobiographical fragment has been
subject to considerable over-interpretation by Luther scholars. It must
be remembered that the fragment forms part of a preface, addressed
to the *pius lector* who is about to read the first volume of Luther's
collected Latin works. What would Luther wish such a reader to know?
It is clear that Luther's object in writing the preface is to acquaint
the reader with the *historia negotii evangelici* of 1517-19, in order that

[164] Bizer, *Fides ex auditu*, pp. 172-8.
[165] See W. D. J. Cargill Thompson, 'The Problem of Luther's "Tower Experience"
and its Place in his Intellectual Development', in *Studies in the Reformation: Luther to
Hooker* (London, 1980), pp. 60-80; pp. 79-80. Cargill Thompson does not appear
to take his own suggestion with much seriousness.
[166] Stracke, *Luthers großes Selbstzeugnis*, pp. 122-3.
[167] F. Loofs, *Leitfaden zum Studium der Dogmengeschichte* (Halle, 4th edn, 1906) p. 689.

he may more fully appreciate the significance of what follows within the main body of the work itself. The reader in question may well have been unfamiliar with Luther's background, and thus unable to appreciate the context within which Luther's theology emerged. The purpose of the preface is thus to inform the reader that the writer of the works which he is about to read was once himself a monk and a 'papist', who had profound theological misgivings concerning the accepted theology of his day. In the course of his biblical exposition, he came to acquire new insights which were essentially complete by the time he began to expound the Psalter for the second time. A stumbling block to this development was encountered in the phrase 'the righteousness of God': Luther explains briefly, without adequate documentation, the nature of that difficulty before outlining, with equal brevity, the nature of his solution to this problem, and indicating its Augustinian provenance. In other words, Luther intends the reader to understand that by the end of the period covered by the *historia negotii evangelici* (in other words, by 1519), he was in full possession of the new theology upon which his subsequent actions and publications were based. The preface in no way demands us to conclude that Luther's new theological insights *took place* in 1519, although it does clearly imply that they *were complete* by that date, and that they are incorporated into the substance of the *Operationes in Psalmos*. The *Operationes* do indeed contain his 'new' understanding of *iustitia Dei* — but their leading feature is their exposition of the *theologia crucis*, which, as we shall argue, encapsulates the *cogitationes* which Luther describes in the autobiographical fragment. It is clear that Luther regarded his initial difficulties over *iustitia Dei* as cathartic, and his solution to those difficulties as paradigmatic. In other words, although Luther's discovery of the 'wonderful new definition of righteousness' cannot in any way be regarded as exhausting his early theological insights, it was of decisive importance precisely because the manner in which Luther interpreted the concept was immediately applicable to other related concepts, as the autobiographical fragment indicates, thus providing the model on which his programmatic reinterpretation of such concepts could proceed. As we shall argue in the following chapter, the leading features of the theology of the cross are foreshadowed in this earlier phase of his development.

   Luther's thought over the period 1513-19 demonstrates every evidence of continuous development, rather than cataclysmic alteration. There is no single point at which a dramatic alteration in his theological outlook may be detected. Although this absence is at least partly due to the nature of the material upon which Luther was lecturing at the time, and partly due to Luther's early views on the public nature of scriptural exegesis, it cannot be totally explained upon this basis. The autobiographical fragment indicates that Luther experienced, or at least remembered experiencing, a theological breakthrough in relation to his interpretation of *iustitia Dei*. The evidence unquestionably demonstrates that Luther's interpretation of this concept underwent a radical alteration over the period 1513-16, although in a number of stages. Which, then, of these stages corresponds most closely to Luther's own account of his initial difficulties, and their resolution through his discovery of the *mira et nova diffinitio iustitiae*?

On the basis of his analysis of Luther's discussion of *iustitia Dei* in the *Dictata*, Vogelsang concluded that Luther's discovery must have taken place in 1514, at — or perhaps shortly before — his exposition of Psalm 70 (71). Although this undoubtedly corresponds to a stage in the development of Luther's thinking on the matter, it does not appear to us to represent a breakthrough in any significant sense. When viewed in the light of the soteriology of the *via moderna*, it becomes clear that the alteration which Vogelsang detects, while representing a real development in Luther's thought, must nevertheless be regarded as nothing more than a significant terminological or conceptual clarification within the *existing* framework of his thought. The concept of *iustitia fidei* only resolves Luther's difficulties, as they are stated in the autobiographical fragment, if, *and only if*, faith is understood to be a divine work within man, rather than a human work or activity in itself, unaided by grace — and *this* vital development took place at some point in 1515. Luther's theological breakthrough is indeed related to the realisation that the righteousness which God requires of man is faith — but this fails to resolve his dilemma, *unless* that faith is recognised as originating from God, rather than from man. We therefore conclude that the theological breakthrough in relation to the 'righteousness of God' took place at some point in 1515, possibly having taken place during the final stages of the *Dictata*.

It is our opinion that this breakthrough represents the beginning, rather than the end, of Luther's early theological development, in that it is on the basis of his new understanding of *iustitia Dei* that Luther was obliged to begin the long and painful process of revising his understanding of the manner in which God deals with sinful man in a sinful world. Luther's insight into the true nature of the 'righteousness of God' represents far more than a mere terminological clarification: latent within it is a new concept of God. Who is this God who deals thus with man? Luther's answer to this question, as it developed over the years 1513-19, can be summarised in one of his most daring phrases: the God who deals with sinful man in this astonishing way is none other than the 'crucified and hidden God' (*Deus crucifixus et absconditus*)[168] — the God of the *theologia crucis*. How Luther developed his fundamental insight into the true nature of the 'righteousness of God' into the *theologia crucis*, with all that this entails, is the subject of the following chapter.

---

[168] The phrase dates from 1518, and may be found in the *Resolutiones disputationum de indulgentiarum virtute*, WA 1.613.23-8: 'Theologus crucis (id est de *deo crucifixo et abscondito* loquens) poenas, cruces, mortem docet esse thezaurum omnium preciosissimum et reliquias sacratissimas, quas ipsemet dominus huius theologiae consecravit benedixitque non solum tactu suae sanctissimae carnis, sed et amplexu suae supersanctae et divinae voluntatis, easque hic reliquit vere osculandas, quaerendas, amplexandas' (our italics). For an excellent discussion of this aspect of Luther's theology, see Pierre Bühler, *Kreuz und Eschatologie. Eine Auseinandersetzung mit der politischen Theologie, im Anschluß an Luthers theologia crucis* (Tübingen, 1981), pp. 91-132.

5

Crux sola est nostra theologia:
The Emergence of the Theology
of the Cross 1514-19

ON 26 April 1518 Luther presided over the opening disputation of
the chapter of the Augustinian Order at Heidelberg.[1] The
disputation concerned a series of theses which Luther had drawn up
for the occasion at the invitation of Johannes von Staupitz. In the
course of these theses, the main elements of Luther's emerging *theologia
crucis* become clear.[2] The most significant statements relating to this
theology are to be found in Theses 19 and 20:

19. The man who looks upon the invisible things of God as they are
    perceived in created things does not deserve to be called a theologian.
    (*Non ille dignus theologus dicitur, qui invisibilia Dei per ea, quae facta sunt,
    intellecta conspicit.*)
20. The man who perceives the visible rearward parts of God as seen in
    suffering and the cross does, however, deserve to be called a theologian.
    (*Sed qui visibilia et posteriora Dei per passiones et crucem conspecta intelligit.*)[3]

[1] See K. Bauer, 'Die Heidelberger Disputation Luthers', *Zeitschrift für Kirchengeschichte* 21 (1900), pp. 233-68; 299-329. This study requires supplementation at
points — e.g., on the theological faculty at Heidelberg: see H. Bornkamm, 'Die
theologische Fakultät Heidelberg', in *Aus der Geschichte der Universität Heidelberg und
ihrer Fakultäten* (Ruperto-Carlo Sonderband: Heidelberg, 1961), pp. 135-54.
[2] For an excellent study, see W. von Loewenich, *Luthers Theologia Crucis* (München,
4th edn, 1954) pp. 11-20. The English translation of this work is seriously inaccurate
at several points of importance: *Luther's Theology of the Cross* (Belfast, 1976). The
important study of Eduard Ellwein should also be noted: 'Die Entfaltung der theologia
crucis in Luthers Hebräerbriefvorlesung', in *Theologische Aufsätze. Karl Barth zum 50.
Geburtstag*, ed. E. Wolf (München, 1936), pp. 382-404, especially pp. 398-401.
[3] WA 1.354.17-21. The translation of Thesis 20 in the English version of
Loewenich's study is seriously inaccurate (*Luther's Theology of the Cross*, p. 18): *posteriora
Dei* is there translated as 'the manifest things of God', which is clearly unacceptable.

For Luther, the sole authentic *locus* of man's knowledge of God is the cross of Christ, in which God is to be found revealed, and yet paradoxically hidden in that revelation. Luther's reference to the *posteriora Dei* serves to emphasise that, like Moses, we can only see God from the rear: we are denied a direct knowledge of God, or a vision of his face (cf. Exodus 33. 23: *videbis posteriora mea, faciem autem meam videre non poteris*). The cross does indeed reveal God — but that revelation is of the *posteriora Dei*. In that it is the *posteriora Dei* which are made visible, this revelation of God must be regarded as an indirect revelation — but a genuine revelation nonetheless.

God is revealed in the *passiones et crucem* — and yet he is hidden in this very revelation. In the very things which human wisdom regards as the antithesis of deity — such as weakness, foolishness and humility — God stands revealed in the 'humility and shame of the cross'.[4] We may summarise the leading features of the *theologia crucis* as follows:[5]

(1) The *theologia crucis* is a theology of revelation, which stands in sharp contrast to speculation. Those who speculate on the created order (*ea quae facta sunt*) have, in effect, forfeited their right to be called 'theologians'. God has revealed himself, and it is the task of the theologian to concern himself with God as he has chosen to reveal himself, instead of constructing preconceived notions of God which ultimately must be destroyed.

(2) This revelation must be regarded as indirect and concealed. This is one of the most difficult aspects of the *theologia crucis* to grasp: how can one speak of a *concealed* revelation? Luther's allusion to Exodus 33.23 in Thesis 20 is the key to understanding this fundamental point: although it is indeed God who is revealed in the passion and the cross of Christ, he is not immediately recognisable *as God*. Those who expect a direct revelation of the face of God are unable to discern him in his revelation, precisely because it is the *posteriora Dei* which are made visible in this revelation. In that it is God who is made known in the passion and cross of Christ, it is *revelation*; in that this revelation can only be discerned by the eye of faith, it is *concealed*. The 'friends of the

---

Not only is the important allusion to Exodus 33.23 overlooked: on the basis of this translation, it is impossible to speak of the *hiddenness* of God's revelation — yet it is clear that this is precisely what Luther intended to convey by the phrase.

[4] WA 1.362.12-13.
[5] Cf. von Loewenich, *Luthers Theologia Crucis*, p. 18.

cross' know that beneath the humility and shame of the cross lie concealed the power and the glory of God — but to others, this insight is denied.

(3) This revelation is to be recognised in the sufferings and the cross of Christ, rather than in human moral activity or the created order. Both the moralist and the rationalist expect to find God through intelligent reflection upon the nature of man's moral sense or the pattern of the created order: for Luther, 'true theology and knowledge of God are found in Christ crucified'. The cross shatters human illusions concerning the capacity of human reason to discern God in this manner.[6]

(4) This knowledge of God who is hidden in his revelation is a matter of faith.[7] Revelation of the *posteriora Dei* is addressed to faith, which alone recognises it as a revelation *of God*. Luther illustrates this point with reference to John 14.8. Philip here asks Jesus to show him the Father — which, according to Luther, makes him a 'theologian of glory', in that he considers that God may be found and known apart from Christ. Jesus then explains to him that there is no knowledge of God other than that which may be found in his own person: 'Whoever has seen me, has seen the Father' (John 14.9). For Luther, the 'theologian of the cross' is he who, through faith, discerns the presence of the hidden God in his revelation in Christ and his passion and cross — and who is thus able to acknowledge the truth of Isaiah's *dictum*: 'Truly you are a hidden God!'[8] The concept of a hidden God (*absconditus Deus*) lies at the centre of the theology of the cross: *vivimus in abscondito Dei, id est, in nuda fiducia misericordiae eius.*[9] For Luther, Philip represents the tendency of the *theologia gloriae* to seek for God apart from Christ, unaware that God is revealed in him, although concealed in that revelation.

(5) God is particularly known through suffering. Although this is essentially a reference to the *passiones Christi*, a far deeper spiritual truth is involved: a fundamental contention of the *theologia crucis* is not merely that God is known *through* suffering (whether that of Christ or of the individual), but that God *makes himself known* through

---

[6] WA 1.362.30-31: 'Per crucem destruuntur opera et crucifigitur Adam, qui per opera potius aedificatur.'

[7] Cf. P. Althaus, 'Theologie des Glaubens', *Zeitschrift für systematische Theologie* 2 (1924), pp. 281-322.

[8] WA 1.362.14: 'Vere absconditus tu es Deus.'

[9] WA 1.357.3-4.

suffering. For Luther, God is active in this matter, rather than passive, in that suffering and temptation are seen as means by which man is brought to God. This brings us to the dialectic between the *opus proprium Dei* and the *opus alienum Dei*, which Luther introduces in his explanation of Thesis 16. The basic paradox involved is illustrated with reference to the justification of an individual. In order that a man may be justified, he must first recognise that he is a sinner, and humble himself before God. Before man can be justified, he must be utterly humiliated — and it is God who both humiliates and justifies. 'Thus an action which is alien to God's nature (*opus alienum Dei*) results in an action which belongs to his very nature (*opus proprium Dei*): God makes a person a sinner in order that he may make him righteous.' The *opus alienum* is a means to the end of the *opus proprium*. The significance of suffering, whether this is understood as *passiones Christi* or human *Anfechtung*, is that it represents the *opus alienum* through which God works out his *opus proprium*. In his important study on *Anfechtung*, Beintker demonstrated that Luther regards God himself as the source of *Anfechtung*: God assaults man in order to break him down and thus to justify him.[10] Similarly, studies on Luther's understanding of the role of the Devil in the Christian life have demonstrated that he regarded the Devil as God's instrument, who performs the *opus alienum Dei* on his behalf in order that the *opus proprium* may be realised.[11] Far from regarding suffering or evil as a nonsensical intrusion into the world (which Luther regards as the opinion of a 'theologian of glory'), the 'theologian of the cross' regards such suffering as his most precious treasure, for revealed and yet hidden in precisely such sufferings is none other than the living God, working out the salvation of those whom he loves.

The same themes are repeated and developed in the *Operationes in Psalmos*, dating from the same period of Luther's career. God's revelation in the cross of Christ must be regarded as a hidden revelation, which defies the attempts of reason to master it: *crucis sapientia nimis*

---

[10] H. Beintker, *Die Überwindung der Anfechtung bei Luther: Eine Studie zu seiner Theologie nach den Operationes In Psalmos 1519-21* (Berlin, 1954), pp. 38-56; 99-104; 106-7; 132-44.

[11] H.-M. Barth, *Der Teufel und Jesus Christus in der Theologie Martin Luthers* (Göttingen, 1967), pp. 165-6; 183; 188; 200-201. Similar conclusions were drawn earlier by P. T. Bühler, *Die Anfechtung bei Martin Luther* (Zürich, 1944).

hodie est abscondita in mysterio profundo. [12] Human wisdom takes offence
at the cross of Christ, which stands in contradiction to accepted human
standards of wisdom. [13] Human reason cannot understand the ways
of God, and thus finds itself driven to despair. [14] Through the
experience of the *opus alienum Dei*, the sinner finds himself driven to
despair, his confidence in himself totally shaken; finding himself under
the wrath of God, he counts himself as damned. Yet through this
experience of the strange work of God, the sinner is enabled to appropriate the proper work of God: by experiencing the 'delicious despair'
of *Anfechtung*, the sinner learns to trust only in God, as known in the
cross of Christ, and thus comes to be justified. As Luther remarks,
Anfechtung, 'in so far as it takes everything away from us, leaves us
nothing but God: it cannot take God away from us, and actually brings
him closer to us'. [15] It is through undergoing the torment of the cross,
death and hell that true theology and the knowledge of God come
about. 'The cross alone is our theology' (*CRUX sola est nostra
theologia*). [16] It is only by experiencing the wrath of God in this manner
that a man becomes a 'theologian of the cross'. It is precisely this
consideration which underlies Luther's celebrated statement concerning the qualifications of a true theologian: 'living, or rather dying
and being damned make a theologian, not understanding, reading
or speculating' (*vivendo immo moriendo et damnando fit theologus, non
intelligendo, legendo aut speculando*). [17]

These, then, are the main features of the *theologia crucis* as they are
developed in the Heidelberg disputation of 1518, and the *Operationes*
of 1518-21. In the present chapter, we shall subject these features to
further analysis, and indicate how they are related within the context
of Luther's thought at the time. Before undertaking such an analysis,
however, we propose to return to the question of the origins of the
theologia crucis. What considerations led Luther to formulate such a
theology? In the following section, we shall develop the thesis already
referred to earlier in this study: namely, that the main features of
the *theologia crucis* are foreshadowed in Luther's resolution of his earlier
difficulties concerning the 'righteousness of God'.

[12] WA 5.84.40. For a useful discussion, see E. G. Rupp, *The Righteousness of God:
Luther Studies* (London, 1953), pp. 227-41.
[13] WA 5.107.5-9; 5.263.17-18.
[14] WA 5.615.17-22.
[15] WA 5.165.39-166.1.
[16] WA 5.176.32-3.
[17] WA 5.163.28-9.

THE FORESHADOWING OF THE THEOLOGY
OF THE CROSS IN LUTHER'S DISCOVERY
OF THE 'RIGHTEOUSNESS OF GOD'

As shown in the previous chapter, by late 1514 Luther had arrived at the fundamental insight that the proper disposition for justification is humility. *This* is the righteousness which God demands of man *ex pacto suo* if he is to be justified — the *humilitas fidei*. It is only when the sinner, in his total humilitation, cries out to God for grace that he can be justified. Before grace can be given to the sinner, he must be forced to admit the total inadequacy of his own soteriological resources, and turn to God in emptiness and prayer. Although a decisive modification to this understanding of the proper disposition for justification appears at some stage during 1515, in that the *humilitas fidei* is recognised to be itself a gracious work of God within man, the overall structure of Luther's early scheme of justification remains essentially the same: before man can be raised to the heights, he must first be forced to descend to the depths; before he can be elevated by God, he must first humiliate himself; before he can be saved, he must first be damned; before he can live in the spirit, he must first be put to death in the flesh.

As we indicated in the previous chapter, there are two aspects to Luther's discovery of the 'righteousness of God'. The first relates to the *nature* of this righteousness: Luther discovered a 'wonderful new definition of righteousness' which stood in diametrical opposition to human understandings of *iustitia*. The second relates to the *mode* by which this righteousness comes about within the individual: man cannot perform good works which are capable of earning justification on a *quid pro quo* basis, but he can totally abase himself, and cry out to God for grace. It is this second aspect of the matter which we shall consider first, before turning to deal with the significance of the *nature* of *iustitia Dei* for the development of Luther's theology of the cross.

God humiliates man, in order that he may justify him; he makes man a sinner, in order that he may make him righteous — and both aspects of this matter are increasingly seen by Luther as works *of God*. Although Luther initially appears to have believed that man humbled himself, there are clear indications in the later stages of the *Dictata* that he is moving towards a more theocentric understanding of the various aspects of justification. God induces in man a state of total humiliation — a term which Luther prefers to 'humility', on account of the latter's associations with the monastic virtue of humility — and then accepts this as the righteousness which he demands of man if he is to be justified. Once Luther has grasped the fact that it is God who takes the initiative in justification, and that he must be regarded as active rather than passive at every stage in the process, he is increasingly obliged to recognise the problems which are raised by this assertion. It is not man who humbles himself — it is God who humbles him. Even in the earlier stages of the *Dictata*, where Luther allows man a greater role in his own justification, God is still seen as instigating man's humiliation, even if man himself must cooperate with God if this humiliation is to be properly effected.

How does God humiliate man? Through the experience of the wrath of God, the threat of hell and eternal damnation, through *Anfechtung* and suffering. It is through experiencing the wrath of God that man is humbled, and forced to concede that he cannot, by himself, stand in the presence of God — and thus he turns to God in his helplessness and hopelessness, and by doing so, is justified. Paradoxically, it is thus through God's wrath that his mercy is able to operate, in that man would not seek that mercy unless he knew how much he needed it. It is considerations such as this which lead Luther to distinguish two aspects of the work of God in justification. Even at the earliest stages of the *Dictata*, Luther may be found to employ the concepts of the *opus alienum* and *opus proprium* to deal with this paradox.[18] Similar considerations underlie his important distinction between the 'wrath of severity' (*ira severitatis*) and the 'wrath of mercy' (*ira misericordiae*).[19] While the impenitent taste nothing but the severity of the wrath of God, the penitent recognise the merciful intention which lies behind it, in that they discern that it is intended to move them to repentance, humility and faith, and thus to receive the grace of God.[20] God, having ordained that he will bestow grace upon the sole precondition of humility, is obliged to stand by his primordial decision — and thus, if man is to receive grace, he must meet this condition. The intent underlying the *opus alienum Dei* is to enable man to fulfil this

[18] WA 3.246.19-20; 4.87.22-5. For a useful discussion, see H. Bandt, *Luthers Lehre vom verborgenen Gott: Eine Untersuchung zu dem offenbarungsgeschichtlichen Ansatz seiner Theologie* (Berlin, 1958), pp. 54-82.
[19] WA 3.69.24; 3.153.30-32.
[20] WA 3.330.26-28. Other similar phrases should be noted — e.g., 'iudicium benignum et salutare' (WA 3.462.2).

precondition, and thus to receive the grace of the merciful God who is hidden in his strange work. As we showed on the basis of our analysis of the soteriology of the *Dictata* in the previous chapter, Luther appears to interpret *fides Christi* as *sibi iniustus esse et ita coram Deo humilis*, where *fides Christi* is the righteousness which God requires of man if he is to be justified. If man is to recognise his own unrighteousness, and thus to be moved to humility, he must first be forced to concede his own utter unworthiness, and the futility of his situation, if left to his own devices. The merciful intention of the *opus alienum* thus becomes clear, even although this may only be recognisable to faith. It is this dialectic between the *opus alienum* and the *opus proprium* which underlies Luther's reflections upon the *iudicium Dei*: the Word of God, by passing its severe judgement upon man, makes him a sinner, and thus executes the *opus alienum* — but in that this moves man to cry out to God for mercy and grace (which are immediately forthcoming!), it indirectly executes the *opus proprium*. It is of considerable significance that Luther later illustrates the concepts of the *opus alienum* and *opus proprium* in the Heidelberg disputation with specific reference to the justification of the sinner: 'thus an action which is alien to God's nature results in an action which belongs to his very nature: God makes a person a sinner, in order to make him righteous.' The fundamental insight, recognised by faith alone, is that God's wrath is his penultimate, and not his final, word.

God's mercy is thus latent under his wrath, although this insight is denied to all save believers. The dialectic between the *opus alienum* and *opus proprium* leads Luther to assert that God's works are hidden 'under the form of their opposite' (*abscondita sub contrariis*). This hiddenness of God in his revelation is, as Luther emphasises, discernable only within the context of faith. In the wrath of God, we see the means by which his mercy is brought into play; in his damnation of man, we see the means by which he saves him. Luther states this principle with increasing frequency in the course of the *Dictata*,[21] often in relation to the specific question of justification:

It is clear that these are hidden inside, but more amazingly, that they are hidden under the form of the opposite (*sub contrario suo abscondita sunt*). So whoever totally humiliates himself in the eyes of the world (*coram mundo*) is totally exalted in the sight of God (*coram Deo*).[22]

---

[21] e.g., WA 4.82.17-18; 4.243.7-13; 4.451.25-7.
[22] WA 4.449.35-7.

The *locus* of this disclosure is supremely the cross of Christ. Luther's use of I Corinthians 1.27-8 is of particular interest in this respect, as it is this passage concerning the 'word of the cross' which explicitly contrasts human and divine concepts of wisdom and strength. Luther's exposition of Psalm 95 (96) is of particular significance here: a series of antitheses is developed, based upon the hidden revelation of God in the cross of Christ: the man who weakens himself is made strong; the man who makes himself foolish is made wise; the man who condemns himself is the man who is saved.[23] The *opus alienum* is the destruction of human preconceptions of divine justice, wisdom and strength; the *opus proprium* is the establishment of the righteousness, the wisdom and the power of God within man in their place.[24] Before God can build, he must first destroy.

It will be clear that Luther's early insistence upon the necessity of destroying human preconceptions of *iustitia* through the *opus alienum Dei* leads us on to consider the *nature* of the 'righteousness of God'. In the opening of the *scholia* of his lectures on Romans, Luther states his conviction that the letter represents a programmatic assault upon human preconceptions of wisdom and righteousness:

The purpose of this letter is to break down, to uproot and to destroy all the wisdom and righteousness of the flesh, no matter how great it may be in our own sight or that of other men, and no matter how sincere or heartfelt it may be; and to implant, establish and magnify sin, no matter how much we may insist that it does not exist, or fail to recognise its existence.[25]

It is therefore clear that Luther presupposes a radical dichotomy between human and divine conceptions of *iustitia*: indeed, as we have argued in the previous chapter, it was Luther's earlier failure to recognise this dichotomy which led to his difficulties over the phrase 'the righteousness of God'. For Luther, the essence of *fides Christi* (the only *iustitia* which he recognises as being valid *coram Deo*) is the sinner's recognition of his total *un*righteousness. As Vogelsang has correctly stated, Luther arrived at this insight concerning the nature of the righteousness which is required of man by God during, or possibly before, his exposition of Psalm 71 (72). In the course of that exposition,

---

[23] WA 4.110.34-111.19.
[24] e.g., see the *catena* of scriptural citations assembled at WA 4.111.21-6.
[25] WA 56.157.2-6; cf. WA 56.3.6-13.

he not merely elaborates on the contrast between human and divine judgement, but also indicates where the latter may be found:

It is therefore called the judgement of God (*iudicium Dei*), because it is contrary to the judgement of men (*contrarium est iudicio hominum*), condemning what men choose, and choosing what men condemn. And this judgement has been shown to us in the cross of Christ (*hoc iudicium est in cruce Christi nobis ostensum*). [26]

How is this judgement revealed in the cross? Luther points to the suffering of Christ upon the cross, and his apparent abandonment by God, and argues that in the weakness, the folly and the injustice of this appalling spectacle, the judgement of God against human understandings of strength, wisdom and justice may be discerned. It is through suffering (*passio*) such as that of Christ upon the cross that man is brought to realise the seriousness of his predicament: through realising the force of the divine judgement passed against him, he is saved. *Infirmitas, passio, crux, persecutio, etc. Hec sunt arma Dei, hec virtutes et potentiae, per que nos salvat et iudicat.* [27] The dialectic between the *opus alienum* and *opus proprium* has its focal point in the cross of Christ. Nevertheless, this dialectic is only discernible to faith: the unbeliever misinterprets the *opus alienum* as the *opus proprium*, unable to distinguish *ira severitatis* and *ira misericordiae*. Just as God cannot be discerned empirically or by the powers of human reason in the human figure of Jesus, [28] but is only seen therein by faith, so human reason is outraged and confounded by the *iustitia, sapientia* and *virtus* revealed in the cross of Christ. It is only when man is totally humiliated that he learns to recognise the futility of his own powers of reason in matters of faith, [29] and so turns to the cross of Christ.

With these considerations in mind, let us return to the *crux interpretativum* with which Luther had such difficulty. As the autobiographical fragment of 1545 indicates, Luther found Romans 1.17 a stumbling block: 'The righteousness of God is revealed in it.' In the previous chapter, we considered at some length the difficulties Luther encountered with the first part of this sentence, *iustitia Dei*. But what of the second part of the sentence, *revelatur in illo*? In what

[26] WA 3.463.15-18. Cf. WA 5.168.25.
[27] WA 3.301.36-7
[28] WA 3.124.33-5; 4.6.40-7.3.
[29] WA 4.83.3-9. Cf. WA 3.548.6-9; 4.82.37-83.2.

sense is the 'righteousness of God' (however this may be interpreted) *revealed?* It will be clear that Luther's theological breakthrough is intimately related to the idea of a *hidden* revelation — the 'righteousness of God' really is revealed in the cross of Christ, but it can only be discerned by the eye of faith. It is revealed in a manner similar to the *posteriora Dei*, as described in Thesis 20 of the Heidelberg Disputation: a *real* revelation of God, it is nevertheless not recognisable as a revelation of *God*, because it contradicts preconceptions of what form that revelation should take. Similar remarks apply to the hidden revelation of the wisdom, the strength, the glory and the salvation of God, as described in the autobiographical fragment: all *really* are revealed — but they are revealed *sub contrariis*. In this sense, as we noted in the previous chapter, Luther's comments concerning these amount to a programmatic description of the *theologia crucis*. It is not enough to recognise that all these *come from* God: it is necessary to appreciate that all are revealed *abscondita sub contrariis*. In the injustice, the shame, the weakness, the folly and the condemnation of the cross are revealed, and yet hidden, the righteousness, the glory, the wisdom, the strength and the salvation of God. As we have already indicated, Luther recognised an intimate relationship between human understandings of *iustitia* and *sapientia*, so that his sustained critique of the role of reason in matters theological, which becomes evident from 1515 onwards, is ultimately a consequence and an expression of his conviction that human reason cannot comprehend the manner in which God has effected the salvation of mankind. In the cross of Christ, this tension reaches breaking point, and a near-permanent divorce between the spheres of faith and reason results. Reason is scandalised by the cross; faith embraces it with joy.

Underlying the *theologia crucis* and the discovery of the 'righteousness of God' is a radical critique of the analogical nature of theological language.[30] Within the earlier medieval period in general, the concept of *iustitia Dei* had been constructed on the assumption that it was analogous to *iustitia*. While the difficulties encountered in transferring the term *iustus* from a *human* context (as in the statement, 'Socrates is just') to a *divine* context (as in the statement, 'God is just') were

[30] See A. E. McGrath, ' "The Righteousness of God" from Augustine to Luther', *Studia Theologica* 36 (1982), pp. 63-78; also 'Divine Justice and Divine Equity in the controversy between Augustine and Julian of Eclanum', *Downside Review* 101 (1983), pp. 312-19.

fully appreciated,[31] it was nevertheless assumed that the term bore a related meaning in each of these contexts. Although the epistemological presuppositions of the concept were greatly weakened through the critique of Henry of Ghent's theory of the divine attributes, initially by Godfrey of Fontaines, and subsequently (and more radically) by William of Ockham,[32] the essentially analogical relationship between *iustitia Dei* and *iustitia hominum* was upheld. Similarly, although the theologians of the *via moderna* emphasised the contingency of the established order of salvation (and hence of the analogical nature of theological language in general), the analogy between human and divine concepts of *iustitia* was upheld. Although there was clearly a disparity between the human and divine understandings of terms such as *iustitia, sapientia, virtus*, etc., there remained an essential underlying continuity. The *theologia crucis* represents a programmatic critique of the analogical nature of theological language. The concept of *absconditas sub contrario*, which is an essential feature of both the *theologia crucis* and the earlier theological breakthrough, represents the most radical critique of the principle of analogy in theological discourse yet known, and, at least in this respect, parallels the origins of dialectical theology in the early twentieth century.[33] While we would be guilty of a serious anachronism if we were to dub Luther a 'theologian of the Word of God', given the twentieth-century connotations of this phrase, the fact remains that Luther insists that the word to which all theology must be related is the word of the cross. *Crux probat omnia!*[34] All responsible Christian discourse about God must be based upon the cross, and must be subject to criticism upon this basis.[35] For Luther, the rejection of the analogical nature of theological language[36] represents

---

[31]   e.g., Alan of Lille, *Theologicae Regulae* 26; MPL 210.633D: '"Deus est iustus." Hoc nomen "iustus" transfertur a sua propria significatione ad hoc ut conveniat Deo, sed res nominis non attribuitur Deo.' See G. R. Evans, 'The Borrowed Meaning: Grammar, Logic and the Problem of Theological Language in Twelfth-Century Schools', *Downside Review* 96 (1978), pp. 165-75.

[32]   McGrath, '*The Righteousness of God*', pp. 69-70.

[33]   See Karl Barth's remarkable essay of 1916, 'Die Gerechtigkeit Gottes', originally published in *Neue Wege* 10 (1916), pp. 143-54; reprinted in *Das Wort Gottes und die Theologie: Gesammelte Vorträge* (München, 1929), pp. 5-17.

[34]   WA 5.179.31.

[35]   See the brilliant exposition of Jürgen Moltmann, *Der gekreuzigte Gott: Das Kreuz Christi als Grund und Kritik christlicher Theologie* (München, 4th edn, 1981).

[36]   Bizer has drawn attention to a passage in the *Operationes* which closely parallels the 1545 autobiographical fragment, and which explicitly states the problem of analogy which is at issue: WA 5.144.1-22.

an admission that man lives in theological twilight, in a world of half-light and half-truths. His preconceptions of God in general, and his righteousness in particular, are unreliable and confused and, like a broken bone which has set incorrectly, must be broken before they can be healed. The word of the cross reveals the gulf between the preconceived and the revealed God, and forces man to abandon his preconceptions if he is to be a 'theologian of the cross'. While this insight is initially associated with Luther's early difficulties concerning the predication of human concepts of righteousness to God, his resolution of these difficulties is essentially methodological, and thus comes to be extended to *every* divine attribute. Luther's critique of the analogical predication of human concepts of *iustitia* in particular to God foreshadows his critique of the predication of human concepts of qualities in general — and thus foreshadows the *theologia crucis* in this vital respect.

Iustitia Dei revelatur in illo. How is *iustitia Dei* revealed in the gospel? And how is this 'righteousness of God' revealed in the cross of Christ? Luther's early difficulties with questions such as these, recorded in the autobiographical fragment and elsewhere, were resolved through his realisation that, while the 'righteousness of God' was indeed revealed in the suffering of Christ on the cross, it was a hidden revelation which contradicted his preconceptions of the form which it should take, and which thus inhibited him from recognising it when confronted by it. Luther's critique of the analogical nature of theological language, his concept of the hiddenness of God in his self-revelation, and his growing recognition that the sufferings of Christ on the cross constituted the centre and the foundation of Christian theology, are inextricably linked in his theological breakthrough, as they are in the *theologia crucis*. Although these insights appear to have arisen through his deliberations concerning the 'righteousness of God', it is clear, as the autobiographical fragment indicates, that they were directly applicable to other crucial divine attributes: the 'power of God', the 'wisdom of God', the 'strength of God' and the 'glory of God' are all revealed, and yet hidden, in the cross of Christ. They need not be, and they must not be, sought elsewhere.

On the basis of the analysis presented in the present section, it will be clear that the five leading features of the *theologia crucis* are foreshadowed in Luther's discovery of the 'righteousness of God'. Although the precise relationship of these elements has yet to be explored fully, and although the full implications of the existential character of faith and the hiddenness of God's self-revelation in the cross have yet to be appreciated, it is evident that the characteristic die of Luther's *theologia crucis* has already been cast by late 1515. It is for this reason that we regard Luther's discovery of the 'righteousness of God' as being a catalyst for the development of the *theologia crucis*: Luther's solution to his initial difficulties over the true meaning of *iustitia Dei* was not complete in itself, but was pregnant with potential conceptual elaboration. That elaboration took place over the years 1516-18, and led to the statement of that theology which is for ever associated with the name of Martin Luther — the 'theology of the cross'. It is to an analysis of the leading features of this theology that we now turn.

THE CRUCIFIED AND HIDDEN GOD

God is revealed in the cross of Christ. Yet, as the Christian contemplates the appalling spectacle of Christ dying upon the cross, he is forced to concede that God does not appear to be revealed there at all. This insight is fundamental to a correct appreciation of the significance of Luther's theology of the cross. The God who is crucified is the God who is hidden in his revelation. Any attempt to seek God elsewhere than in the cross of Christ is to be rejected out of hand as idle speculation: the theologian is forced, perhaps against his will, to come to terms with the riddle of the crucified and hidden God. 'Truly you are a hidden God' (Isaiah 45.15).

For Luther, the cross mediates an indirect and hidden revelation of God. God cannot be known directly — for example, through intelligent contemplation of the created order — but discloses himself to us in the cross. Luther is, of course, too faithful to the thought of St Paul to reject the idea of a *natural* knowledge of God. In the lectures on Romans of 1515-16, Luther readily concedes that man has a natural knowledge of God.[37] This knowledge, however, is limited, and cannot be applied theologically without supplementation and modification on the basis of divine revelation. If a theology were constructed on the basis of this natural knowledge of God, Luther insists that the inevitable consequence would be nothing less than idolatry and

[37] WA 56.176.15-32. See R. Josefson, *Den naturliga teologins problem hos Luther* (Uppsala, 1943).

162   *The Breakthrough*

heresy.[38] Luther's discussion of the nature and significance of such a natural knowledge of God, as we encounter it in the Romans lectures, is not particularly lucid. The same general principles, however, are explained at greater length in the Jonah lectures of 1526.

The difficulty which Luther has to resolve here is posed by Jonah 1.5-16: how can the pagan mariners know that God is able to save them from their plight? Commenting on these verses, Luther observes that 'all mankind can speak of God, and human reason knows that God is greater than all created things'. Although the crew of the stricken ship cannot be said to have faith in God, they nevertheless possess the fundamental insight that God is able to save them.[39] Luther then comments:

So let us here also learn from nature and reason what is to be thought about God. For these people believe that God is such that he can rescue them from all evil. It follows that human reason must confess that all good comes from God; for he who can save us from all evil and misfortune can also give all good and happiness. The light of natural reason, in so far as it reaches concerning God as good, gracious, merciful and tender, has reached a deep understanding.[40]

In effect, Luther allows that man naturally possesses certain insights concerning God. Nevertheless, these insights exist at the purely cognitive level, and provide no incentive whatsoever to believe in God's personal assistance. As Luther points out with some force in the great Galatians commentary of 1535, it is one thing to be aware of God's general attributes, and quite another to understand God's particular intentions for mankind.[41] In other words, men have a natural *noticia* of God (that is, certain insights concerning his *esse*), but are unable to discern his specific intentions towards mankind by the same means (that is, they are ignorant concerning his *velle*). The transition from the cognitive to the existential level, which Luther insists to be an essential element of faith, cannot be made on the basis of reason alone.

[38] WA 56.177.11-33.
[39] WA 19.205.28-206.6.
[40] WA 19.206.7-14. Cf. B. Lohse, *Ratio und Fides. Eine Untersuchung über die Ratio in der Theologie Luthers* (Göttingen, 1958), pp. 59-64; D. Löfgen, *Die Theologie der Schöpfung bei Luther* (Göttingen, 1960), *passim*; H. Olsson, *Schöpfung, Vernunft und Gesetz in Luthers Theologie* (Uppsala, 1971), pp. 150-1; 177.
[41] WA 40 I.608.6-10.

Faith is ultimately grounded in a knowledge of the divine *velle*, rather than the divine *esse*. *Omnes sunt ignari, quid deus velit, i.e., habuistis aliquam noticia dei, divinitas nota, sed non de voluntate.* [42]

The point at issue here is familiar to those acquainted with the *Anknüpfungspunkt* controversy between Emil Brunner and Karl Barth in the early twentieth century. [43] Whereas divine revelation may end up by drastically modifying man's innate concept of God, it is, according to Brunner, necessary that such an innate concept exist in the first place, in order that man can make sense of revelation when he encounters it. It is necessary to have a 'point of contact' by which divine revelation can be appropriated, whatever the subsequent effect of that divine revelation may be. Luther's concession of a natural knowledge of God is in no way inconsistent with his *theologia crucis*, providing merely the point of contact betwen man and the revelation which is addressed to him. The theology of the cross, as we have emphasised, is a theology of revelation, and, as such, cannot be divorced from the question of the *preconditions of revelation*. According to Luther, it is natural that man may have preconceptions of God, through which divine revelation may be appropriated: nevertheless, the effect of that revelation is to *destroy* such preconceptions, and replace them with the 'crucified God'. As we have already noted, man's natural conception of God is highly confused and unreliable, and must be replaced by God's revelation of himself in the cross of Christ: that

[42] WA 40 I.608.6-7. A similar point appears to emerge from Calvin's discussion of God, according to Dowey: see E. A. Dowey, *The Knowledge of God in Calvin's Theology* (New York, 1952), pp. 41-86; 148-53; 221-42. Here a distinction is drawn between the natural knowledge of God the creator (*cognitio Dei creatoris*) and the revealed knowledge of God the redeemer (*cognitio Dei redemptoris*): only the latter may be regarded as *saving* knowledge. Cf. P. Brunner, 'Allgemeine und besondere Offenbarung in Calvins Institutio', *Evangelische Theologie* 1 (1934), pp. 189-215. For a critique of Dowey's views, see T. H. L. Parker, *Calvin's Doctrine of the Knowledge of God* (Edinburgh, 2nd edn, 1969).

[43] The basic documents are Emil Brunner's *Natur und Gnade*, reprinted in *Ein offenes Wort. Vorträge und Aufsätze 1917-1962* (2 vols: Zürich, 1981) Vol. I pp. 333-75, and Karl Barth's *Nein! Antwort an Emil Brunner* (Theologische Existenz heute 14 [1934]). The two are collected and translated into English in *Natural Theology* (London, 1946). Cf. E. Brunner, 'The New Barth: Observations on Karl Barth's Doctrine of Man', *Scottish Journal of Theology* 4 (1951), pp. 123-35. It is interesting to note that Bandt's *Luthers Lehre vom verborgenen Gott* appears to have been written with this controversy in mind: in his foreword, Bandt makes his disagreement with Barth clear. For a critical evaluation of the use made of Calvin in this controversy, see Dowey, *Knowledge of God*, pp. 247-9.

natural conception of God nevertheless serves a valuable purpose, in that it provides the means by which 'true theology and the knowledge of God' may come about.

In order for this true knowledge of God to come about, man's preconceptions of God must first be destroyed through the cross. Fundamental to this process is the notion that God is hidden in his revelation, a concept which is usually regarded as being encapsulated in the phrase *Deus absconditus*.[44] Before discussing the nature of the hiddenness of the divine self-revelation in the cross, it is necessary to appreciate that Luther scholars appear to have greatly impeded the proper interpretation of Luther on this point by their elevation of the term *Deus absconditus* to a programmatic statement of the *theologia crucis* as it bears on divine revelation. It seems that this represents an instance in which a tool of Luther research has finally become its master. Since the important study of Ferdinand Kattenbusch, which appeared in 1920, there has been a general tendency on the part of Luther scholars to impose a far greater precision on the term *Deus absconditus* than Luther himself intended. Luther uses the term considerably less frequently than might be imagined, and frequently employs variants (for example, *Deus nudus*) to express substantially the same ideas. While it is certainly true to state that Luther employs the notion of the hiddenness of God in the *theologia crucis*, that 'hiddenness' is expounded in several different ways. The variety of senses in which Luther uses the term *Deus absconditus* underlies the absence of a general consensus on the part of contemporary Luther scholars as to the precise meaning of the term. Indeed, there are excellent reasons for suggesting that Luther uses the term *Deus absconditus* in two main senses, which have little in common apart

[44] See F. Blanke, *Der verborgene Gott bei Luther* (Berlin, 1928); H. Bornkamm, 'Der verborgene und der offenbare Gott', *Theologische Rundschau* 16 (1944), pp. 38-52; W. Koehler, *Der verborgene Gott* (Heidelberg, 1946); J. Richter, 'Luthers "Deus absconditus" — Zuflucht oder Ausflucht?', *Zeitschrift für Religions- und Geistesgeschichte* 7 (1955), pp. 289-303; R. Koehler, 'Der *Deus Absconditus* in Philosophie und Theologie', ibid., 7 (1955) pp. 46-58; A. Adam, 'Der Begriff "Deus Absconditus" bei Luther nach Herkunft und Bedeutung', *Luther-Jahrbuch* 30 (1963), pp. 97-106; H. Grass, 'Der verborgene und der offenbare Gott bei Luther', *Reformation und Gegenwart: Vorträge und Vorlesungen von Mitgliedern der theologischen Fakultät Marburg zum 450 Jubiläum der Reformation* (Marburg, 1968), pp. 57-69; B. A. Gerrish, ' "To the Unknown God": Luther and Calvin on the Hiddenness of God', *Journal of Religion* 53 (1973), pp. 263-92. The two outstanding studies are those of Bandt, *Luthers Lehre vom verborgenen Gott*, and J. Dillenberger, *God Hidden and Revealed: The Interpretation of Luther's Deus Absconditus and its Significance for Religious Thought* (Philadelphia, 1953).

from the general idea of 'hiddenness'.[45]

(1) *Deus absconditus* is the God who is hidden *in* his revelation. The revelation of God in the cross lies *abscondita sub contrario*, so that God's strength is revealed under apparent weakness, and his wisdom under apparent folly. We have already discussed this theme at some length in the present chapter, and do not propose to repeat what has already been said. Nevertheless, it must be appreciated that this understanding of the 'hiddenness' of divine revelation means that *Deus absconditus* and *Deus revelatus* are identical.[46] In the single event of revelation, the eye of faith discerns the *Deus revelatus*, where sense-perception can only find the *Deus absconditus*. Both the *deus absconditus* and *Deus revelatus* are to be found in precisely the same event of revelation: which of the two is recognised depends upon the perceiver. For example, consider the wrath of God revealed in the cross. To reason, God thus appears wrathful; to faith, God's mercy is revealed in this wrath. There is no question of God's mercy being revealed independently of his wrath, or of an additional and subsequent revelation of God's mercy which contradicts that of his wrath. In the one unitary event of revelation in the cross, God's wrath and mercy are revealed simultaneously — but only faith is able to recognise the *opus proprium* as it lies hidden under the *opus alienum*; only faith discerns the merciful intention which underlies the revealed wrath; only faith perceives the real situation which underlies the apparent situation.

(2) *Deus absconditus* is the God who is hidden *behind* his revelation. This understanding of the hiddenness of God becomes increasingly significant in Luther's controversy with Erasmus in *de servo arbitrio* (1525),[47] where it appears to function as a purely polemical device to discredit Erasmus' apparently legitimate exegesis of scripture. Luther argues that, in addition to the *Deus revelatus*, we must recognise that there are certain aspects of God's being which will always remain hidden from us. The *Deus absconditus* is thus understood as the God who will forever remain unknown to us, a mysterious and sinister being whose intentions remain concealed from us. This understanding

---

[45] See Bandt, *Luthers Lehre vom verborgenen Gott*, pp. 19-23.

[46] F. Kattenbusch, 'Deus absconditus bei Luther', in *Festgabe für D. Dr. Julius Kaftan zu seinem 70. Geburtstag* (Tübingen, 1920), pp. 170-214; p. 204.

[47] See E. Grislis, 'Martin Luther's View of the Hidden God. The Problem of the *Deus Absconditus* in Luther's Treatise *De servo arbitrio*', *McCormick Quarterly* 21 (1967), pp. 81-94; K. Schwarzwäller, *Theologia Crucis: Luthers Lehre von Prädestination nach De servo arbitrio 1525* (München, 1970).

of *Deus absconditus* is closely linked to the riddle of divine predestination, where faith is forced to concede the existence of a concealed (*occulta*) will of God. Beginning from the plausible premise that there is much more to God than we can ever know from his self-revelation, Luther draws a distinction between the God who is known through his self-revelation (*Deus revelatus*) and the God who is permanently hidden from us (*Deus absconditus*). There is thus a serious tension between the *Deus revelatus* and the *Deus absconditus*: indeed, on the basis of some of Luther's ominous hints, the two may even stand in total antithesis. Although Luther concedes that this problem may well be noetic rather than ontic (that is, corresponding to our perception of the situation, rather than the situation itself), he is nevertheless forced to concede that behind the merciful God who is revealed in the cross of Christ there may well be a hidden God whose intentions are diametrically opposite. In the present study, we are concerned with Luther's development up to the year 1519, when this second understanding of *Deus absconditus* has yet to make its appearance. For the purposes of our study, we can agree with Bandt when he states that, 'in the final analysis, there is no hiddenness of God for Luther other than the hidden form of his revelation'.[48] Nevertheless, by 1525 this conclusion is no longer valid, and Luther's doctrine of God appears to have reached an impasse: God wills many things which he does not disclose in his Word,[49] and there is every reason to suppose that the hidden and inscrutable will of God may stand in contradiction to his revealed will. 'God does not will the death of a sinner *in his Word* — but he does it by that inscrutable will.'[50] The *Deus incarnatus* must find himself reduced to tears as he sees the *Deus absconditus* consigning men to perdition.[51] Not only do such statements suggest that Luther has abandoned his earlier principle of deriving theology solely on the basis of the cross: they also suggest that the cross is not the final word of God on anything. While we cannot pursue the question of the origins of this second understanding of the *Deus absconditus*, it seems to us that it is not a necessary consequence of the first, discussed above. The origins of the concept appear to lie in Luther's thirty-sixth proposition. Thus when Erasmus states that God does not

---

[48] Bandt, *Luthers Lehre vom verborgenen Gott*, p. 94.
[49] WA 18.685.27-8: 'Multa quoque vult, quae verbo suo non ostendit nobis.'
[50] WA 18.685.28-9.
[51] WA 18.689.32-3.

desire the death of a sinner, Luther counters by arguing that while this may be true of the *revealed* God, it is not necessarily true of the *hidden* God. This argument inevitably makes theology an irrelevancy, if any statements which can be made on the basis of divine revelation may be refuted by appealing to a hidden and inscrutable God, whose will probably contradicts that of the revealed God. Although this tension between *Deus revelatus* and *Deus absconditus* may appear to be similar to that between the *potentia Dei ordinata* and the *potentia Dei absoluta* of later 'Nominalism', it is clear that this comparison cannot be maintained: as we have emphasised (see pp. 55-8), the theologians of the *via moderna* insisted that there was only *one* will and *one* power within God — and this is the revealed and ordained will of God, as established in the present order of salvation. Luther does not revert to the theology of the *via moderna* at this point, despite superficial similarities. His dilemma is his own creation, and his failure to resolve it in *de servo arbitrio* an indictment of his abandonment of his own principle: *Crux sola est nostra theologia!*

In a sermon delivered on 24 February 1517, Luther remarked: 'Man hides his own things, in order to conceal them; God hides his own things, in order to reveal them.'[52] This is an excellent summary of Luther's early understanding of the significance of the hiddenness of God's revelation. God works in a paradoxical way *sub contrariis*: his strength lies hidden under apparent weakness; his wisdom under apparent folly; his *opus proprium* under his *opus alienum*; the future glory of the Christian under his present sufferings. It will therefore be clear that there is a radical discontinuity between the *empirically perceived situation* and the *situation as discerned by faith*. To the eye of reason, all that can be seen in the cross is a man dying in apparent weakness and folly, under the wrath of God. If God *is* revealed in the cross, he is not recognisable *as God*. Empirically, all that can be discerned are the *posteriora Dei*. Reason therefore, basing itself upon that is empirically discernible, deduces that God cannot be present in the cross of Christ, as the perceived situation in no way corresponds to the preconceived situation. The 'theologian of glory' expects God to be revealed in strength, glory and majesty, and is simply unable to accept the scene of dereliction on the cross as the self-revelation of God.

In the *Dictata*, we find Luther emphasising that faith stands in total

[52] WA 1.138.13-15.

contradiction to the perception of the senses. [53] Basing himself upon Hebrews 11.1, Luther insists that faith is characterised by its ability to see past *visibilia* and recognise the *invisibilia* which lie behind them. Empirical verification of the conclusions reached by faith is utterly impossible, in that sense-perception necessarily contradicts it. [54] Whereas worldly wisdom deals with visible things — and hence can call upon the evidence of sense-perception in support of its conclusions — faith is denied this possibility. [55] In a remarkable sermon, delivered on 30 November 1516, Luther points to the crucifixion as a paradigm for the relation between faith and sense-perception: just as Christ was raised up from the ground upon the cross, so that his feet did not rest upon the earth, so the faith of the Christian is denied any foothold in experience. [56] Although an earlier generation of theologians detected a hidden neo-Platonism behind Luther's statements on faith, this opinion is no longer taken seriously. It is clear that Luther's dialectic between the worlds of sense-perception and faith is intended to convey his basic conviction that God is at work in the world, and supremely in the cross of Christ — but that this work lies concealed from the senses. It is faith, and faith alone, which recognises the *posteriora Dei* for what they are, having abandoned any hope of knowing God through the unaided power of reason. Reason can only confuse the *opus alienum* with the *opus proprium*, the *Deus absconditus* with the *Deus revelatus*, failing to recognise that the latter lies hidden beneath the former. It is interesting to observe how closely Luther's early doctrine of faith is related to his Christology. It is through faith alone that the invisible things about Christ, which distinguish him from all other men, can be discerned. [57] Indeed, knowledge of *invisibilia* is intimately linked to knowledge of Christ, for this very reason. This serves to emphasise the point we wish to make: Luther's doctrine of faith does not concern a hidden metaphysical realm concealed under that of the senses, but concerns the manner in which God is at work in his world, which is crystallised, concentrated, and focused on the death of Christ on the cross.

On the basis of these considerations, it will be clear that the Christian

---

[53] WA 3.474.14-19. For an excellent discussion of Luther's doctrine of faith, see von Loewenich, *Luthers Theologia Crucis*, pp. 54-147.
[54] WA 56.48.18-24.
[55] WA 56.543.12-14; 463.3-5.
[56] WA 1.102.39-41.
[57] WA 3.230.25-7. Cf. WA 3.508.1-5; 3.176.4-10.

life is characterised by the unending tension between faith and experience. For Luther, experience can only stand in contradiction to faith, in that revealed truth must be revealed under its opposite form. This dialectic between experienced perception and hidden revelation inevitably leads to radical questioning and doubt on the part of the believer, as he finds himself unable to reconcile what he believes with what he experiences. The best discussion of this tension which we possess from Luther's own hand is to be found in the *Operationes in Psalmos*, dating from the close of the period covered by our study. Before examining the contents of this work, it is important to appreciate the nature of the context within which it was written.

The *Operationes* date from a time when Luther's life was widely regarded as being already forfeited. The shadow of the cross darkens the pages of the work, as Luther wrestles with the relationship between the sufferings of Christ upon the cross and those which he himself expected to undergo in the near future. Where was God in all this? It must never be forgotten that Luther was not speculating about the nature of God in the comfort of a university senior common room: he himself was under threat of death for his theology, and in this very threat he saw a paradigm of the hiddenness of God's self-revelation both in Christ and the Christian life. When Luther speaks of *mors*, *tribulatio*, *passio*, and so on, he speaks as one who believed himself to be close to experiencing them in their full terror, and as one who recognised in the grim scene at Calvary the fact that God had worked through such experiences in the past, and would work through them in the future. Thus when Luther insists that faith turns away from outward appearances and clings to God without wavering,[58] the apparent hopelessness and helplessness of his own situation cannot have been far from his mind. The total stultification of the world through the cross and resurrection of Christ is the foundation upon which Luther based his theology: *CRUX sola est nostra theologia!*[59] Perhaps the most severe test which the *theologia crucis* ever had to face was whether it would satisfy Luther himself as death drew near in the aftermath of Leipzig, and it appears that Luther found in the *angefochtene Christus* a spiritual solace which was more than capable of meeting his needs.

The existential nature of Luther's concept of faith has frequently

---

[58] WA 5.53.31-3.
[59] WA 5.176.32-3. The capitals are Luther's.

been emphasised,[60] and is particularly associated with the notion of *Anfechtung*. The German term is not easy to translate, because of the overtones now associated with it ('assault' is probably more illuminating than 'temptation', although the latter is more accurate. For Luther, death, the devil, the world and Hell combine in a terrifying assault upon man,[61] reducing him to a state of doubt and despair.[62] *Anfechtung* is thus a state of hopelessness and helplessness,[63] having strong affinities with the concept of *Angst*.[64] The terms which Luther himself uses when discussing *Anfechtung* illuminate the various aspects of the concept: it is a form of temptation (*tentatio*),[65] which takes place through an assault upon man (*impugnatio*),[66] which is intended to put him to the test (*probatio*).[67] It must be emphasised that Luther does not regard *Anfechtung* as a purely subjective state of the individual. Two aspects of the concept can be distinguished, although they are inseparable: the *objective* assault of spiritual forces upon the believer, and the *subjective* anxiety and doubt which arise within him as a consequence of these assaults. Most significantly of all, as we have already noted, God himself must be recognised as the ultimate source of *Anfechtung*: it is his *opus alienum*, which is intended to destroy man's self-confidence and complacency, and reduce him to a state of utter despair and humilitation, in order that he may finally turn to God, devoid of all the obstacles to justification which formerly existed. The believer, recognising the merciful intention which underlies *Anfechtung*, rejoices in such assaults, seeing in them the means by which God indirectly

---

[60] L. Pinomaa, *Der existentielle Charakter der Theologie Luthers* (Helsinki, 1940).

[61] P. T. Bühler, *Die Anfechtung bei Luther* (Zürich, 1942), pp. 1-2.

[62] Bühler, *Anfechtung bei Luther*, p. 79.

[63] Bühler, *Anfechtung bei Luther*, p. 89. Cf. H. Appel, *Anfechtung und Trost im Spätmittelalter und bei Luther* (Leipzig, 1938); F. K. Schumann, *Gottesglaube und Anfechtung bei Luther* (Leipzig, 1938); H. Thielicke, *Theologie der Anfechtung* (Tübingen, 1949).

[64] E. Vogelsang, *Der angefochtene Christus bei Luther* (Berlin/Leipzig, 1932), pp. 7; 15; 18. The existential interpretation of *Anfechtung* in relation to Luther's doctrine of justification can, however, be misleading: see R. Lorenz, *Die unvollendete Befreiung vom Nominalismus: Martin Luther und die Grenzen hermeneutischer Theologie bei Gerhard Ebeling* (Gütersloh, 1973), pp. 131-44. The study of Gerhard Ebeling, 'Gewissheit und Zweifel: Die Situation des Glaubens im Zeitalter nach Luther und Descartes', *Zeitschrift für Theologie und Kirche* 64 (1967), pp. 282-324 is important in this connection.

[65] See Beintker, *Die Überwindung der Anfechtung bei Luther*, pp. 58-60.

[66] WA 5.381.18-19; 619.27.

[67] WA 5.470.10, 33. Cf. 5.203.35. Other terms are also used: e.g. *persecutio, tribulatio, percussio, mortificatio, perditio,* etc. For a useful discussion, see Beintker, *Die Überwindung der Anfechtung bei Luther*, pp. 64-6.

effects and ensures his salvation. It is for this reason that Luther is able to refer to *Anfechtung* as a "delicious despair". *Anfechtung*, it must be appreciated, is not some form of spiritual growing pains, which will disappear when a mystical puberty is attained, but a perennial and authentic feature of the Christian life. In order for the Christian to progress in his spiritual life, he must continually be forced back to the foot of the cross, to begin it all over again (*semper a novo incipere*) — and this takes place through the continued experience of *Anfechtung*. The correlation between the present suffering of the Christian and the cross is safeguarded by the *angefochtene Christus*, who disclosed both the necessity and the ultimate purpose of *Anfechtung*. The obvious similarities here between Luther and certain mystics, such as Tauler, have often been noted,[68] although the interpretation of such similarities is considerably more complicated than might at first appear to be the case.[69] Nevertheless, we remain convinced that all the evidence indicates that, while Luther may have used terms originating from mysticism and other forms of late medieval piety to articulate and develop his basic theological insights, these insights cannot be regarded as *having arisen* through the influence of mysticism, but originate from reflections such as those which we have documented in the present study.

It will be clear that there is a direct relationship between *Anfechtung* and the hiddenness of God's self-revelation, in either of the two

[68] E. Vogelsang, 'Luther und die Mystik', *Luther-Jahrbuch* 19 (1937) pp. 32-54; idem., 'Die unio mystica bei Luther', *Archiv für Reformationsgeschichte* 35 (1938), pp. 63-80. These papers represented a significant shift from the previously prevailing consensus, exemplified by H. Bornkamm, *Protestantismus und Mystik* (Gießen, 1934).
[69] The basic criticism which can be directed against many studies of the relationship between Luther and mysticism is that they tend to assume that a reference to, or a citation from, a mystic such as Tauler implies that Luther agreed with the mystic, or used the terms involved (e.g. *Gelassenheit*) in exactly the same sense. See H. A. Oberman, '*Simul Gemitus et Raptus*: Luther und die Mystik', in *Kirche, Mystik, Heiligung und das Natürliche bei Luther: Vorträge des Dritten Internationalen Kongresses für Lutherforschung*, ed. I. Asheim (Göttingen, 1967), pp. 20-59. The approach suggested by Oberman has been adopted by several scholars, e.g. K.-H. zur Mühlen, *Nos extra nos: Luthers Theologie zwischen Mystik und Scholastik* (Tübingen, 1972). The results of this approach suggest that Luther appropriates ideas from mysticism, and reshapes them to suit the purposes of his own theology of justification. Thus Luther's use of mystical terms proves considerably less than might at first be thought. For further studies on Luther and mysticism, see S. E. Ozment, 'Eckhart and Luther: German Mysticism and Protestantism', *The Thomist* 42 (1978), pp. 259-80, and references therein. His earlier study, *Homo Spiritualis: A Comparative Study of the Anthropology of Johannes Tauler, Jean Gerson and Martin Luther (1509-1516) in the Context of their Theological Thought* (Leiden, 1969), is still invaluable.

meanings of the term. If God is understood to be hidden *in* his revelation, the believer will always be prone to doubt as to whether the *opus proprium* really does lie behind the *opus alienum*, or whether God really is hidden, and not simply absent altogether. The possibility of *Anfechtung* is, however, enormously increased if God is understood to be hidden *behind his revelation*. Although Luther insisted that the object of faith is always the word of God, by 1525 he had been forced to concede that God might not have spoken his final word in Christ. [70] The notion of a hidden and inscrutable God, who predestines men to death without cause, looms large in the 1525 treatise *de servo arbitrio*. In a highly perceptive essay, Pannenberg pointed out the intimate relationship between *Anfechtung* and the idea of predestination. [71] Precisely because the 1525 Luther permitted no solution to the riddle of predestination, there was no means available to the believer by which his *Anfechtung* could be relieved. This development, however, dates from after the period covered by our study, and we do not propose to consider it further here.

Although Luther considers all *Anfechtung* to originate from God, whether directly or indirectly, he makes a distinction between *satanic Anfechtung* and *divine Anfechtung*. [72] The former relates particularly to fundamental matters of faith, such as doubt about one's election, or whether Christ really did die *pro nobis*. [73] The latter, however, is much more closely associated with the doctrine of justification, [74] and is specifically linked with the dialectic between law and gospel, between the *opus proprium* and the *opus alienum*, between the *deus absconditus* and *deus revelatus*. The individual finds himself under the judgement of God, as revealed in his word, and is terrified of the wrath of God. He recognises himself as a guilty criminal, standing in terrible isolation before the tribunal of an eternal and angry God, convinced that he can expect nothing other than eternal damnation as his portion, and that there is no one upon whom he can call for support or assistance.

---

[70] WATr 5.5658A.
[71] W. Pannenberg, 'Der Einfluß der Anfechtungserfahrung auf den Prädestinationsbegriff Luthers', *Kerygma und Dogma* 3 (1954), pp. 109-39.
[72] Beintker, *Die Überwindung der Anfechtung bei Luther*, pp. 80-2.
[73] Beintker, *Die Überwindung der Anfechtung bei Luther*, pp. 82-6. Attention must be directed towards the misuse of Luther's *pro nobis* principle in contemporary theology, where it is frequently confused with the Kantian subjectivity of experiential knowledge: see H. J. Iwand, 'Wider den Mißbrauch des pro me als methodisches Prinzip in der Theologie', *Theologische Literaturzeitung* 69 (1954), pp. 453-6.
[74] Beintker, *Die Überwindung der Anfechtung bei Luther*, pp. 86-93, especially pp. 92-3.

Through this realisation he is moved to flee to God against God (*ad Deum contra Deum*),[75] to receive the mercy which lies hidden under this terrible wrath.

How is this crisis of *Anfechtung* resolved?[76] For Luther, the solution lies in the crucified Christ, who suffered precisely the same *Anfechtung* on our behalf. Christ became sin on our behalf, in order that his righteousness might become our righteousness.[77] We have already noted the concept of *iustitia Christi aliena*, which is so central a feature of Luther's teaching on justification from 1515 onwards, in the previous chapter. Underlying this 'marvellous exchange' (*commercium admirabile*) is a well-established late medieval Augustinian tradition, particularly associated with Johannes von Staupitz,[78] but which can be found in earlier works, such as those of Agostino Favaroni.[79] The mystery of the incarnation lies in the fact that Christ took upon himself all our sin, that we might possess his righteousness: *adeo in omnia nostra immersus est Christus.*[80] Luther uses the analogy of a human marriage to make this point: *sponsus et sponsa fiunt una caro.*[81] As we contemplate the grim spectacle of the *angefochtene Christus* on the cross, we come to realise that Christ did not undergo *Anfechtung* for his own benefit, but for ours: *cum non pro sua, sed pro nostra hac ipsa, necessitate haec mala suceperit, volens et sciens per gratiam.*[82] Reason is totally unable to comprehend this astonishing mystery, by which we are made the righteousness of God. Through faith, the believer enters into a spiritual marriage with Christ, as a result of which this marvellous exchange

[75] WA 5.204.26-7. The sense of the phrase is as follows: experienced *Anfechtung* originates from God, and appears to reveal the wrath of God against man, thus suggesting that God is opposed to man — whereas in fact, his wrath directed against man is the means by which his mercy may be exercised. Man thus flees *ad deum* (the reality) *contra deum* (the appearance).

[76] This question is, in fact, too complex to discuss in the very limited space available. The reader is referred to the excellent discussion in Beintker, *Die Überwindung der Anfechtung bei Luther*, pp. 115-78.

[77] WA 5.607.32-7.

[78] D. C. Steinmetz, *Luther and Staupitz: An Essay in the Intellectual Origins of the Protestant Reformation* (Durham, N.C., 1980), p. 106.

[79] As noted by H. A. Oberman, 'Headwaters of the Reformation: *Initia Lutheri — Initia Reformationis*', in *Luther and the Dawn of the Modern Era*, ed. H. A. Oberman (Leiden, 1974), pp. 40-88; p. 73, where Favaroni's astonishing conclusion that '*Christus hodie peccat*' is noted.

[80] WA 5.605.11.

[81] WA 5.608.16.

[82] WA 5.606.16-17.

of attributes takes place. Just as the believer is *simul iustus et peccator*, so he is equally caught up in the dialectic between faith and *Anfechtung*, a dialectic which will never be resolved in this life.[83] Nevertheless, where there is true faith, *Anfechtung* can only serve to strengthen it, as it is recognised as the *opus alienum* concealing the *opus proprium*.

It will be clear that the theology of the cross is thus a theology of faith, and *of faith alone*. The correlative to *Crux sola* is *sola fide*, as it is through faith, and *through faith alone*, that the true significance of the cross is perceived, and through faith alone that its power can be appropriated. 'The reason why some do not understand how faith alone justifies is that they do not understand what faith is.'[84] By 1519, the two main elements of Luther's mature understanding of the nature of faith have become clear. First, faith is hearing the word of promise (*fides ex auditu*). The Word of God, and especially the preached Word, is the means of grace by which the sinner is justified. We have already emphasised the intimacy of the link between the Word of God and the cross, within the context of the *theologia crucis*. Second, faith is the bond which unites the believer with Christ, in a spiritual marriage which far transcends any mere external or forensic imputation of the righteousness of Christ to the believer. The following passage from the great Galatians commentary of 1535 is instructive:

Faith justifies because it grasps and possesses this treasure, the presence of Christ. But how he is present is beyond understanding...And so it is Christ, who is grasped by faith, who is the Christian righteousness, on account of which God reckons us to be righteous and grants us eternal life.[85]

Faith thus has a dual function within the *theologia crucis*. It is only through faith that the true significance of the cross is perceived, and it is only through faith that its power can be appropriated. Faith has both cognitive and existential elements. Unless a man has faith, he will never understand the true meaning of the cross, and its mystery

[83] See Beintker, *Die Überwindung der Anfechtung bei Luther*, pp. 181-95, especially pp. 192-5, for an excellent discussion.

[84] WA 6.94.7-8: 'Quod autem aliqui non intelligunt, quomodo sola fides iustificat, in causa est, quod quid fides sit non cognoverint' (*Resolutio disputationis de fide infusa et acquisita* [1520]).

[85] WA 40 I.229.22-9. For an excellent discussion of Luther's concept of faith, see B. A. Gerrish, 'By faith alone: Medium and Message in Luther's Gospel', in *The Old Protestantism and the New: Essays on the Reformation Heritage* (Edinburgh, 1982), pp. 69-90.

will remain forever hidden from him. Equally, unless he has faith, the perceived significance of the cross cannot be appropriated, and translated into the real and redeeming presence of Christ within the believer, in the *commercium admirabile*. Faith recognises in the apparent debacle of the cross the means by which God is effecting the salvation of mankind, and faith appropriates this salvation through uniting the believer to Christ in a spiritual union, whereby his righteousness becomes ours. Everything which is concerned with the *theologia crucis* hinges upon faith. Only those who have faith understand the true meaning of the cross. Where the unbeliever sees nothing but the helplessness and hopelessness of an abandoned man dying upon a cross, the theologian of the cross (*theologus crucis*) recognises the presence and activity of the 'crucified and hidden God' (*Deus crucifixus et absconditus*),[86] who is not merely present in human suffering, but actively works through it. It is with *this* God, and none other, that Christian theology must come to terms. As Luther himself emphasised, faith is the only key by which the hidden mystery of the cross may be unlocked: 'The cross is the safest of all things. Blessed is the man who understands this.'[87]

[86] WA 1.613.23-4. For this phrase in its full context, see note 168 of the previous chapter.
[87] WA 5.84.39-40.

6

The Origins and Significance of the Theology of the Cross

IN the present study, we have been concerned primarily with the gradual emergence of the theology of the cross, as Luther gradually broke free from the matrix of later medieval theology. In consequence, we have been more concerned with the origins of the *theologia crucis* than with a detailed analysis of the concept as such. In view of the complexity of the historical and theological issues that underlie the prsent study, this concluding chapter is intended to draw together the various strands of the discussion so that the emergence of the *theologia crucis* may be seen in its proper context.

The essential thesis of the present study is that Luther's theological development over the period 1509-19 is a continuous process, rather than a series of isolated and fragmented episodes, and that one aspect of this development — namely, his discovery of the 'righteousness of God' — is of fundamental importance within this overall process. The question of the true meaning of the 'righteousness of God' is a fundamental aspect of the Christian doctrine of justification, and it is evident that there was widespread confusion within the later medieval church on precisely this doctrine. Luther's early difficulties over this doctrine reflect a general lack of clarity on the matter at the time, and cannot be taken as an indication of his theological incompetence or ignorance. The question then arises as to what Luther's early understanding of justification actually was. The conclusion of the present investigation is that up to 1514 Luther must be regarded as holding a doctrine of justification which, in all its essential features, corresponds to the teaching of the *via moderna*. This conclusion is dictated by two convergent lines of evidence.

Historically, there is sufficient circumstantial evidence to warrant the conclusion that Luther was a representative of the *via moderna* (see chapter 2 in particular). Thus his teachers at Erfurt were all noted representatives of this school, and the texts which he was obliged to study also originate from this school. It is significant in this connection that Luther does not demonstrate first-hand knowledge of theologians of the *via antiqua*. Of course, if it could be shown that Luther had been influenced by the *schola Augustiniana moderna*, deriving from Gregory of Rimini, this conclusion would have to be radically revised. Nevertheless, we wish to emphasise that there is no convincing evidence of such influence. Luther was not familiar with the works of Gregory of Rimini until 1519 — well after the *theologia crucis* was formulated. Furthermore, although there is sufficient evidence to allow us to concede the existence of a *schola Augustiniana moderna* within the Augustinian Order during the later medieval period, all the available evidence indicates that (1) this school was *not* represented at the Augustinian priory at Erfurt, and (2) that Johannes von Staupitz cannot be regarded as its representative at Wittenberg. Although there is a suggestion that the mysterious *via Gregorii*, which came to be represented on the Wittenberg faculty of arts in 1508, in the term during which Luther arrived to lecture as a member of that faculty, is actually the *schola Augustiniana moderna*, the evidence appears decidedly in favour of its being none other than the *via moderna*. The influence of Trutvetter in Luther's appointment to this position further suggests affinity with this *via*. Although this evidence is circumstantial, it has cumulative force, particularly when linked with the theological evidence, which we now consider.

Theologically, there is every indication that Luther remained a faithful adherent of the *via moderna* up to 1514, particularly in relation to the doctrine of justification (see chapter 3). Of decisive importance in this respect is his use of the concept of *covenantal causality*, characteristic of the *via moderna*. Luther's early discussion of the axiom *facientibus quod in se est Deus non denegat gratiam* reproduces the characteristic features of this theology of justification, as do the analogies he employs to explain it. Most significantly, Luther's early difficulties concerning the 'righteousness of God' are immediately explicable in the light of the covenant theology of the *via moderna*, whereas they can only be explained with difficulty if it is assumed that Luther is familiar with other theological systems (see chapter 4). It is interesting to note that, in the Romans lectures of 1515-16, Luther frequently criticises positions (such as the axiom *facientibus quod in se est*) which he himself had held several years earlier, while attributing them to theologians of the *via moderna*.

The evidence and discussion of earlier chapters indicates that on both historical and theological grounds there is sufficient evidence to permit us to state that at the beginning of the period covered by the present study Luther was a theologian of the *via moderna*, at least in his theology of justification. This establishes the *terminus a quo*, and the *terminus ad quem* is the *theologia crucis*. How did the transition between them take place?

This brings us to the question of the nature and significance of Luther's discovery of the righteousness of God, probably one of the most vexed areas of Luther scholarship. In chapter 5 of the present study, we argue that Luther's theological breakthrough is essentially *methodological* in character, and is thus capable of being applied to divine attributes other than righteousness, as Luther himself indicates in the 1545 autobiographical fragment. Furthermore, an analysis of the nature of Luther's insights concerning the true nature of *iustitia Dei* shows that, in every respect, the *theologia crucis* is foreshadowed. In other words, Luther's theological breakthrough — which we date in 1515 — contains within itself the germs of the theology of the cross. The period between 1515 and 1518 may therefore be considered as the period within which Luther explored the consequences of his new understanding of *iustitia Dei*. This approach to the matter remains faithful to the autobiographical fragment itself, and casts further light upon it. For example, we have already pointed out how the *Operationes in Psalmos* are permeated with the theology of the cross. It is this theology, far more than the new interpretation of *iustitia Dei*, which is the hallmark of the work. It would seem fair to suggest that the '*cogitationes*' with which Luther approached the *Operationes* are those encapsulated in the *theologia crucis*, rather than just in the single theologoumenon of the 'righteousness of God'. It seems to us that this approach to the matter allows the 'theological' approach to the discovery (which places it in 1514-15) to be reconciled with the 'historical' (which places it in 1518-19). The former is thus understood to refer to the decisive and catalytic step, and the latter to the *terminus* of the process of theological reflection and analysis thus initiated. Far from representing a 'pre-reformation' element in Luther's thought,[1] the *theologia crucis* encapsulates the very essence of his 'reformation' thought.

---

[1] As suggested by O. Ritschl, *Dogmengeschichte des Protestantismus* I/1 (Leipzig, 1912), pp. 40-84.

What, then, is the significance of this theology of the cross? For the theologians of the liberal Protestant era, it had little, if any significance,[2] being seen as little more than an ascetical or ethical principle,[3] a relic of a bygone age. The shattering of liberal Protestant values and aspirations through the devastation and dereliction of the First World War, however, gave a new urgency and relevance to Luther's insights. It is no accident that the first serious studies of Luther's *theologia crucis* date from the period immediately after this war.[4] Those who still considered Luther's *theologia crucis* to be of ephemeral significance found themselves stultified when the unthinkable happened, and the horrors of a second World War were unleashed upon Europe. Luther's theology of the cross assumed its new significance because it was the theology which addressed the question which could not be ignored: is God *really* there, amidst the devastation and dereliction of civilisation? Luther's proclamation of the hidden presence of God in the dereliction of Calvary, and of the Christ who was forsaken on the cross, struck a deep chord of sympathy in those who felt themselves abandoned by God, and unable to discern his presence anywhere. One such individual was Karl Goerdeler, executed as a conspirator against Hitler in the darkest days of the war. In 1955, the distinguished German historian Gerhard Ritter published details of Goerdeler's final days in his death cell, giving us a distressing account of the agonising doubt and despair of a Christian who found his faith increasingly called into question by the horror to which he had been a witness. Shortly before his execution he wrote thus:

In sleepless nights I have often asked myself whether a God exists who shares in the personal fate of men. It is becoming hard to believe this. For this God must for years have allowed rivers of blood and suffering, and mountains

---

[2] Thus T. Harnack, *Luthers Theologie mit besonderer Beziehung auf seine Versöhnungs- und Erlösungslehre* (2 vols: Erlangen, 1862-8).

[3] Thus H. Hering, *Die Mystik Luthers im Zusammenhang seiner Theologie* (Leipzig, 1879), pp. 86-90; A. W. Dieckhoff, *Luthers Lehre in ihrer esten Gestalt* (Rostok, 1887).

[4] e.g., W. von Loewenich, *Luthers Theologia Crucis* (München, 1929). The fourth edition (1954) has been used in the present study. The important study of B. Steffen, *Das Dogma vom Kreuz. Beitrag zu einer staurozentrischen Theologie* (Gütersloh, 1920), should be noted. For a useful guide to the *Zeitgeist* at this point, see F. Gogarten, *Der Zerfall des Humanismus und die Gottesfrage* (Stuttgart, 1937). For more recent evaluations, see H. A. Oberman, 'De aangevochten God: De betekenis van de reformation voor onze tijd', *Rondom het Woord* 21 (1979), pp. 30-4, and especially the penetrating study of Pierre Bühler, *Kreuz und Eschatologie: Eine Auseinandersetzung mit der politischen Theologie, im Anschluß am Luthers theologia crucis* (Tübingen, 1981), pp. 63-285.

of horror and despair for mankind to take place...He must have allowed millions of decent men to die and suffer without lifting a finger. Is this meant to be a judgement?...Like the Psalmist, I am angry with God, because I cannot understand him...And yet through Christ I am still looking for the merciful God. I have not yet found him. O Christ, where is truth? Where is there any consolation?[5]

The *theologia crucis*, with its concept of *Deus crucifixus et absconditus*, appeared to many to address itself to the central question posed by Goerdeler, which as Ritter suggests, captured the *Zeitgeist*. In the face of the repeated failure of the bourgeois optimism of liberal Protestant theology to deal with such questions, and the situations which occasioned them, Luther's concept of the 'crucified and hidden God' of Calvary assumed a new relevance and urgency. Rarely, if ever, has a sixteenth-century idea found such a powerful response in twentieth-century man. Jürgen Moltmann unerringly puts his finger on the point at issue:

Since I first studied theology, I have been concerned with the theology of the cross...It is the basic theme of my theological thought. No doubt this goes back to the period of my first concern with questions concerning Christian faith and theology in real life, as a prisoner of war behind barbed wire...Shattered and broken, the survivors of my generation were then returning from camps and hospitals to the lecture room. A theology which did not speak of God in terms of the abandoned and crucified one would not have got through to us then.[6]

Die Weltgeschichte ist das Weltgericht. The patent absurdity of much Christian thinking about man and God has been shown up by the history of the world during the present century, especially by the two world wars. As a result of these, the twentieth century has seen increasing recognition of, and respect for, Luther's theological insights, and supremely his theology of the cross.

[5] Ritter's report appeared in *Monat*, 1955. We have taken this excerpt from J. Richter, 'Luthers "Deus absconditus" — Zuflucht oder Ausflucht?', *Zeitschrift für Religions- und Geistesgeschichte* 7 (1955), pp. 289-303; pp. 289-90. Richter considers that this questioning demonstrates the inadequacy of the Ritschlian concept of God (pp. 290-91), and cites U. Neuenschwander, *Die neue liberale Theologie* (Bern, 1953) in support of this contention.

[6] J. Moltmann, *Der gekreuzigte Gott. Das Kreuz Christi als Grund und Kritik christlicher Theologie* (München, 4th edn, 1981), p. 7. Note his explicit references to Reformation theology therein.

The *theologia crucis* passes judgement upon the church where she has become proud and triumphant, or secure and smug, and recalls her to the foot of the cross, there to remind her of the mysterious and hidden way in which God is at work in his world. The scene of total dereliction, of apparent weakness and folly, at Calvary is the theologian's paradigm for understanding the hidden presence and activity of God in his world and in his church. Where the church recognises her hopelessness and helplessness, she finds the key to her continued existence as the church *of God* in the world. In her very weakness lies her greatest strength. The 'crucified and hidden God' is the God whose strength lies hidden behind apparent weakness, and whose wisdom lies hidden behind apparent folly. The theology of the cross is thus a theology of hope for those who despair, then as now, of the seeming weakness and foolishness of the Christian church. How can it survive, let alone prosper? For Luther, the answer was clear, and it is fitting that we end the present study by permitting him to state it:

It is not we who can sustain the church, nor was it those who came before us, nor will it be those who come after us. It was, and is, and will be, the one who says: 'I am with you always, even to the end of time.' As it says in Hebrews 13: 'Jesus Christ, the same *yesterday, today* and *for ever.*' And in Revelation 1: '*Who was*, and *is*, and *is to come.*' Truly he is that one, and no one else is, or ever can be.

For you and I were not alive thousands of years ago, yet the church was sustained without us — and it was done by the one of whom it says, '*Who was*', and '*Yesterday*'. . . The church would perish before our very eyes, and we along with it (as we daily prove), were it not for that other man who so obviously upholds the church and us. This we can lay hold of and feel, even though we are reluctant to believe it. We must give ourselves to the one of whom it is said: '*Who is*', and '*Today*'.

Again, we can do nothing to sustain the church when we are dead. But he will do it, of whom it is said: '*Who is to come*', and '*For ever*'.[7]

---

[7] WA 54.470.8-26. This is taken from Luther's preface to the second volume of the Wittenberg edition of his German works, which appeared in 1548. As this preface was published posthumously, there will always be a certain element of doubt as to its authenticity. The theological sentiments expressed are, of course, unquestionably Luther's.

Select Bibliography

A. Adam, 'Der Begriff "Deus absconditus" bei Luther nach Herkunft und Bedeutung', *Luther-Jahrbuch* 30 (1963), pp. 97-106.

P. Althaus, 'Theologie des Glaubens', *Zeitschrift für systematische Theologie* 2 (1924), pp. 281-322.

——, *Die lutherische Rechtfertigungslehre und ihre heutigen Kritiker* (Berlin, 1951).

H. Appel, *Anfechtung und Trost im Spätmittelalter und bei Luther* (Leipzig, 1938).

R. Arbesmann, *Der Augustiner-Eremitenorder und der Beginn der humanistischen Bewegung* (Würzburg, 1965).

H. Bandt, *Luthers Lehre vom verborgenen Gott. Eine Untersuchung zu dem offenbarungsgeschichtlichen Ansatz seiner Theologie* (Berlin, 1958).

H. -M. Barth, *Der Teufel und Jesus Christus in der Theologie Martin Luthers* (Göttingen, 1967).

——, 'Martin Luther disputiert über den Menschen. Ein Beitrag zu Luthers Anthropologie', *Kerygma und Dogma* 27 (1981), pp. 154-66.

G. Bauch, 'Die Anfänge des Studiums der griechischen Sprache und Literatur in Nord-Deutschland', *Gesellschaft für deutsche Erziehungs- und Schulgeschichte* 6 (1896), pp. 47-98.

——, 'Christoph Scheurl in Wittenberg', *Neue Mitteilungen aus dem Gebiet historischer-antiquarischer Forschungen* 21 (1903), pp. 33-42.

——, 'Die Einführung des Hebräischen in Wittenberg mit Berücksichtigung der Vorgeschichte des Studiums der Sprache in Deutschland', *Monatschrift für Geschichte und Wissenschaft des Judentums* 48 (1904), pp. 22-32; 77-86; 145-60; 214-23; 283-99; 328-40; 461-90.

K. Bauer, 'Die Heidelberger Disputation Luthers', *Zeitschrift für Kirchengeschichte* 21 (1900), pp. 233-68; 299-329.

——, *Die Wittenberger Universitätstheologie und die Anfänge der deutschen Reformation* (Tübingen, 1928).

O. Bayer, *Promissio: Geschichte der reformatorischen Wende in Luthers Theologie* (Göttingen, 1971).

H. Beintker, *Die Überwindung der Anfechtung bei Luther: Eine Studie zu seiner Theologie nach den Operationes in Psalmos 1519-1521* (Berlin, 1954).

E. Bizer, *Fides ex auditu: Eine Untersuchung über die Entdeckung der Gerechtigkeit Gottes durch Martin Luther* (Neukirchen, 3rd edn, 1966).

F. Blanke, *Der verborgene Gott bei Luther* (Leipzig, 1928).

H. Boehmer, *Luthers erste Vorlesung* (Leipzig, 1924).

H. Bornkamm, 'Luthers Bericht über seine Entdeckung der Gerechtigkeit Gottes', *Archiv für Reformationsgeschichte* 37 (1940), pp. 117-28.

——, 'Iustitia Dei in der Scholastik und bei Luther', *Archiv für Reformationsgeschichte* 39 (1942), pp. 1-46.

——, 'Der verborgene und der offenbare Gott', *Theologische Rundschau* 16 (1944), pp. 38-52.

——, 'Thesen und Thesenanschlag Luthers', in *Geist und Geschichte der Reformation*, ed. H. Liebing and K. Scholder (Berlin, 1966), pp. 179-218.

——, 'Iustitia Dei beim jungen Luther', in *Der Durchbruch der reformatorischen Erkenntnis bei Luther*, ed. B. Lohse (Darmstadt, 1968), pp. 115-62.

C. Boyer, 'Luther et "De Spiritu et Littera" de Saint Augustin', *Doctor Communis* 21 (1968), pp. 167-87.

A. Brandenburg, *Gericht und Evangelium: Zur Worttheologie in Luthers erste Vorlesung* (Paderborn, 1960).

M. Burchdorf, *Der Einfluß des Erfurter Humanismus auf die Entwicklung Luthers bis 1510* (Leipzig, 1928).

W. D. J. Cargill Thompson, 'The Problem of Luther's "Tower Experience" and its Place in his Intellectual Development', in *Studies in the Reformation: Luther to Hooker* (London, 1980), pp. 60-80.

W. J. Courtenay, 'Covenant and Causality in Pierre d'Ailly', *Speculum* 46 (1971), pp. 94-119.

——, 'The King and the Leaden Coin: The Economic Background of "sine qua non" Causality', *Traditio* 28 (1972), pp. 185-209.

——, 'Nominalism and Late Medieval Thought: A Bibliographical Essay', *Theological Studies* 33 (1972), pp. 716-34.

——, 'Nominalism and Late Medieval Religion', in *The Pursuit of Holiness in Late Medieval and Renaissance Religion*, ed. C. Trinkaus and H. A. Oberman (Leiden, 1974), pp. 26-59.

H. Denifle, *Luther und Luthertum in der erste Entwicklung* (Mainz, 2nd edn, 1904-6).

W. Dettloff, *Die Lehre von der Acceptatio Divina bei Johannes Duns Skotus* (Werl, 1954).

——, *Die Entwicklung der Akzeptations- und Verdienstlehre von Duns Skotus bis Luther* (Münster, 1963).

G. Ebeling, *Evangelische Evangelienauslegung: Eine Untersuchung zu Luthers Hermeneutik* (München, 1942).

——, 'Gewißheit und Zweifel: Die Situation des Glaubens im Zeitalter nach Luther und Descartes', *Zeitschrift für Theologie und Kirche* 64 (1967), pp. 282-324.

——, 'Die Anfänge von Luthers Hermeneutik', in *Lutherstudien I* (Tübingen, 1971), pp. 1-68.

——, 'Luthers Psalterdruck vom Jahre 1513', in *Lutherstudien I* (Tübingen, 1971), pp. 69-131.

M. Elze, 'Züge spätmittelalterlicher Frömmigkeit in Luthers Theologie', *Zeitschrift für Theologie und Kirche* 62 (1965), pp. 381-402.

H. Entner, 'Der Begriff "Humanismus" als Problem der deutschen Literaturgeschichtsschreibung', *Klio* 40 (1962), pp. 260-70.

——, 'Probleme der Forschung zum deutschen Frühhumanismus 1400-1500', *Wissenschaftliche Zeitschrift der Ernst-Moritz-Arndt-Universität Greifswald* 15 (1966), pp. 587-90.

C. Feckes, *Die Rechtfertigungslehre des Gabriel Biel und ihre Stellung innerhalb der nominalistischen Schule* (Münster, 1925).

H. Feld, *Martin Luthers und Wendelin Steinbachs Vorlesungen über den Hebräerbrief* (Wiesbaden, 1971).

——, *Die Anfänge der modernen biblischen Hermeneutik in der spätmittelalterlichen Theologie* (Wiesbaden, 1977).

M. Ferdigg, 'De Vita et Operibus et Doctrina Joannis de Paltz, O.E.S.A.', *Analecta Augustiniana* 30 (1967), pp. 210-321; 31 (1968), pp. 155-318.

F. Frey, *Luthers Glaubensbegriff: Gottesgabe und Menschentat in ihrer Polarität* (Leipzig, 1939).

W. Friedensburg, *Geschichte der Universität Wittenberg* (Halle, 1917).

——, *Urkundenbuch der Universität Wittenberg, Teil I. (1502-1611)* (Magdeburg, 1926).

B. A. Gerrish, *Grace and Reason: A Study in the Theology of Martin Luther* (Oxford, 1962).

——, 'To the Unknown God: Luther and Calvin on the Hiddenness of God', *Journal of Religion* 53 (1973), pp. 263-92.

W. Graf, *Doktor Christoph Scheurl von Nürnburg* (Leipzig, 1930).

L. Grane, *Contra Gabrielem: Luthers Auseinandersetzung mit Gabriel Biel in der Disputatio contra scholasticam theologiam* (Gyldendal, 1962).

——, 'Gregor von Rimini und Luthers Leipziger Disputation', *Studia Theologica* 22 (1968), pp. 29-49.

——, 'Augustins "Expositio quarundam propositionum ex epistola ad Romanos" in Luthers Römerbriefvorlesung', *Zeitschrift für Theologie und Kirche* 69 (1972), pp. 304-30.

——, *Modus loquendi theologicus: Luthers Kampf um die Erneuerung der Theologie 1515-1518* (Leiden, 1975).

H. Grass, 'Der verborgene und der offenbare Gott bei Luther', in *Reformation und Gegenwart. Vorträge und Vorlesungen von Mitgleidern der Theologischen Fakultät Marburg zum 450. Jubiläum der Reformation* (Marburg, 1969), pp. 57-69.

M. Greschat, 'Der Bundesgedanke in der Theologie des späten Mittelalters', *Zeitschrift für Kirchengeschichte* 81 (1970), pp. 44-63.

A. Gyllenkrok, *Rechtfertigung und Heiligung in der frühen evangelischen Theologie Luthers* (Uppsala/Wiesbaden, 1952).

B. Hägglund, *De homine: Människouppfattningen i äldre luthersk tradition* (Lund, 1952).

——, *Was ist mit Luthers 'Rechtfertigungs'-Lehre gemeint?* (Ratzeburg, 1982).

A. Hamel, *Der junge Luther und Augustin* (2 vols: Gütersloh, 1934-5).

B. Hamm, *Promissio, Pactum, Ordinatio: Freiheit und Selbstbindung Gottes in der scholastischen Gnadenlehre* (Tübingen, 1977).

G. Hammer, 'Militia franciscana seu militia Christi: Das neugefundene Protokoll einer Disputation des sächsischen Franziskaner mit Vertretern der Wittenberger theologischen Fakultät am 3. und 4. Oktober 1519', *Archiv für Reformationsgeschichte* 69 (1978), pp. 51-81; 70 (1979), pp. 59-105.

T. Harnack, *Luthers Theologie mit besonderer Beziehung auf seine Versöhnungs- und Erlösungslehre* (2 vols: Erlangen, 1862-66).

S. H. Hendrix, *Ecclesia in via: Ecclesiological Developments in the Medieval Psalms Exegesis and the Dictata super Psalterium (1513-1515) of Martin Luther* (Leiden, 1974).

H. Hermelink, *Die theologische Fakultät in Tübingen vor der Reformation 1477-1534* (Stuttgart, 1906).

E. Hirsch, 'Initium Theologiae Lutheri', in *Der Durchbruch der reformatorischen Erkenntnis bei Luther*, ed. B. Lohse (Darmstadt, 1968), pp. 84-95.

E. Hochstetter, 'Nominalismus?', *Franciscan Studies* 9 (1949), pp. 370-403.

K. Holl, *Gesammelte Aufsätze zur Kirchengeschichte* (3 vols: Tübingen, 4th edn, 1928).

K. Honzelmann, *Urfassung und Drucke der Ablassthesen Martin Luthers und ihre Veröffentlichung* (Paderborn, 1966).

E. Iserloh, *Luther zwischen Reform und Reformation: Der Thesenanschlag fand nicht statt* (Münster, 3rd edn, 1968).

W. Joest, *Gesetz und Freiheit: Das Problem des Tertius usus legis bei Luther und die neutestamentliche Parainese* (Göttingen, 1951).

R. Josefson, *Ödmjukhet och tro: En studie in den unge Luthers teologi* (Stockholm/Uppsala, 1939).

——, *Den naturliga teologins problem hos Luther* (Uppsala, 1943).

E. Jüngel, 'Die Welt als Wirklichkeit und Möglichkeit', in *Unterwegs zur Sache* (München, 1972), pp. 206-31.

H. Junghans, 'Der Einfluß des Humanismus auf Luthers Entwicklung bis 1518', *Luther-Jahrbuch* 37 (1970), pp. 37-101.

E. Kähler, *Karlstadt und Augustin: Der Kommentar des Andreas Bodenstein von Karlstadt zu Augustins Schrift De Spiritu et Litera* (Halle, 1952).

——, 'Die 95 Thesen: Inhalt und Bedeutung', *Luther: Zeitschrift der Luther-Gesellschaft* 38 (1967), pp. 114-24.

P. Kalkoff, 'Die Stellung der deutschen Humanismus zur Reformation', *Zeitschrift für Kirchengeschichte* 46 (1927), pp. 161-231.

E. Kleineidam, *Universitas Studii Erfordensis: Überblick über die Geschichte der Universität Erfurt im Mittelalter* (Leipzig, 1969).

G. C. Knod, *Deutsche Studenten in Bologna (1289-1562): Biographischer Index zu den Acta nationis Germanicae universitatis Bononienses* (Berlin, 1899).

W. Koehler, *Der verborgene Gott* (Heidelberg, 1946).

P. O. Kristeller, *Renaissance Thought and its Sources* (New York, 1979).

M. Kroeger, *Rechtfertigung und Gesetz: Studien zur Entwicklung der Rechtfertigungslehre beim jungen Luther* (Göttingen, 1968).

W. Link, *Das Ringen Luthers um die Freiheit der Theologie von der Philosophie* (München, 2nd edn. 1955).

W. von Loewenich, 'Zur Gnadenlehre bei Augustin und Luther', in *Von Augustin zu Luther* (Witten, 1959), pp. 75-87.

——, *Luthers Theologia Crucis* (München, 4th edn, 1954).

B. Lohse, *Ratio und Fides: Eine Untersuchung über die Ratio in der Theologie Luthers* (Göttingen, 1958).

——, *Mönchtum und Reformation: Luthers Auseinandersetzung mit dem Mönchsideal des Mittelalters* (Göttingen, 1963).

H. Lutz, 'Humanismus und Reformation: Alte Antworten auf neue Frage', *Wort und Wahrheit* 27 (1972), pp. 65-77.

A. E. McGrath, 'The Anti-Pelagian Structure of "Nominalist" Doctrines of Justification', *Ephemerides Theologicae Lovanienses* 57 (1981), pp. 107-19.

——, '"Augustinianism"? A Critical Assessment of the so-called "Medieval Augustinian Tradition" on Justification', *Augustiniana* 31 (1981), pp. 247-67.

——, 'Humanist Elements in the Early Reformed Doctrine of Justification", *Archiv für Reformationsgeschichte* 73 (1982), pp. 5-20.

——, 'Forerunners of the Reformation? A Critical Examination of the Evidence for Precursors of the Reformation Doctrines of Justification", *Harvard Theological Review* 75 (1982), pp. 219-42.

——, '"The Righteousness of God" from Augustine to Luther', *Studia Theologica* 36 (1982), pp. 63-78.

——, 'Divine Justice and Divine Equity in the Controversy between Augustine and Julian of Eclanum', *Downside Review* 101 (1983), pp. 312-19.

——, 'Mira et nova diffinitio iustitiae: Luther and Scholastic Doctrines of Justification', *Archiv für Reformationsgeschichte* 74 (1983), pp. 37-60.

——, 'Der articulus iustificationis als axiomatischer Grundsatz des christlichen Glaubens', *Zeitschrift für Theologie und Kirche* 81 (1984), pp. 383-94.

——, *Iustitia Dei. A History of the Christian Doctrine of Justification* (3 vols: Cambridge, forthcoming).

H. J. McSorley, *Luther Right or Wrong? An Ecumenical-Theological Study of Luther's Major Work, The Bondage of the Will* (Minneapolis/New York, 1969).

B. Moeller, 'Die deutschen Humanisten und die Anfänge der Reformation', *Zeitschrift für Kirchengeschichte* 70 (1959), pp. 46-61;

K. -H. zur Mühlen, *Nos extra nos: Luthers Theologie zwischen Mystik und Scholastik* (Tübingen, 1972).

A. V. Müller, *Luthers theologische Quellen: Seine Verteidigung gegen Denifle und Grisar* (Gießen, 1912).

T. Muther, *Die Wittenberger Universität- und Fakultätstatuten von Jahre MDVIII* (Halle, 1867).

R. Newald, *Probleme und Gestalte des deutschen Humanismus* (Berlin, 1963).

F. Nitzsch, *Luther und Aristoteles* (Kiel, 1883).

H. A. Oberman, '*Facientibus quod in se est Deus non denegat gratiam*: Robert Holcot O.P. and the Beginnings of Luther's Theology', *Harvard Theological Review* 55 (1962), pp. 317-42.

——, *The Harvest of Medieval Theology: Gabriel Biel and Late Medieval Theology* (Cambridge, Mass., 1963).

——, 'Wir sind Pettler. Hoc est verum. Bund und Gnade in der Theologie des Mittelalters und der Reformation', *Zeitschrift für Kirchengeschichte* 78 (1967), pp. 232-52.

——, 'Simul gemitus et raptus: Luther und die Mystik', in *Kirche, Mystik, Heiligung und das Natürliche bei Luther: Vorträge des Dritten Internationalen Kongresses für Lutherforschung*, ed. I. Asheim (Göttingen, 1967), pp. 20-59.

——, 'Headwaters of the Reformation: *Initia Lutheri — Initia Reformationis*', in *Luther and the Dawn of the Modern Era*, ed. H. A. Oberman (Leiden, 1974), pp. 40-88.

——, 'Reformation: Epoche oder Episode?', *Archiv für Reformationsgeschichte* 68 (1977), pp. 56-111.

——, *Werden und Wertung der Reformation: Vom Wegestreit zum Glaubenskampf* (Tübingen, 1977).

H. Olsson, *Schöpfung, Vernunft und Gesetz in Luthers Theologie* (Uppsala, 1971).

S. E. Ozment, *Homo Spiritualis: A Comparative Study of the Anthropology of Johannes Tauler, Jean Gerson and Martin Luther (1509-1516) in the Context of their Theological Thought* (Leiden, 1969).

——, 'Eckhart and Luther. German Mysticism and Protestantism', *The Thomist* 42 (1978), pp. 259-80.

W. Pannenberg, 'Der Einfluß der Anfechtungserfahrung auf den Prädestinationsbegriff Luthers', *Kerygma und Dogma* 3 (1957), pp. 109-39.

R. Paqué, *Das Pariser Nominalistenstatut: Zur Entstehung des Realitätsbegriffs der neuzeitlichen Naturwissenschaft* (Berlin, 1970).

N. Paulus, *Der Augustiner Bartholomäus Arnoldi von Usingen: Luthers Lehrer und Gegner* (Freiburg, 1893).

O. H. Pesch, 'Zur Frage nach Luthers reformatorischer Wende', in *Der Durchbruch der reformatorischen Erkenntnis bei Luther*, ed. B. Lohse (Darmstadt, 1968), pp. 445-505.

A. Peters, 'Luthers Turmerlebnis', in *Der Durchbruch der reformatorischen Erkenntnis bei Luther*, ed. B. Lohse (Darmstadt, 1968), pp. 243-88.

G. Pfeiffer, 'Das Ringen des jungen Luther um die Gerechtigkeit Gottes', in *Der Durchbruch der reformatorischen Erkenntnis bei Luther*, ed. B. Lohse (Darmstadt, 1968), pp. 163-202.

L. Pinomaa, *Der Zorn Gottes in der Theologie Luthers: Ein Beitrag zur Frage nach der Einheit des Gottesbildes bei Luther* (Helsinki, 1938).

——, *Der existenzielle Charakter der Theologie Luthers: Das Hervorbrechen der Theologie der Anfechtung und ihre Bedeutung für das Lutherverständnis* (Helsinki, 1940).

G. Plitt, *Jodokus Trutvetter von Eisenach, der Lehrer Luthers in seinem Wirken geschildert* (Erlangen, 1876).

R. Prenter, *Der barmherzige Richter: Iustitia Dei passiva in Luthers Dictata super Psalterium 1513-1515* (København, 1961).

H. Preuss, 'Das Frömmigkeitsmotiv von Luthers Tessaradeks und seine mittelalterlichen Wurzeln', *Neue kirchliche Zeitschrift* 26 (1915), pp. 217-43.

J. S. Preus, *From Shadow to Promise: Old Testament Interpretation from Augustine to the Young Luther* (Cambridge, Mass., 1969).

S. Raeder, *Das Hebräische bei Luther untersucht bis zum Ende der ersten Psalmenvorlesung* (Tübingen, 1961).

——, *Die Benutzung des masoretischen Textes bei Luther in der Zeit zwischen der ersten und zweiten Psalmenvorlesung* (Tübingen, 1967).

——, *Grammatica Theologica: Studien zu Luthers Operationes in Psalmos* (Tübingen, 1977).

J. Richter, 'Luthers "Deus absconditus" — Zuflucht oder Ausflucht?', *Zeitschrift für Religions- und Geistesgeschichte* 7 (1955), pp. 289-303.

G. Ritter, *Studien zur Spätscholastik I: Marsilius von Inghen und die okkamistische Schule in Deutschland* (Heidelberg, 1921).

——, *Studien zur Spätscholastik II: Via antiqua und via moderna auf deutschen Universitäten des XV. Jahrhunderts* (Heidelberg, 1922).

——, 'Die geschichtliche Bedeutung des deutschen Humanismus', *Historische Zeitschrift* 127 (1922-3), pp. 393-453.

E. G. Rupp, *The Righteousness of God: Luther Studies* (London, 1953).

U. Saarnivaara, *Luther discovers the Gospel: New Light upon Luther's Way from Medieval Catholicism to Evangelical Faith* (St Louis, 1951).

R. Schäfer, 'Zur Datierung von Luthers reformatorischer Erkenntnis', *Zeitschrift für Theologie und Kirche* 66 (1969), pp. 151-70.

O. Scheel, *Martin Luther: Vom Katholizismus zur Reformation* (2 vols: Tübingen, 1921).

E. Schott, *Fleisch und Geist nach Luthers Lehre, unter besonderer Berücksichtigung des Begriffs 'Totus Homo'* (Leipzig, 1930).

F. K. Schumann, *Gottesglaube und Anfechtung bei Luther* (Leipzig, 1938).

C. Stange, 'Über Luthers Beziehungen zur Theologie seines Ordens', *Neue kirchliche Zeitschrift* 11 (1900), pp. 574-85.

——, 'Luther über Gregor von Rimini', *Neue kirchliche Zeitschrift* 13 (1902), pp. 721-7.

D. C. Steinmetz, *Misericordia Dei: The Theology of Johannes von Staupitz in its Late Medieval Setting* (Leiden, 1968).

——, *Luther and Staupitz: An Essay in the Intellectual Origins of the Protestant Reformation* (Durham, N.C., 1980).

E. Stracke, *Luthers großes Selbstzeugnis 1545 über seine Entwicklung zum Reformator historisch-kritisch untersucht* (Leipzig, 1926).

D. Trapp, 'Augustinian Theology of the Fourteenth Century', *Augustiniana* 6 (1956), pp. 146-274.

W. Urban, 'Die "via moderna" an der Universität Erfurt am Vorabend der Reformation', in *Gregor von Rimini: Werk und Wirkung bis zur Reformation*, ed. H. A. Oberman (Berlin/New York, 1981), pp. 311-30.

P. Vignaux, *Justification et prédestination au XIVe siècle* (Paris, 1934).

——, *Luther Commentateur des Sentences* (Paris, 1935).

E. Vogelsang, *Die Anfänge von Luthers Christologie nach der ersten Psalmenvorlesung* (Berlin/Leipzig, 1929).

——, *Der angefochtene Christus bei Luther* (Berlin/Leipzig, 1932).

——, 'Luther und die Mystik', *Luther-Jahrbuch* 19 (1937), pp. 32-54.

——, 'Die Unio Mystica bei Luther', *Archiv für Reformationsgeschichte* 35 (1938), pp. 63-80.

H. Volz, *Martin Luthers Thesenanschlag und dessen Vorgeschichte* (Weimar, 1959).

——, 'Luthers Randbemerkungen zu zwei Schriften Gabriel Biels: Kritische Anmerkungen zu Hermann Degerings Publikation', *Zeitschrift für Kirchengeschichte* 81 (1970), pp. 285-327.

H. Wendorf, 'Der Durchbruch der neuen Erkenntnis Luthers im Lichte der handschriftliche Überlieferung', *Historische Vierteljahrschrift* 27 (1932), pp. 124-44; 285-327.

E. Wolf, *Staupitz und Luther: Ein Beitrag zur Theologie des Johannes von Staupitz und deren Bedeutung für Luthers theologische Werdegang* (Leipzig, 1929).

——, 'Die Rechtfertigungslehre als Mitte und Grenze reformatorischer Theologie', *Evangelische Theologie* 9 (1949-50), pp. 298-308.

——, 'Zur wissenschaftsgeschichtlichen Bedeutung der Disputationen an der Wittenberger Universität im 16. Jahrhundert', in *Peregrinatio II: Studien zur reformatorischen Theologie, zum Kirchenrecht und zur Sozialethik* (München, 1965), pp. 38-51.

A. Zumkeller, *Dionysius de Montina: Ein neuentdeckter Augustinertheologe des Spätmittelelters* (Würzburg, 1948).

——, 'Hugolino von Orvieto über Prädestination, Rechtfertigung und Verdienst', *Augustiniana* 4 (1954), pp. 109-56; 5 (1955), pp. 5-51.

——, 'Das Ungenügen der menschliche Werke bei den deutschen Predigern des Spätmittelalters', *Zeitschrift für katholischen Theologie* 81 (1959), pp. 265-305.

——, 'Die Augustinertheologen Simon Fidati von Cascia und Hugolin von

Orvieto und Martin Luthers Kritik an Aristoteles', *Archiv für Reformationsgeschichte* 54 (1963), pp. 13-37.

——, 'Die Augustinerschule des Mittelalters: Vertreter und philosophisch-theologische Lehre (Übersicht nach dem heutigen Stand der Forschung)', *Analecta Augustiniana* 27 (1964), pp. 167-262.

——, 'Der Wiener Theologieprofessor Johannes von Retz und seine Lehre von Urstand, Erbsünde, Gnade und Verdienst', *Augustiniana* 22 (1972), pp. 118-84; 540-82.

——, 'Johannes Klenkok O.S.A. im Kampf gegen den "Pelagianismus" seiner Zeit: Seine Lehre über Gnade, Rechtfertigung und Verdienst', *Recherches Augustiniennes* 13 (1978), pp. 231-333.

——, 'Die Lehre der Erfurter Augustinertheologen Johannes von Dorsten über Gnade, Rechtfertigung und Verdienst', *Theologie und Philosophie* 53 (1978), pp. 27-64; 127-219.

——, 'Der Augustinertheologe Johannes Hiltalingen von Basel über Urstand, Erbsünde, Gnade und Verdienst', *Analecta Augustiniana* 43 (1980), pp. 57-162.

——, 'Erbsünde, Gnade und Rechtfertigung im Verständnis der Erfurter Augustinertheologen des Spätmittelalters', *Zeitschrift für Kirchengeschichte* 92 (1981), pp. 39-59.

——, 'Der Augustiner Angelus Dobelinus, erster Theologieprofessor der Erfurter Universität über Gnade, Rechtfertigung und Verdienst', *Analecta Augustiniana* 44 (1981), pp. 69-147.

Glossary of Theological Terms

The use of technical theological terms in a study of this type is inevitable, unless a serious diminution in the accuracy and value of the resulting analysis is to occur. Although the theological terms used in the present study are explained as and when they first occur, the following glossary is provided to permit the reader who is unfamiliar with such theological terms to familiarise himself with them. The reader who desires a more detailed analysis of late medieval theological terms is referred to Johannes Altensteig, *Vocabularius Theologiae* (Hagenau, 1517).

Acceptatio Divina. The act of God by which he grants man his claim to eternal life. The term refers to the divine decision to grant man this claim, rather than to any quality within man upon which this claim may be based (this latter being referred to as the *ratio acceptationis*). From the time of Duns Scotus onwards, the term *acceptatio divina* is usually employed by those theologians who wish to emphasise that the divine decision to accept man is not necessarily dependent upon any quality he possesses: God may accept a man to eternal life, in principle, without reference to his merit or possession of a habit of grace.

Anfechtung. Luther's term, discussed in chapter 5 of the present study, for spiritual assaults upon man and the resulting doubt and anxiety which they occasion. The German word is probably best translated as 'temptation', although this does not convey the full meaning of the word. Luther frequently uses the term to emphasise the existential aspect of Christian faith.

Deus absconditus. Luther's term, discussed in chapter 5 of the present study, to refer to the hiddenness of God within his self-revelation. The term appears to have two main senses: God, as he is hidden *in* his revelation, and God, as he is hidden *behind* his revelation. Since 1920, much attention has been focused by Luther scholars on this aspect of Luther's theology of the cross, with a probable distortion of the significance of the concept.

Ex puris naturalibus. The abilities of man in his natural state, without the assistance of grace.

Facere quod in se est. Literally, 'doing what lies within one's powers', or 'doing one's best'. The requirement laid upon man by God, according to the theologians of the *via moderna* and the young Luther, if he is to dispose himself to receive the gift of grace. God's gift of grace is understood to be conditional upon man's preparing himself for its reception.

Habitus. A permanent state or disposition within the believer, to be distinguished from a transitory act. The habit of grace is thus understood to be a created form within the soul of the believer, as distinct from the external influence of grace. In earlier medieval theology, the habit of grace was understood to have a status intermediate between that of God and man.

Meritum de condigno. Merit in the strict sense of the term — i.e., a human moral act which is preformed in a state of grace, and which is worthy of divine acceptation on a *quid pro quo* basis.

Meritum de congruo. Merit in a very weak sense of the term. A human moral act which is performed outside a state of grace which, although not meritorious in the strict sense of the term, is nevertheless deemed 'appropriate' or 'congruous' by God in relation to the bestowal of the first (i.e., justifying) grace. Within the context of the theology of the *via moderna*, man's doing *quod in se est* is regarded as meritorious *de congruo*, under the terms of the *pactum*, so that the notion of congruous merit provides the link between the moral and meritorious realms.

Opus alienum Dei. Luther's term for actions performed by God which apparently contradict his nature, and yet which ultimately lead to a conclusion in keeping with that nature. Thus the wrath of God is seen as his 'alien work', yet in that this wrath leads to the repentance of the sinner, and hence his salvation, it is seen not to contradict his revealed character.

Opus proprium Dei. Luther's term for actions performed by God which are evidently consonant with his self-revelation. The tension between the *opus alienum* and *opus proprium* is an important feature of the *theologia crucis*, discussed in chapter 5.

Pactum. The term used by the theologians of the *via moderna* and the young Luther to refer to the established order of salvation, by which God has committed himself to bestow grace upon man, provided that he fulfils certain preconditions (i.e., that he does *quod in se est*). The idea of a 'covenant' (*pactum, foedus, testamentum*) was an obvious choice for a theological term to express the divine reliability.

Potentia Dei absoluta. The absolute power of God, by which he was free to do anything which did not involve self-contradiction. The concept is used to refer to the divine omnipotence, as distinct from the presently established order.

Potentia Dei ordinata. The ordained power of God, referring to the established order of salvation which, although contingent (in that it is not the consequence of absolute necessity) is utterly reliable. Often referred to by theologians of the *via moderna* in phrases such as *de facto, stante lege*, etc. Discussed in chapter 2 of the present study.

Index